THE PRINTED WORD

THE
PRINTED
WORD

An Instrument of Popularity

———◆———

CHRISTOPHER SMALL

ABERDEEN UNIVERSITY PRESS

First published 1982
Aberdeen University Press
A member of the Pergamon Group

© Christopher Small 1982

The publisher acknowledges the
financial assistance of the
Scottish Arts Council in the
publication of this volume

British Library Cataloguing in Publication Data
Small, Christopher
    The printed word
    1. Mass Media   2. Printing—History
    I. Title
    302.2'32 (expanded)   HM258

    ISBN 0-08-025766-6   (hard)
    ISBN 0-08-025767-4   (flexi)

PRINTED IN GREAT BRITAIN
THE UNIVERSITY PRESS
ABERDEEN

Contents

Contents

For wise M.S.S.S., who knows
That life is more than verse, or prose

I
THE EXPLOSIVE DEVICE

THE invention of printing is, obviously, a crucial event in modern history: 'modern times', that vaguely-defined period, can be said to have begun with it. The five European centuries since Gutenberg set up his press in Mainz (c.1450) have been shaped in profound and varied ways by the device, in essence extremely simple, of reproducing a text, in identical and virtually unlimited number, by means of movable type; the same device, modified and extended, has been a potent instrument in spreading European power and influence throughout the world.

The connection with European history and the domination of European culture is a point to be noted at the outset, for printing was not originally a European technique. But though the Chinese knew how to print and make paper many hundreds of years earlier they did not develop the technique, or allow the technique to develop them, as did the men of fifteenth century Europe. Many reasons have been adduced for the difference, both complimentary to the Chinese and disparaging. They are outside the scope of this essay; though it may be noted that among the most important were certainly the nature of Chinese as a written language—comprising over 40,000 characters in a full modern dictionary—and the attitude towards it expressed in the traditions of Chinese society. China had literary traditions far older and more extensive than has Europe; it has been calculated that written Chinese produced 'a greater volume of recorded literature than any other language before modern times'. But it was regarded in a particular and strongly conservative fashion: 'The Chinese language had the character of an institution, rather than a tool, of society.'[1] The distinction has implications which will be returned to. What is immediately to the point is to ask not why China did not go on, from the use of movable type at least as early as the thirteenth century, rapidly to become a print-dominated civilisation, but why Europe did.

Whether Johann Gutenberg or another produced the first European book printed by movable type is disputed and not perhaps very important. What is certain is that printing, like certain other technical innovations— the making and military use of gunpowder, for example—was a rapid and

[1] Notes begin on p. 160.

1

spectacular success. Half a century after the appearance of Gutenberg's
42-line Latin Bible, generally reckoned to be the first printed book in the
European, modern sense, there were hundreds of printing-shops in cities
all over the continent: a map of their distribution shows the heaviest concentrations in Italy and the Low Countries, but there is a general scatter
through nearly all the countries of the Western world—the world, that is,
of Western Christendom.[2] Thousands of books, tens of thousands and
even, according to one calculation, millions[3] of copies, were already being
turned out; however primitive the means, compared with later refinements, the possibility of mass production was present from the beginning.
This in itself gave the printed word what may be thought its most significant characteristic, the triumph of mere number, or multiplication, over
any restriction that may be placed on it. The story is told of a printer in
Paris who, learning that the newly-printed *Colloquies* of Erasmus might be
condemned as heresy, rushed through an edition of 24,000 copies, circumventing in advance any attempt at suppression.[4] In the contemporary contests between authority anxious to control opinion and authors trying to
disseminate heretical or unorthodox notions the printing press gave dissi-
dence a new and enormous advantage—something which, as we shall see,
was to remain an attribute of words in print for a long time, if not quite to
this day. The very term 'publisher', in the sense of someone making
writings available to the public at large, only begins to be used at this time;
and the whole idea of the book as communication and store of thought and
information began rapidly to alter. When books were reproduced only in
manuscript and the number of copies was strictly limited the potential
readership was so to speak *linear*: a book might have an indefinitely extended succession of readers through time (and books were made, as
material objects, to last) but only as handed on from one person to another.
Not only and obviously did this make it unlikely that literacy should be
other than a specialised skill, but it strongly tended to make books the
transmitters of tradition rather than the means of disseminating novelty.
Printed books, on the other hand, could be and were spread abroad
laterally, to many readers at once, with quite new and different effects: the
proliferation of presses and bookseller-publishers from Northern Europe to
Spain had consequences quite without precedent, 'ensuring a wider diffusion of ideas than Europeans had ever been able to conceive as possible'.[5]

The dissemination, or sowing of ideas was not of course impossible
before the advent of print. It was carried out, slowly, by writing, and
rapidly by speech: by proclamation, performance, and all levels of discussion from formal debate to mere gossip, by teaching and by preaching,

words as the communication of man's thoughts were *words of mouth*. There is no reason to believe that simply as spreaders abroad of whatever can be conveyed by speech they were less effective. In many ways probably 'word of mouth' was—and is—the most rapid and economical means of making something widely known; it is notorious that certain kinds of news especially, the kind known as rumour, spreads faster by mouth to ear—like wildfire, as the saying goes—than anything that has to be read. There are differences, and possible disadvantages attached to such a mode of learning from others that will be returned to later; in the meantime it may be noted that this 'primitive' way of getting news, or knowledge, around persists to this day, and is enshrined in common use of the verb *to hear*. 'Have you heard?' is the usual way of asking whether a particular item of news has been received; even, exactly describing the old word-of-mouth process, 'Have you heard tell?' The information alluded to may very well have been transmitted in the first place by print (or, recently, by the peculiar hybrid significantly called broadcasting) but the association of intimacy and immediacy with direct speech persists, as an attribute at least of particular kinds of information. Most commonly this is current news, often contained in a newspaper. This curious and remarkable institution, in the form familiar to us which is so much the creation of printing that it is known simply by the technical name for the print-machine itself, 'the press', will be discussed in due course. At this point it is perhaps worth remarking that newspapers, although the offspring of print, have commonly occupied an anomalous position between printed information, what is set down 'in black and white', and word of mouth. Another common phrase, strictly a colloquialism—i.e. one used in everyday speech—refers vividly if awkwardly to this dual ancestry when someone, often in the very act of reading a newspaper, remarks, 'I see where it says. . . .'

Books, of course, or more simply writing, had always important advantages as a means of communication. Books are accurate—that is to say, they are not subject to the unavoidable modification which oral information suffers in passing from hearer to hearer. They constitute a permanent record which can be checked: what a man merely says, even with oaths, he can later deny, but what he has set down is there in evidence. Speaking to the Jews, people of the Book, Pilate—a functionary in a system very much maintained by writing—said, 'What I have written I have written.' Books have been able to overcome both space and time. They can be sent—though slowly, and until the coming of electronic communication, never any faster than word of mouth can travel—where their authors cannot go; they can outlast a man's personal life, and transmit his thoughts to future generations, in theory at least, without limit. Because they can be read over and over, and compared one with another, they are far more suitable than speech for conveying complex ideas.

This is not to deny the great and nowadays scarcely credible feats of memory which were common before the general use of writing, or before it developed at all: at different times and in different societies and parts of the world it is demonstrable that entire cultures, both 'the arts' and 'the sciences', to make an artificial distinction, were transmitted from generation to generation very largely by spoken words alone. It is also true that when and where books began to be relied on as 'memory banks', the powers of individual and collective memory decayed. In the final section of the *Phaedrus* Plato turns to 'the question of the propriety and impropriety of writing' and, himself a writer, comes down unequivocally in condemnation of writing as an inferior mode of communication. His Socrates recounts an Egyptian myth in which Thoth, credited with the invention of writing, is rebuked by the supreme god, Thamus: Thoth claims that the art of writing is 'a sure receipt for memory and wisdom', but Thamus says, 'Those who acquire it will cease to exercise their memory and become forgetful; they will rely on writing to bring things to their remembrance by external signs instead of on their own internal resources. What you have discovered is a receipt for recollection, not for memory.' This Platonic paradox applies to writing as such, but it is worth extending it to the operations of print, where its comment has, perhaps, even more force. Thamus goes on to say, 'As for wisdom, your pupils will have the reputation for it without the reality: they will receive a quantity of information without proper instruction, and in consequence be thought very knowledgeable when they are for the most part quite ignorant. And because they are filled with the conceit of wisdom instead of real wisdom they will be a burden to society.' With this Socrates contrasts his own method of person-to-person dialogue, communication of 'the kind that is written on the soul of the hearer together with understanding; that knows how to defend itself, and can distinguish between those it should address and those in whose presence it should be silent'. Writing may be allowed as a diversion and aid to recollection in the forgetfulness of old age, 'but finer still is the serious treatment . . . which you find when a man employs the art of dialectic, and, fastening upon a suitable soul, plants and sows in it truths accompanied by knowledge'.[6] This distinction is worth bearing in mind now, when the transmission in former times of the equivalent of whole volumes of information and tradition, all by word of mouth, is something we can barely understand. The point that Plato fastens upon is the selectiveness of verbal teaching, by which knowledge is transmitted only to suitable persons, a chosen few; while writing, an inanimate go-between, cannot choose or control its readers in any way. It is a problem which has troubled men, especially those of a Platonic or authoritarian cast of mind, ever since books were around and liable to fall into the hands of 'the wrong sort' of reader.

The invention of printing enormously exacerbated the problem. Originally described simply as mechanical handwriting, 'ars artificialiter scribendi', it hugely and precipitately enhanced the latent powers of written communication. The transformation from 'lineal' to 'lateral' was more than mere multiplication, though it was multiplication that brought it about: almost at once the effect Plato feared and deplored, of indiscriminate distribution, began to show as never before. Books, with their power (which often appeared to be magic) to outreach and outlast the frailties of mortal memory, were powerful transmitters and sustainers of tradition, and had hitherto operated in the main within a minority only; there was a 'clerkly culture' nourished by reading and writing, and there was a 'popular' or illiterate culture transmitted by word of mouth. Print began at once to demolish the distinction; books suddenly took on the possibility of becoming a means, if not at once the chief means, of dissemination to all and sundry. The very possibility helped to create the feeling that all and sundry—the whole human landscape, stony and fertile ground, in which the word could now be sown—not only might but ought to have the chance to receive it.

The connections are subtle and not easily disentangled, but it is certainly not accidental that the rise, or rather the explosion of printing and that other explosion which shook Europe to its foundations, the Reformation, belonged to the same time. That the first book printed by the new means of movable type was (probably) a Bible may have been accidental, but it was certainly symbolic, and much more direct and dynamic connections and interactions were soon to show. That the so-called Revival of Learning was partly dependent on the first use of print is clear, since by means of printed reproductions scholars were brought far more widely in contact with classic texts, long buried in medieval libraries, and, in turn, with each other, than would otherwise have been possible. If Erasmus is thought of, however ambiguously, as one of the fathers of the Reformation, then his paternity was largely realised through print. 'More than any other humanist,' says a modern historian of the Reformation, 'he wrote books which penetrated the homes and studies of northern readers',[7] and they were able to do so because they were printed and sold in large numbers. Erasmus was not alone, as he himself acknowledged: 'All over the world' (he wrote in 1517) 'as if on a given signal, splendid talents are stirring and conspiring together to revive the best learning. For what else is this but a conspiracy when all these great scholars from different lands share out the work among themselves?'[8] And, one might add, what communicated the signal but print?

Other writers, on both 'sides', enjoyed the same advantage: arguments and counter-arguments were, by means of print, unloosed from monastic studies and ecclesiastical courts and made available to all educated persons. Nor was the process all one of division and side-taking. The Reformation split Europe, but part of the whole movement that produced it was the spread and inter-connection of learning which, across boundaries, enlarged the all-embracing 'Commonwealth of Letters'. Erasmus, again, can be taken as witness, in his *Adages*: the library of Ptolemy, he said, 'was contained between the narrow walls of its own house', but the printer was 'building up a library which has no other limits than the world itself.'[9]

There were very soon more 'educated persons' around, and many of these were of a new sort, created by the new technique itself: 'Printing, with its rapidly accumulating technical improvements, engendered a new kind of intellectual: the bookseller-cum-printer-cum-publisher.'[10] This new breed of 'non-clerical clerks' were men who often combined the necessary practical knowledge and business acumen of their trade with wide learning, especially of languages, being familiar with Latin and Greek as well as their national tongues. The great master-printers, such as Manutius Aldus in Venice, Robert Estienne in Paris, Christophe Plantin in Antwerp, or Johannes Oporinus in Basel, were polymaths active in the world of affairs and also close associates of the scholars whose work they published. Whether or not in sympathy with the reformers—sometimes in secret, as Plantin was a member of the clandestine 'Family of Love'—they were deeply engaged in a traffic of learning, always partly an underground movement. On one hand a printer might give practical help and succour, as the Huguenot Andreas Wechel—printer first in Paris and later in Frankfurt—is said to have harboured Giordano Bruno. On the other, scholars might work directly for the press: 'It was not unusual to see humanists of all ranks and every level of renown take service under the entrepreneurs of the book trade and work as correctors in a printing workshop for a few months, or a few years: neither Erasmus nor Bude (the French scholar, librarian to François I) scorned these chores.'[11]

The documents they helped to print, to translate and comment upon, were part of the essential material out of which reforming ideas arose; and these, of course, were themselves spread with unprecedented rapidity by means of the press. Whether or not the original *95 Theses on Indulgences* which Luther nailed to the door of All Saints' Church in Wittenberg were handwritten, they were very soon in print and (translated into the vernacular) carried the igniting spark of the Reformation throughout Germany. They may indeed have done so beyond their author's first intention. It has been argued that Luther thought at first only of a limited disputation, but the scope of his challenge to Papal authority was taken out of his hands: 'by a stroke of magic he found himself addressing the whole world.'[12] Thereafter his writings were printed in huge numbers; it has been calculated that between 1517, when the *Theses* were first published, and his stand at the Diet of Worms in 1521, some 300,000 copies of his different works to that date were printed and sold.[13] He came himself to see the part played by printing, describing it as 'God's highest and extremest grace, whereby the business of the Gospel is driven forward'.[14]

Perhaps the most significant point about this series of events is that the *Theses*, and many of the pronouncements that followed them, including the appeal *To the Christian Nobility of the German Nation* which was the chief manifesto of the German Reformation, were printed in the vernacular— either translated from Latin or written from the start in German. The connection between printing, as a German invention, and its use in forwarding a national Reformation, was not lost on contemporaries: the sixteenth century historian Johann Sleidan, writing less than 100 years after Gutenberg, declared, 'As if to proffer proof that God has chosen us to accomplish a special mission, there was invented in our land a marvellous new and subtle art, the art of printing. This opened German eyes even as it is now bringing enlightenment to other countries. Each man became eager for knowledge, not without feeling a sense of amazement at his former blindness.'[15] But even this boast, with its strong nationalist undertones, recognised what was happening in 'other countries'; and the alliance between print, national language, and religious reform did not stop at national-linguistic boundaries.

The idea, so powerful a mover of the Reformation, that the laity should have direct access to the things of God and not depend on priestly mediation was, of course, largely—though not entirely—a question of language. If there was to be a priesthood of all believers, it was needful for believers to know what they were preaching; they must be able to read, and learn, in their mother-tongue. The strong demand for renderings of Scripture in 'the vulgar tongues' antedated printing—as it antedated or foreshadowed the Reformation itself—but it found an incomparably effective instrument in the combination of scholarship and print which made new translations, in most initial cases 'from the original tongues' of Greek and Hebrew, generally available. Looking back from the late sixteenth century the English Protestant John Foxe had no doubt about it: 'Although through might [i.e. force] be stopped the mouth of John Hus, God hath opened the press to preach, whose voice the Pope is never able to stop with all the puissance of his triple crown', and again, 'The Lord began to work for his Church not with sword and target to subdue his exalted adversary, but with printing, writing, and reading.'[16] It was the printed, vernacular Bible that he was above all thinking of.

The first versions in English, attributed to John Wycliffe and his followers, were widely circulated but can have been read only by a small minority. (Even so it included, according to Thomas More, 'good and catholic folk' as well as heretics.) Its existence was enough to bring about ecclesiastical prohibition, in the so-called Constitutions of Oxford, which forbade anyone to translate the Bible or even to read a translation without express authority from a bishop.

But a century later, though the Constitutions were still in force, they were quite unable to prevent the spread and use of printed Bibles in English, simply because authority was circumvented by mere number. Caxton, who brought printing to England in the late fifteenth century, printed no English Bibles, being prevented by the official ban, but copies of William Tyndale's New Testament, translated and printed abroad between 1523 and 1526, were soon arriving in England in such numbers that their distribution could not be stopped. There is an amusing anecdote of this bafflement by the contemporary Edward Halle, who describes how the bishop of London, Tonstall (to whom Tyndale had in the first instance applied, unsuccessfully, for permission to make his translation) attempted to corner the edition at its source on the Continent, and commissioned a London merchant, Packington, to buy up the whole stock, 'whatever they cost you'. Packington in due course informed Tyndale that he had now 'gotten thee a merchant which with ready money shall despatch thee of all thou have, if you think it so profitable to yourself'.

'Who is the merchant?' said Tyndale. 'The bishop of London,' said Packington. 'Oh, that is because he will burn them,' said Tyndale. 'Yea, marry,' quoth Packington. 'I am the gladder,' said Tyndale; 'for these two benefits shall come thereof: I shall get money of him for these books, to bring myself out of debt, and the whole world shall cry out upon the burning of God's word. And the overplus of the money, that shall remain to me, shall make me more studious to correct the said New Testament, and so newly to imprint the same once again; and I trust the second will much better like you than ever had the first.' And so forward went the bargain: the bishop had the books, Packington had the thanks, and Tyndale had the money.[17]

Such a tale, whether true in all its detail or not, could only be told of a printed book. Books had become, not just the repositories of ideas, but ammunition in ideological warfare—which was, of course, soon to become actual war, in deadly earnest. Nevertheless, it took some time for censorious authority to grasp the fact that now it was futile to seize and destroy the offending product—the book in question, which could always be reproduced—and that it was necessary also to suppress or control the means of production, the press itself. Even then, with many presses in existence, the survival of no more than one copy could very soon lead to a new flood of the objectionable material.

The notion that printing is of its very nature seditious can thus be seen to have early roots; though authority also began to make use of print at an early stage, both in the mass-production of orders and instructions—printed missals and breviaries, not to mention Papal Bulls themselves—and in answering, in print, with counter-arguments and polemics of its own. Thomas More could see, as apparently Bishop Tonstall could not, that Tyndale's Bible could not be physically destroyed, and so set about discrediting it in published controversy. The only answer to print is more print, a fact which in itself is likely to foster a judicious, even sceptical frame of mind, as contradictory opinions can be questioned where they are set down 'in black and white' and compared one with another.

In Germany itself, the heartland of the Reformation, much of the early printing enterprise seems to have been firmly in the hands of authority of one kind or another, Papist or anti-Papist. Treatises setting forth the rights and privileges of princes have a large place along with theological argument. In one notorious example Luther himself produced, in reaction to the peasant risings of 1524-5, what may be taken as a classic counter-revolutionary broadside. His tract, 'Against the robbing and murdering hordes of peasants', was written while the peasant forces led by Thomas Müntzer were at the height of their short-lived success, and was not published until after the massacre of Frankenhausen; it is supposed that Luther later repented of it. But it may be said to have lived on, a model of its kind, not only as justifying and encouraging the ferocity of the princes' revenge, but as one of the first expressions in print of a particular frame of mind, using the arguments and even many of the phrases of any number of such incitements to 'meet terror with terror' that frightened authority has had recourse to since: '. . . any man against whom it can be proved that he is a maker of sedition is outside the law of God and Empire, so that the first who can slay him is doing right and well. For if a man is an open rebel every man is his judge and executioner, just as when fire starts, the first to put it out is the best man. . . . Therefore let everyone who can smite, slay and stab, secretly or openly, remembering that nothing can be more poisonous, hurtful or devilish than a rebel. It is just as when one must kill a mad dog: if you do not strike him he will strike you, and a whole land with you.'[18]

To return to the printing of the English Bible, of greater significance for the early history of printing itself: here again authority sought to take control, but in a way that was to prove in the long run exceedingly danger-ous to itself. The sequence of events may briefly be rehearsed. After Henry VIII's quarrel with the Pope the Constitutions of Oxford were revoked and two versions of the Bible in English—Myles Coverdale's and the pseudony-mous 'Matthew's Bible'—were circulating freely by 'the king's most gracious licence', and with the recommendation of Archbishop Cranmer that it should 'be sold and read of every person'. A year later, in 1538, the clergy of every parish in England were instructed to 'provide . . . one book of the whole Bible of the largest volume in English, and the same set up in some convenient place within the said church that ye have cure of, whereas your parishioners may most commodiously resort to the same and read it.'[19] The injunction to 'expressly provoke, stir, and exhort every person to read the same' was only qualified by the warning to 'avoid all contention and alterca-tion therein, but to use an honest sobriety in their inquisition of the true sense of the same, and to refer the explication of obscure places to men of higher judgment in Scripture'.

It was not necessarily the same English Bible that was thus made available for mass study, since there were by that time several, mostly overlapping editions in circulation; even the so-called Great Bible, an authorised revision by Coverdale, was subsequently re-revised by him. The increasing capri-ciousness of royal authority, as Henry VIII advanced into paranoia, produced such quirks of policy as the prohibition in 1546 of Tyndale's and Coverdale's New Testament while the Great Bible itself was still 'appointed to the use of churches' throughout England. The close connection between the status of Scripture and politics is illustrated in the presentation of the Great Bible—equipped at this stage with Cranmer's recommendation as the all-sufficient source of knowledge and wisdom for everyone:

Here may all manner of persons: men, women; young, old; learned, unlearned; rich, poor; priests, laymen; lords, ladies; officers, tenants, and mean men; virgins, wives, widows; lawyers, merchants, artificers, husbandmen, and all manner of persons of what estate or condition soever they be; may in THIS BOOK learn all things, what they ought to believe, what they ought to do, and what they should not do, as well concerning Almighty God as also concerning themselves, and all others.[20]

It was, perhaps, the sixteenth century English equivalent of the Soviet Great Encyclopaedia, also the repository of everything the good and obedient citizen is expected to know. Like that publication, it was subject to alteration, and not only by scholars. The first edition of 1539 carries a splendidly decorated title-page which shows King Henry delivering the Word of God with his right and left hands to Cranmer and Thomas Cromwell (identified by coats of arms) who in turn deliver it to the clergy and laity, while an admiring crowd cry 'God Save the King' and God Himself looks down approvingly from above. But by the end of the following year Cromwell had fallen from favour, and his coat of arms was silently removed.[21]

In the further turns and reversals of religious politics the vernacular Bible continued to undergo change both in status and content—the latter altering through successive versions and editions chiefly in response to advances in scholarship, but also in deference to political climate. (In Elizabeth's reign, for example, the new and unpopular version known as the Bishop's Bible was prepared, at the queen's behest, chiefly because the glosses to the much more widely-read Geneva Bible were obnoxious to royal authority.) In Scotland the Geneva Bible, first published in 1560, arrived at the same time that Reformation itself was established, and remained the chosen version of the newly triumphant Kirk; this despite the fact that the marginalia, some of them probably supplied by John Knox himself, were as much disliked by James VI as by Elizabeth. Although unquestionably superior as a translation, the Geneva Bible was denounced by James as the worst he had ever seen, and there can be no doubt that it was the extensive marginal commentary, with its uncompromising Calvinist attitude to worldly princes—to James 'very partial, untrue, seditious and savouring too much of dangerous and traitorous conceits'— that chiefly offended him; nor that this was an important stimulus, after James had become king of England as well, for the production, with royal approval and backing, of the new, un-glossed Authorised Version.

Throughout these changes Bible-reading in the vernacular continued to expand; it is notable that even during the reign of Mary Tudor and the temporary re-establishment of Roman Catholicism in England the 'Great Bible' was not proscribed and remained in many parish churches; and by the end of the century English Roman Catholics—by that time persecuted in turn—were supplied with their own version in the so-called Douai Testament, the Old Testament following soon after. In mere bulk terms, taking into account the multiplicity of transcribed texts and translations, and successive editions of different versions—over 140 of the Geneva Bible alone between 1560 and 1644—the Old and New Testaments must vastly have outweighed all other writings to which print was applied in the first two centuries of its use. Whether as an instrument of royal policy or of incipient rebellion—as, in the group Bible-readings organised by Knox in Scotland before 1560, 'it was transforming the Protestant lords, lairds, merchants, artisans, and husbandmen into brethren of a revolutionary party'[22]—the printed Bible was a potent political weapon; it was so because it was in print, and because it was in print and everywhere available, it was helping to transform the nature of political movements themselves. Its availability and familiarity had far-reaching consequences, not only on the large historical scale, in directly influencing the movements of Reformation and Counter-Reformation, but in ways not so easy, perhaps, to define, in the development of popular attitudes to the whole business of publication, of assumptions about literature and the significance of print itself.

Among the first attractions of printed books was simply their novelty, and what was in them might also be expected to be new. It was 'New Learning' that the first of them propagated, and the Bible, itself by definition the bearer of Good News, had a special place in the process. The revived evangelism of both Reformation and Counter-Reformation excited whole populations with a desire to know more directly what this good news was; for Protestants at least the suspicion that it had been concealed from them by centuries of 'priest-craft' produced a hunger for the original source, to be known and judged by the individual, which preaching alone, however 'Bible-based', could no longer satisfy. For thousands of the newly literate—the 'unlearned' for whom in the preface to his Greek New Testament in 1516 Erasmus had said scripture should be available, 'even all women', and others yet further beyond the pale, 'not merely the Scots and Irish, but even . . . Turks and Saracens'[23]—the printed and translated Bible was the first and may have remained the only book they read in their lives; though reading it will in many have created an appetite for more. Perhaps a typical state of mind was expressed in the celebrated inscription of an English shepherd, Robert Williams, in 1546, when in the to and fro of Henrician policies the vernacular Bible was forbidden reading for 'the unlearned'. Williams, a mere farm-servant, was not among those licensed to read, and though protesting—'I prey God amende that blyndnes'—was at least ostensibly obedient. But he bought another book instead, in which he signed his name and made these observations while 'keppynge shepe uppon Seynbury hill'. It was a brand-new translation of an Italian humanist treatise on *Inventions of Things*.[24]

To sum up this rapid survey of the first impact of printing on European society—The device of movable type was in every sense a revolutionary invention: the first and for a long time yet the only application of machine methods to mass production; a direct contributor almost from the outset to intellectual, political and religious upheavals; the agent in more indirect ways of great changes in men's whole attitude to knowledge, its transmission and reception. But as a disturbing force of huge power it was from the start ambiguous in effect; capable, like other new tools suddenly placed in men's hands, of being used in apparently quite opposite ways. Among works printed in the first hundred years after Gutenberg were not only the *Theses against Indulgences* but the Indulgences themselves; not only Erasmus's *In Praise of Folly* but the master-handbook of witch-hunters, the *Malleus Maleficarum*; the *Cosmographia* of Ptolemy and the letter of Columbus which changed the very shape of the world; the *Institutions* of Calvin and the *Restitutio Christianismi* of Servetus whom Calvin burnt, together with all but three copies of the work which thereby survived him; the records of the Inquisition and, at the end of his life and almost exactly 100 years after the beginnings of printing in Europe, the *De Revolutionibus Orbium Coelestium* of Copernicus; at different dates from the same printer in Rome Machiavelli's *The Prince* and Ignatius Loyola's *Spiritual Exercises*.

In this process the printed and, especially, the vernacular Bible had a unique and central place, but one that also is ambiguous in implication; profoundly seditious, yet used as the seal of authority; the common treasure of all, yet the most fruitful source of division and strife; vehicle of the Word made Flesh, yet tending more than any of the former vagaries of religious teaching to make flesh word, to isolate words from feelings and to appropriate all value to itself; instrument for the destruction of idolatry, replacing all others with the idolatry of the Book.

II
'TEEMING FREEDOM'

AT this point, where print can be seen beginning to exert its immense influence on European society as a whole, some distinctions seem to be called for. What are the departments of 'the printed word' chiefly to be examined?—for clearly it will be impossible to survey them all. Lines will have to be drawn which are doubtless unjustified; for it is obvious, looking over the whole field of words in print from the telephone directory to poetry, that there are no logical and consistent boundaries to be seen. If there are categories, one merges with another; elements of one kind appear embedded among those which have been called intrinsically different; if rules are laid down, numerous exceptions will certainly occur. We are talking about 'the printed word', not 'literature'; if it were possible to exclude the latter, it would certainly be convenient.

However, this begs a huge question, and there are traps in wait for anyone who asks, What is literature? that should make a prudent person recoil. The present approach does, it is true, seem to offer a way out: for since literature, lettered communication, existed before the invention of printing, we may say that literature is also what survived it. It could be defined as the element in writing which was not either greatly affected or actually brought into being by the coming of print. But such a formula will not take us very far. On the one hand, although the changes brought about by printing, briefly sketched already, were immediate and spectacular, a great deal of what was initially put into print was already in circulation, or at least in existence, as manuscript. It was there, it was 'literature', and whether it was a work of classical antiquity or something as recent as *The Canterbury Tales*, its content was not altered by being printed. But its function, its place in society, certainly was; merely being in print made a difference. And on the other hand when, later, authorship began to catch up with the new facility offered to it, and completely new writing of all sorts became the main material of the printing presses, the prospect of appearing in print became part of the circumstances of literary creation. It would be difficult to say of more than a very few examples that they were completely untouched in their composition by the fact of printing, the

14

continually expanding new readership it promised, and the subtle but real influence on thinking of its common utterance as the printed word.

Poetry is a case in point. It is on the face of it most obviously unaffected by being printed, since it is still closely related, even after centuries of being written down, to another mode of communication altogether, of speech and song. Poets, moreover, can be thought of as too private, writing for an intimate circle or for themselves alone, to be interested in the possibilities of immediate publicity afforded by print. The poet has time, he can wait; he may be genuinely indifferent to fame or may think of a more distant and abstract glory in posterity or even eternity. For him whose words will (so he boasts) outlast marble and bronze, the doubtful permanency of print would seem to have few attractions. So one might suppose; yet poets, ever since they have had the chance, have rarely been indifferent to printed publication. Shakespeare may have cared little what happened to his plays beyond their actual performance, and was evidently willing to leave their publication to a doubtful, posthumous futurity; but his non-dramatic poetry he wished to see in print, and he took care that it should be printed correctly. (*Venus and Adonis* and *The Rape of Lucrece* were 'intended for a sophisticated reading public, and hence qualified as literature'—so a modern scholar puts it, with the significant corollary, 'therefore he saw them through the press personally'.)[25] Literature, by now at any rate, is synonymous with print, and it seems reasonable to a twentieth-century commentator that a poet, because he is a poet, should care especially how his work is printed. Indeed, there are not wanting nowadays poets who maintain that the look of their work on the page, the direct product of typography, is more important for them than it can ever be for a writer of prose. Poets may be private, but they are also performers and always have been, whether reciting in antique illiterate courts or at modern poetry readings; the vastly larger public commanded by print has, we may be sure, had its effect not only on the reception, but also on the performance. Without print could *Childe Harold* have made Byron famous overnight; and without the kind of readership implied by that fame, would not *Don Juan* have been very different?

It is impossible to abstract a writer from his times, which include cumulatively the times that have gone before him; thanks to printing these include a vastly greater cloud of literary witnesses, 'influences' and examples than would otherwise have been the case, contributing in all manner of minute and untraceable as well as large and obvious ways to the knowledge and feelings of 'his' age. (As T. S. Eliot replied to the observation that writers nowadays know so much more than their predecessors, 'Yes, and *they* are what we know'.) No writer, no work since 1500 can be altogether separated from the effects of printing, even if that work had never been printed, nor intended for it; what is not for printing acquires a new and perhaps a stronger character of privacy just because print is the normal destiny of writing. Such a very singular writer as William Blake, in conscious revolt against the received values and customs of his age, set out actually to circumvent the printing process by engraving his books himself. But he must be related if only by negatives to the print-made world which he rejected, the world of 'single vision and Newtonian night'. And even for him, striving to present his visions directly and without mechanical inter-mediations, prophetic speech was not inconsistent with book-production.

In his picture of 'a printing-house in Hell' (from *The Marriage of Heaven and Hell*) it is psychic powers which, in a vivid symbolic hierarchy of living creatures, dragons, serpents, eagles and lions, bring 'knowledge' to birth. When their creation is finally 'received by men . . . [in] the forms of books and . . . arranged in libraries', the implication is clear that book-making, or writing in itself, diminishes primal inspiration. But still it is seen to be necessary; and later, in the prologue to *Jerusalem*, Blake made what are perhaps the highest claims put forward by anyone for the printed page:

> Reader, lover of books, lover of heaven,
> And of that God from whom all books are given,
> Who in mysterious Sinai's awful cave
> To man the wondrous art of writing gave.
> Again he speaks in thunder and in fire—
> Even from the depths of Hell his voice I hear,
> Within the unfathomed caverns of my ear.
> Therefore I print, nor vain my types shall be;
> Heaven, Earth & Hell henceforth shall live in harmony.[26]

Another attempt to segregate 'literature' can be made by thinking of it as the heights only of the whole extent of print: at these heights, it may be said, certain qualities appear which, like snow on the hilltops, are the same however different the lower slopes and plains from which they arise, and irrespective of whether the hills stand in deserts or the most populous land-scape. These qualities are also those, though given other forms, which can be identified in the most lasting works of pre-printing ages. But even if metaphors of 'high' and 'low' are allowed (and they are always dubious), such an exalted view is little help in separating plains from peaks; there are too many interconnections 'up' and 'down', and however determined one may be to remain on flat ground and ignore the lofty sublime it is never possible for long. Print is continually mixing the levels. To take the example of Shakespeare again, as poet for a select circle and dramatist for all: while it may be true that one kind of writing was intended for a particular, 'sophisticated' readership and another not originally for reading at all, once both were in print the distinction disappeared. Heminge and Condell having done their work, all Shakespeare is equally accessible to all who can read.

What printing has done, indeed, is to break down divisions and distinctions, as appears if we turn to the dictionary for help. There is a whole range of definitions of 'literature', from (*Oxford English Dictionary*) 'literary culture' and 'writings esteemed for beauty of form or emotional effect' to 'any printed matter'. This last is the most recent usage given (1895), and though it embraces rather than excludes the others, it does make them seem old-fashioned, even obsolete. 'Belles-lettres', 'polite learning', 'the profession of a man of letters'—do not these have a dusty and antique sound? The 'man of letters' himself is said to be defunct, and doubtless it is true, in the sense that might be applied, for instance, to Samuel Johnson. But Johnson, though supremely a literary man, is too big to fit inside the phrase, and literature also is too large to be confined. For him it meant learning itself, as well as the means of learning—'Has he much literature?', he would ask, meaning is such a person well-read?—and for him, as a means to erudition, literature certainly also meant 'any printed matter', or any sort of book. So unavoidably, it must be for us; we cannot so label it as to rule anything out.

But what can possibly be avoided is a certain point of view, the very attitude which would place letters or literary culture apart from the whole mass. The whole subject really is the diffusion of letters or, in a word, popularity. Popularity sums up the whole story of print: what printing has done to render all 'literature'—that is, everything written which is not merely private, and in course of time that as well—the province of all; what the possibility of universal availability has done to the acts of writing and reading.

There is a vivid, indeed prophetic description of the process in Rabelais, whose own lifetime coincided very nearly with the introduction and first spread of printing. Gargantua's letter to Pantagruel speaks of the 'revival of learning' and its vulgarisation at the same time:

> Now is it that the minds of men are qualified with all manner of discipline, and the old sciences revived, which for many ages were extinct. . . . Printing likewise is now in use, so elegant, and so correct, that better cannot be imagined,

although it was found out but in my time by divine inspiration, as by a diabolical suggestion on the other side was the invention of Ordnance. All the world is full of knowing men, of most learned schoolmasters, and vast Libraries; and it appears to me as a truth, that neither in Plato's time, nor Cicero's, nor Papinian's, there was ever such conveniency for studying, as we see at this day there is: nor must any adventure henceforward to come in public, or present himself in company, that hath not been pretty well polished in the shop of Minerva: I see robbers, hangmen, freebooters, tapsters, ostlers, and such-like of the very rubbish of the people, more learned now than the Doctors and Preachers were in my time.

What shall I say? the very women and children have aspired to this praise and celestial Manna of good learning. . . . [27]

Rabelais equated, or balanced the invention of printing with that of gunpowder, and he was not the only man of his time to do so. Both were put to use with great rapidity, both had, so to speak, the same levelling tendency and both spread their effects in the same impartial way. 'Ordnance' made undefendable the strongholds of great lords, but thereby it increased the power of kings; it made armoured chivalry as absurd as Don Quixote, but it also rendered obsolete the weapons of the poor.

Print also, it seems, was a neutral force, also from the beginning at the service of princes and an instrument of centralised power. Rulers acquired cannon and printing-presses at nearly the same time, and used both as tools of policy. Luther's ferocious pamphlet against the peasant risings of 1525 has already been mentioned, but it may be further noted that it was published—serving usefully as justification in retrospect for the cruelties of repression—*after* the cannonade of the princes' forces had scattered Thomas Müntzer's followers at Frankenhausen. The wars of Francois I against the Papacy produced from that great early patron of printing the *Lettres au Pape* which have been described as the model, in 'studious suppressio veri and suggestio falsi . . . for many a White Book'.[28] All over Europe monarchs aspiring to absolutism set up printing establishments under their direct control. Yet at the same time the control itself, and the importance rulers attached to it, showed up certain quite different potentialities in print. Royal printing presses and royal censorship were set up at the same time, the latter offering a backhanded tribute to the powers of print in fostering unorthodoxy and disaffection.

In times when it was generally dangerous to hold or propagate wrong opinions printing itself, let alone authorship, was a hazardous trade. Etienne Dolet, burned for heresy and blasphemy at Paris in 1541, suffered not only on his own account but as the owner of a printing press which had issued his own and other obnoxious works (among them writings of Rabelais and Erasmus). He is remembered as 'the martyr of the Renaissance', but he might more precisely be called the proto-martyr for the freedom of the press.

Censorship of printing has a history almost as long as printing itself. Indeed Gutenberg's Mainz has the doubtful honour of being its birthplace, when in 1486 the electorate of Mainz and the Imperial city of Frankfurt jointly set up (at ecclesiastical prompting) the first secular censors' office. There will be occasions later to refer to the development of censorship, which appears to be the shadow constantly dogging the progress of the press; it is interesting at this point to see how early it was felt to be necessary, and how soon many of its recurring characteristics were established.

The example of Mainz and Frankfurt was soon followed elsewhere. The concern of authority was firstly to suppress heresy, but the age was one in which—greatly accelerated by printing itself—the boundaries between secular and sacred were breaking down, and as unorthodoxy in one department seemed inevitably to carry its infection into the other it was not long before a general supervision seemed essential. To Pope Paul IV (1555–59) belongs the distinction both of re-establishing the Inquisition while yet a Cardinal and later, in the last year of his reign, of promulgating the first Papal Index of prohibited books. The great book-burning that followed destroyed not only a mass of books of a Protestant tendency—whether on religious subjects or not—but others considered odious on quite other grounds, such as the *Decameron*, and the works of Machiavelli and, again, Rabelais. The destruction was widespread and is reckoned temporarily to have had a disastrous effect on the book-trade in Italy; but as an act of suppression it was unsuccessful. Not one work condemned to the fire was thereby wiped out and lost altogether, although in one instance (of a Lutheran treatise which nevertheless had been sponsored by two cardinals) survival appears to have been by a single copy, 'miraculously' preserved.[29] Print makes such miracles and the discomfiture of book-burners almost inevitable: the whole episode is a prototype of wholesale attempts to purge the printed word, not merely in its arbitrary and often ludicrous condemnations but in its ineffectiveness.

With an historian's hindsight a modern writer may justly remark how 'the defenders of orthodoxy were slow to realise that where they once cut manuscripts to pieces, the printed book was bound to escape their clumsy scissors',[30] and it can be added that their successors often do not seem to have learned the lesson much better. The same writer's description of ecclesiastical censorship in seventeenth century Italy—the endless delays in getting books either licensed or condemned, the absurd elaboration of the rules under which the censors were to operate, and the fact that they were frequently quite unable to understand what they were supposed to be judging—could be applied to every such operation since; with the same generalisation that 'repressive machinery is sometimes more vexatious by its clumsiness than by its violence'. Censorship *after* publication of printed material has always proved not only clumsy, inept (even according to its own rules) and intolerably slow, but in the end unavailing, Censorship *before* any writing is put into print promises a much tighter control, and as will be seen has been an aim of authority in varying degree and by different means for a long time; though to be complete it requires a virtual monopoly of printing which has been achieved only intermittently before the twentieth century.

Authority and sedition are inextricably linked: it can be said that the second is always the child of the first. Nevertheless, if there appears to be something inherently seditious in printing, that need not be understood in a merely negative sense, as reaction against control and suppression. In the past at least it has been seen rather as offering a positive alternative to authoritarian government, in establishing a 'Republic of Letters' more extensive than nation-states, ruled only by the consent and participation of its members, and though without physical force, more powerful. The concept of such a republic, articulated in the writings of the Huguenot Pierre Bayle in the late seventeenth century—whose periodical *Nouvelles de la Republique* counts as the first general survey of European scholarship— has remained as an ideal of intellectual life, open, international, and toler- ant. It has been persuasively argued[31] that the rise of this 'Republic' or 'Commonwealth' as a conscious entity, of indefinite but real dimensions, was closely associated with the printing trade, itself international. The commercial acumen of great printing firms itself played a part:

> From the sixteenth century on, the Republic of Letters expanded in Catholic Europe despite official disapproval, not only because lay rulers were often at odds with churchmen or because censors were overburdened, inefficient, or easily bribed. Expansion occurred also because hard-driving Protestant publishers extended alternative opportunities to writers who found Catholic publication outlets blocked.[32]

But the 'Republic', and the printers who collaborated in extending it, was a larger realm than any dictated by sectional interests, of politics, religion, or trade. In practical terms its capital might seem in Bayle's time to have been

Rotterdam, where he took refuge, or the other great centre of unrestricted printing industry, Amsterdam. But during this period books were often issued as from 'Cosmopolis', 'Utopia', or 'Philadelphia', and these fictitious addresses were not adopted by printers solely for prudential reasons. They announced to readers a different allegiance; the same that was symbolised in the engravings of Minerva used to decorate many books at this time. Minerva was patron of all practical skills and crafts, and was adopted as such by the printing trade (as well as by freemasonry); but especially, as the Roman equivalent of Athena, she was Goddess of Wisdom.[33]

In the symbolism of Minerva, as tutelary deity of the 'Republic of Letters', two powerful and apparently contradictory ideas are combined. As goddess she was the object of a cult, maintained and served by a few, her devotees, to whom her mysteries had been opened; they were the enlightened or illuminated ones, and their associations were half-secret, in the various forms of Illuminati, or Masons, or Families of Love, which spread her arcane wisdom. They did, however, spread it, so that it might become common; and though the 'Republic of Letters' was in the imagination of its members partly a secret society, its purpose was to bring everything into the open, so that all should worship at Wisdom's shrine.

To this end the instrument was at hand in the printing press. The writers and printers who thought of themselves as citizens of the 'Republic' were learned men, but they had no wish (as had some others, such as the alchemists) to keep learning to themselves. Their dream was of universals, universal literacy, universal learning, universal knowledge, crossing all boundaries of language, nationhood, and class. As a programme it could be described in the complete sense as Utopian, but to remember that, as a dream, it certainly existed, helps to make clear what is meant when we speak of 'popularity' and even, as asserted earlier in this chapter, when we propose the formula that popularity and printing are in some sense synonymous. Whatever is in print has the potentiality of becoming popular; and it is this idea, more than any other, which is the revolutionary dynamic within the story of printing. The 'Republic of Letters' embraced all men who wrote, read, printed and published books, but it was the very reverse of what we would nowadays imply by 'a literary society'. In its dream-aspirations 'literature' as the possession of a few would cease to exist.

Print has a built-in tendency to escape from bonds laid upon it. It therefore not only offers a means for free expression and exchange of ideas, but itself becomes associated with the idea of freedom. As an industrial process of some complexity, requiring considerable capital investment, printing appears susceptible to central control and monopoly.

Printing monopolies were indeed established in different countries at an early date, with selective licensing granted directly by a central authority, or on its behalf. But printing has always chafed under such control, both for the commercial reasons which cause any monopoly to be resented, and as reaction against censorship; both motives have reinforced one another, combining in a demand for freedom to print which becomes steadily more conscious and articulate.

In England a print monopoly was formally set up with the foundation of the Stationers' Company, granted its royal charter in 1557, when it was expected, in the last years of Mary Tudor's reign, to act as an auxiliary in heresy-hunting. Continuing under Elizabeth, and serving the new Protestant establishment, it soon became a powerful restrictive force, both in the commercial interests of its members and as a means of government control. No one who was not a member of the Company was permitted to print, and all printed matter had to be registered at Stationers' Hall; the Company was answerable to royal authority for everything so published. As a self-operating mechanism of censorship, driven by self-interest, it was an economical arrangement which was, one may say, typically Elizabethan. It was not, however, wholly effective. Unlicensed publication of different kinds was not uncommon, culminating during Elizabeth's reign in the 'Marprelate' pamphlets which, written by different Puritan partisans under the common pseudonym of 'Martin Marprelate', attacked Church of England episcopacy and simultaneously defied Archbishop Whitgift, the Star Chamber, and the Stationers. This celebrated outbreak of 'underground' printing—the tracts were turned out on secret presses by printers more or less on the run[34]—lasted two years, from 1588 to 1590, the bitter polemics of the 'Marprelates' being answered with equal bitterness and scurrility by officially sanctioned 'Anti-Martinists'. Authority did not catch up with the pamphleteers for another three years, when three of the chief suspects were arrested on other charges; one (the Welsh cleric Penry) was hanged and another died in prison.

The 'Marprelate' affair was in more than one way a precursor of the tumults of the next century in Britain, characterised among other things by a storm of print. It is worth looking in a little more detail at this period, 200 years after Gutenberg, when in one country and for a time at least the potentialities of print for the untrammelled spread of information and opinion showed themselves as never before, only rarely to be equalled since.

We have already glanced in outline at the links between printing and the turmoil throughout Europe of the Reformation, the proliferation on both sides (or more truly on all sides, for there were many more than two) of tracts and counter-tracts, edicts, theses, Bulls, theological speculation and anathematisation, not to mention the printed reproduction of Scripture itself, to which all these others were referred. Yet little of this literature could as yet be called popular. It was in the seventeenth century, and especially in those middle years—less than a generation in temporal extent—which comprehended in Britain what is differently known as the Interregnum, the Great Rebellion, or more recently the English Revolution, that the printed word first came into its own as a genuinely popular medium. Print as the means of spreading ideas among ordinary people assumed at this time a role so important, so indispensable, and so consciously used, that it became inextricably connected with the ideas themselves, and we find the right to print beginning to be claimed as a fundamental liberty, no less than those others which men were putting forward by its aid. Freedom of speech and freedom to print were formulated if not quite for the first time, with an unprecedented breadth of application, and the two went together, so much so that the differences between them (legal and other) were commonly ignored, and men demanded them as though the first naturally included the second.

Britain's 'Century of Revolution' has been extensively studied in recent years, and its every aspect, religious, social, political, philosophical, examined in great detail; and the sources for this study, still by no means fully exploited, exist very largely, and far more copiously than for any earlier period of history, in print. There is thus a curious long-term effect of what at the time was little considered. The idea of history, of human society in a continual condition of change, was still in its infancy. It can be seen assuming modern and sophisticated form in the writings of such as Bacon, Harrington and Hobbes, or towards the end of the period of John Locke. But it can also be detected emerging as a popular notion, and in the characteristic form of a heightened sense of the present: a belief that the present is not or need not be absolutely conditioned by the past, that change is possible, and permissible. 'We are men of the present age', declared one of its spokesmen;[35] and in their vigorous preoccupation with the present and rebellion against the past they provided in unprecedented degree evidence for the future. Two functions of printed communication paradoxically combine: the dissemination of whatever men may be thinking at the time so rapidly and so widely that suppression is difficult or impossible; and its preservation for readers not yet born. Writing itself, of course, had achieved this, and writers knew it, but they were few; now in number and variety more than ever before thousands of men (and women)

were putting their thoughts on record for an unlimited audience, present
and to come. Because they were so zealous to communicate with one, they
still communicate with the other.

Books of all kinds proliferated at this time, the Bible still greatly out-
numbering all others. Near the beginning of the period the succession of
English versions had come to what for long seemed finality with the
publication of the so-called Authorised Version in 1611; the book which can
still rank as the most influential of any in the English language. (The Geneva
Bible, it is true, held its own among the Puritans for some time yet, but by
degrees the 'King James Bible' established itself as supreme authority.) For
King James himself, its royal dedicatee, it was an instrument for reinforcing
religious authority and uniformity no less perhaps than the Prayer Book of
1637, though never imposed like the latter by Act of Parliament. But if the
Prayer Book was an immediate and bitter cause of contention—
even, in the famous story, literally a missile—the vernacular Bible was to
become in a much more powerful sense a weapon of war. The Authorised
Version, printed in successive editions and at a comparatively low price,
came soon into the homes, even the pockets, of 'the very vulgar'; Scripture
was referred to in every argument on every subject, and argument itself
became epidemic, related to all the pressing concerns, high and low, of the
day. So Thomas Hobbes complained that 'every man, nay every boy and
wench that could read English thought they spoke with God Almighty and
understood what he said, when by a certain number of chapters a day they
had read the Scriptures once or twice over'.[36] He might think, as he said
elsewhere, that 'the invention of printing, though ingenious, compared
with the invention of letters, is no great matter',[37] but if print allowed
everyone to read and interpret what was believed to be the word of God
the result would be chaos. For Hobbes the meaning of the Bible (which he
probably did not believe in anyway) must be referred back to authority:
'For, whosoever hath a lawful power over any writing, to make it law, hath
the power also to approve, or disapprove the interpretation of the same.'[38]
This was the view not only taught by the conservative clergy but formerly
accepted by most of their hearers. Now, however, things were changing.
For a man as different from Hobbes as the enthusiast and pamphleteer,
Arise Evans (who certainly did believe in the Bible, every word of it), its
significance had radically altered: 'Afore I looked upon the Scripture as a
history of things that passed in other countries, pertaining to other
persons; but now I looked upon it as a mystery to be opened at this time,
belonging also to us.'[39]

Authority desired that discussion and interpretation of Holy Writ should be confined to the universities and the pulpit; and preaching remained no doubt the means above all others by which ideas were spread, or imposed. But preaching, of course, was no longer the reliable sounding-box that authority desired, and whether orthodox or not, was liable to pass rapidly into print. Vast numbers of sermons were published, often soon after delivery: on the one hand (for example) the 'Repetition Sermon' of the Court divine Thomas Lushington, preached at Oxford in 1624, which—with its remarkable linkage to the news of the day, quite in the modern manner— became a popular pamphlet, reprinted many times during the next 100 years; or on the other the preaching of John Preston, also at the Stuart Court but with the greatest audacity putting the Puritan case under the royal nose, and, again, soon published for a much wider audience. At a humbler level this was the time, leading up to the outbreak of civil war, when, to the indignation of Archbishop Laud, 'lecturers' were introduced into the church at the behest of congregations, by-passing the beneficed clergy whose sermons could be relied on. For Laud the lecturers were 'the people's creatures [who] blow the bellows of sedition'; their very title suggests the close connection between preaching, or agitation, and the printed word.

But if the Bible was at the centre, the explosion of printing, reading, and debate that was about to take place in Britain far outspread its origins. Most typically it took the form of pamphleteering, which flourished during the later years of the Civil Wars and the Commonwealth especially in a manner that has scarcely been repeated since, even in absolute terms, and certainly in proportion to the number of potential readers. Some 22,000 different pamphlets, tracts, and broadsides survive from the period as a whole, and these, of course, are only what remains of a probably much larger number. It has been calculated that over the 20 years of the Civil Wars and 'Interregnum' pamphlets were being turned out at an average rate of three a day.[40] Their readership—one may begin to speak of 'circulation', since it is likely that many copies were passed from hand to hand and read by far more than one person—can only be guessed at; but it must have been a considerable fraction of the population. The extent of literacy at this time is, again, a matter of guesswork, but it was certainly growing, both as a result of deliberate policy—the foundation of new schools which had continued in a more or less haphazard way under the monarchy was directly encouraged by the Commonwealth State[41]—and as a consequence of the flood of reading matter itself. When so much of urgent popular interest was in print, renewing itself and changing all the time, there must have been a powerful motive among the 'unlettered' to gain access to it. It is a fair

assumption that few social groups even in the most isolated places would
not have numbered at least one or two literates among them, who would be
able to transmit anything in print to the rest, at any rate anything in
English. The demand that 'plain English' should be used for all communication took on a new urgency: not only Scripture but the law and indeed all
matters under the sun should be no longer wrapped up in 'learned tongues'
but open to everyone.

The content of this outpouring of print was enormously various, though
a great part of it could be described as theological-political. Its authorship
ran socially from top to bottom—from the *Eikon Basilike*, supposed to have
been written by Charles I awaiting execution, to the works of a man like
Abiezer Coppe, one of the 'Ranters' or extreme antinomians who consorted
with vagabonds and preached the immediate Kingdom of God and the
abrogation of all law.

Many of the surviving pamphlets and broadsheets are anonymous or
pseudonymous, and of the named authors in many cases nothing is known
except their opinions and visions set out in the writings themselves. But
even the briefest survey of them suggests a picture of ideas flying up and
down the country like the sparks of a spreading conflagration. The image
(which was to be seized on later by Shelley) seemed to occur naturally at
the time, and is perhaps archetypal; the words of fire which prophets and
aspirant prophets feel to be on their lips are now carried on a whirlwind of
print. Coppe borrowed from Biblical prophesy the striking visionary description of 'A Flying Fiery Roll' for the titles of his books; the notion of
'Divine Fireworks' (the title of an anonymous broadsheet of the same time,
possibly also by Coppe) was at work in many minds, to the exhilaration of
some and the dismay of others. To a man like Thomas Edwards—Milton's
'shallow Edwards', the conservative Presbyterian divine—the free dissemination and multiplication of opinion was to be deplored and feared: his
book *Gangraena* (1646), warning the Long Parliament of 'Errours, Blas-
phemies and Pernicious Practices of the Sectaries of this time', is a notable
tribute from the opposition to the extent of this whole self-generating
movement. *Gangraena's* 'Catalogue of Errours', by Edwards's own admis-
sion by no means exhaustive, lists 176 different heresies and 'strange
Opinions', with sources noted, mostly from printed examples. Although he
included hearsay and reported speech in his evidence of the 'whirlegig
spirits' abroad it was their expression in print that most appalled him and
that he called upon Parliament to suppress. The existing regulation of publishing by license was, he maintained, quite inadequate because generally
unenforced: there were 'never more dangerous unlicensed Books printed

than since the ordinance against unlicensed printing'. (He was referring to the latest of a series of such decrees, imposed in 1643, but virtually a dead letter.)

Edwards's list, extremely various and including, as he pointed out, many opinions which were mutually contradictory, is of religious rather than political unorthodoxies; but as has already been remarked, there was then no such distinction, almost all political opinion being couched in, and indivisible from, religious terms. The 'gangrene' of opinions extends from the view that 'the Scriptures cannot be said to be the Word of God, there is no Word but Christ', and that 'right Reason is the rule of Faith', which might seem only to threaten ecclesiastical authority, to a direct challenge to property, that 'all the earth is the Saints' and there ought to be community of goods, and the Saints should share in the Lands and Estates of Gentlemen and rich men'. The general import of these 'errors', as the opinions of those who 'deny all principle of Religion (and) are enemies to all holy Duties, Order, Learning, overthrowing all', is revolutionary. The point about them, Edwards insists, is that they are not merely revived ideas that have been around for a long time—'not . . . old errours . . . dead and buried many years ago and now revived by this Discourse', but new: 'a Catalogue of errours now in being, alive in these present times.'

With this frightened warning may be compared the proud boast of the Leveller Richard Overton (already referred to) when he declared in the same year of 1646, in the name of reason and equity, 'whatever our forefathers were . . . we are men of the present age', looking to the same Parliament to which Edwards appealed not to restrict and censor but to make them 'the most absolute free People in the world'.[42] It is the immediacy of these pamphlets that most strikes the reader nowadays. The Levellers' tracts, petitions and manifestoes, following out into democratic demands the principle that 'the great end wherefore God sent man into the world [is] that he should do good in his generation'[43] may have harked back to notions of a Saxon commonwealth before the imposition of 'the Norman yoke', but it is their own times, and their sense of responsibility for those times, that concern them. The yet more radical demands of the 'Diggers'— 'But now the honest man that would have liberty cries down all interests whatsoever, and to this end, he desires common right and equity . . . a just portion for each man to live, so that none need to beg or steal for want, but every one may live comfortably'[44]—or the visionary utterance of a preacher like William Erbery, that 'the great design that God hath to do this day is to undo . . . the mighty ones of the earth, that the outward and inward man should have deliverance at last'[45] are alive with the same urgency, the conviction that all human affairs are the inescapable concern of all men, and the overpowering need to speak. The author of the anonymous pamphlet *Tyranipocrit Discovered* (1649), inveighing against the new tyrannies imposed by the 'tyrannicides', was bound to publish because 'all reasonable men know that to be silent is consenting to a thing'[46] 'But yet', wrote the radical lawyer John Warr, 'the minds of men are the great wheels of things; thence come changes and alterations in the world; teeming freedom exerts and puts forth itself.'[47]

Teeming freedom exerting itself in men's minds demanded or, more strongly, commanded expression. Arise Evans published 'in discharge of his duty to God';[48] George Foster the Quaker not only saw visions but 'was commanded to print them'; Gerrard Winstanley the leader of the Diggers was instructed in a vision to publish it abroad that 'the earth should be made a common treasury of livelihood to whole mankind, without respect of persons'.[49] The men and women so compelled might and did prophesy in the streets like George Fox crying, 'Woe to the bloody city of Lichfield!' or that other and now less well-known Quaker leader James Nayler, who symbolically rode into Bristol upon an ass, in explicit imitation of the Entry into Jerusalem (and suffered cruel punishment for it); or the ecstatic Anna Trapnel, the Baptist prophetess, who sang and prayed aloud.

But they also seized on all the opportunities offered by print and copiously spread their messages further afield by its means: 'testimonies', journals, exhortations were published in great number. For the more politically minded, the liberty to print became very closely associated with 'teeming freedom' itself. 'Let there be liberty of the press for printing', urged the Cromwellian Army chaplain John Saltmarsh, who also held that 'the interest of the people in Christ's kingdom is not only an interest of submission but of consultation, counselling, prophesying, voting';[50] and the radicals in the Army and outside it were acutely aware of the power, on their side, conferred by a free press. The New Model Army had its own press; the Agitators, elected rank-and-filers who for a brief period were on an equal footing with the high officers themselves, had their own printer. One of the key proposals put forward 'for the Managing of the Counsels of the Army' in May 1647 was to 'keep a party of able pen-men at Oxford, where their presses be employed to satisfy and undeceive the people'.[51] One of these able pen-men, the Leveller John Harris, was in fact for a time official printer to the Army.[52]

Outside the Army, though closely in touch with it, the Levellers used both licensed and clandestine presses to turn out their untiring and for a time exceedingly well directed stream of manifestoes, news-sheets, remonstrances, protests and appeals.

Attempts to suppress these brought to the forefront their formula, that liberty of the press was in itself one of the fundamental freedoms they demanded. During the years of their greatest activity, when it seemed for a brief space that they and their followers might indeed add a democratic revolution to the victory of the (quite undemocratic) Parliament, attempts were made to control the press through licensing, but initially these were of little effect, as has been noted already. The complaint of Thomas Edwards was precisely that, and his appeal in *Gangraena* was that Parliament should 'fall upon some effectual ways' of enforcing existing 'ordinances'. To the pamphleteers themselves the ordinances against 'false, scandalous, seditious and libellous works' were no deterrent, though they were a threat, and helped to make clear what a powerful weapon they had in their hands. In a pamphlet of 1646, Richard Overton, himself a printer by trade, wrote that 'this persecuted means of unlicensed printing hath done more good to the people than all the bloody wars; the one tending to rid us quite of all slavery; but the other only to rid us of one, and involve us into another'.[53]

Three years later, when Cromwell was preparing to break the Levellers and the threat of suppression—with severe penalties, including whipping, for publication and distribution of unlicensed prints—became real, the radicals replied with another 'petition' putting the case for a free press as essential to common liberty: 'For whatever specious pretences of good to the Commonwealth have been devised to overawe the Press, yet all times foregone will manifest, it hath ever ushered in a tyranny; men's mouth being to be kept from making noise, whilst they are robbed of their liberties.' The petition linked licensing, or censorship of the press with the obnoxious idea of censorship in general:

... as to the whole course of printing, as justly in our apprehensions may licensers be put over all public or private teaching, or discourses, in divine, moral, natural, civil, or political things, as over the Press; the liberty whereof appears so essential unto freedom as that without it, it's impossible to preserve any nation from being liable to the worst of bondage; for what may not be done to that people who may not speak or write, but at the pleasure of licensers?

As for any prejudice to government thereby, if government be just in its constitution, and equal in its distributions, it will be good, if not absolutely necessary for them, to hear all voices and judgements, which they can never do, but by giving freedom to the Press; and in case any abuse their authority by scandalous pamphlets, they will never want able advocates to vindicate their innocency. And therefore all things being duly weighed, to refer all books and pamphlets to the judgement, discretion, or affection of licensers, or to put the least restraint upon the Press, seems altogether inconsistent with the good of the Commonwealth, and expressly opposite and dangerous to the liberties of the people, and to be carefully avoided, as any other exorbitancy or prejudice in government.[54]

Throughout these tumultuous years, and after them, the issue of censorship was at the centre of the argument about men's rights and freedoms, and of the struggle between different interests and powers which the argument reflected. With the abolition in 1641 of the Prerogative Courts (the Star Chamber and the ecclesiastical High Commission) the draconian control exercised by royal government vanished, and there followed the enormous release of 'men's minds' into print which has been outlined. The freeing of John Lilburne, sentenced by the Star Chamber to prison and flogging at the cart's tail for breach of the old licensing regulations, was symbolic. His fellow-sufferer, John Bastwick, had declared from the pillory that 'were the press upen to us' the kingdom of 'Antichrist'—in this context the rule of Charles I—would be scattered, and so far as the royal power was concerned he was proved right.[55]

But centralised authority was soon trying to snatch this great and unprecedented freedom back. The successive Ordinances for the restoration of licensing were enforced more effectively after the defeat of the Levellers in 1649; and with the Restoration controls almost as rigid as those of earlier Stuart rule were reintroduced, along with other powers designed to wipe out the Interregnum; although, like these, vested in Parliament rather than in royal or church authority. The reversal carried out by the new Licensing Acts was thorough-going, and perfectly conscious. Government bulletins replaced the various 'mercuries' (news-sheets) of the recent past, with the comment of the Licenser of the Press that 'a public mercury should never have my vote; it makes the multitude too familiar with the actions and counsels of their superiors'.[56]Sir Leoline Jenkins, Charles II's Secretary of State from 1680–4, a prime agent in the manoeuvres of those years to instal more absolute royal power, described printing as such, succinctly and disapprovingly, as 'a sort of appeal to the people'.[57]

The same opinion, from the opposite point of view, was put very clearly in an anonymous pamphlet of 1698 when, under the Williamite dispensation, freedom to print was again in dispute. The Stationers' monopoly had been abolished in 1695, and an Act of the following year limited the penalties for seditious printing, but the renewed output of topical prints that immediately followed produced a renewed demand for restriction, especially from the Church of England. To this the pamphlet, in the form of *A Letter to a Member of Parliament*, was a reply:

There's no medium between men's judging for themselves, and giving up their judgment to others. If the first be their duty, the Press ought not to be restrained, because it debars them from seeing those allegations by which they are to inform their judgments. All the arguments that are or can be urged for the regulating the Press have no other foundation than that of the People's being liable to mistake, and subject to be imposed on by fallacious arguments and specious pretences; which instead of proving what they design, only shows the greatest necessity for the freedom of the Press; for the more apt men are to mistake and to be deceived, the less reason there is for their relying on any one Party, but the more to examine with all care and diligence the reasons on all sides, and consequently for the Press being open to all Parties, one as well as the other.

By means of the Press, the writer said, the whole nation, unable 'to assemble in one room', could nevertheless partake in crucial debates,

... which ought not to be denied, as long as everyone in the nation has as much right, not only to judge for himself in religious, as any legislators can have to judge for him in civil matters, but is as much obliged to use all possible means to inform his judgement; and consequently there is as little reason to deny liberty of debating in one case as the other.[58]

Thus at the end of the turbulent century, with certain liberties established—though strictly limited—the writer, taking these for granted, was able to argue for their self-perpetuation: freedom of printing had brought about the liberation of conscience ('The Reformation,' he roundly asserted, 'is wholly owing to the Press') and ought to be maintained to protect its own consequences. It was no temporary expedient of revolutionaries, to be dropped when they themselves had achieved power, but must be a permanent feature of any free society, part of the very definition of such a society, and guarantee of its continuance. Whatever the reactions of Cromwellian, Restoration, and Williamite regimes, none of them overfond of a free Press, the principles on which 50 years earlier its proponents had based their then revolutionary case were become ideas generally, if not universally, received.

It is appropriate here to turn back to the classic statement of those principles, referred to (if not so often honoured) by succeeding ages whenever the issue of Press freedom and censorship has risen afresh. Milton wrote his *Areopagitica* in protest against the Parliamentary Order of 1643 reaffirming the Stationers' monopoly, and laying it down that no book 'shall from henceforth be printed or put to sale unless the same be first approved of and licensed by such person or persons as both or either of the said Houses [of Parliament] shall appoint for the licensing of the same'; granting authority for unlicensed presses to be searched out and destroyed, and for the arrest and examination of authors and printers responsible. His counter-offensive, embarked upon at the 'entreaties and persuasion' of many, took the whole dispute at once beyond consideration of particular 'scandals' or 'seditions' and into a statement of general ethical principles. Its terms are famous but worth repeating: that in the search for truth 'all opinions, yea errors, known, read, and collated, are of main service and assistance'; that 'good and evil we know in the field of this world grow up together almost inseparably' and must be encountered and chosen between freely: 'What wisdom can there be to choose, what continence to forbear, without the knowledge of evil?'

Milton's view of the world and of men is far from Utopian, indeed it is explicitly the reverse: 'To sequester out of the world into Atlantic and Utopian politics, which never can be drawn into use, will not mend our condition: but to ordain wisely as in this world of evil, in the midst of which God hath placed us unavoidably.' The Platonic expedient of banning 'bad' books and banishing such seditious persons as poets from the Republic will do nothing but multiply prohibitions, bringing with it 'so many other kinds of licensing as will make us all both ridiculous and weary, and yet frustrate'; 'if we think to regulate printing, thereby to rectify manners, we must regulate all recreations and pastimes, all that is delightful to man.' 'They are not skilful considerers of human things, who imagine to remove sin by removing the matter of sin.' It followed that censorship of all kinds is odious, absurd, and self-defeating.

It is not by 'a fugitive and cloistered virtue' that men will discover what is good, but by trial, and books 'promiscuously read' allow of it. There are certainly bad books, and books that may have bad influence; just because books are 'not absolutely dead things' they can be potent for evil as for good: 'I know they are as lively, and as vigorously productive, as those fabulous dragon's teeth; and being sown up and down, may chance to spring up armed men.' Yet it is necessary, without good reason to the contrary, to trust both author and reader: 'He who is not trusted with his own actions, his drift not being known to be evil and standing to the hazard of law and penalty, has no great argument to think himself reputed in the Commonwealth wherein he was born, for other than a fool or a foreigner.' Freedom of authorship and freedom of access to what has been written are not simply rights of citizenship but necessities; a man cannot be and act as a citizen without them.

Censorship will crush all originality, all adventurousness of thought: 'I hate a pupil teacher, I endure not an instructor that comes to me under the wardship of an overseeing fist. . . . The State shall be my governors, but not my critics.' It is just because men are roused by the spirit of inquiry, questioning all things, that they need no tutelage:

> Lords and Commons of England, consider what Nation it is whereof ye are, and whereof ye are governors: a Nation not slow and dull, but of a quick, ingenious and piercing spirit, acute to invent, subtle and sinewy to discourse, not beneath the reach of any point, the highest that human capacity can soar to.

Such in 1644 Milton conceived England to be, a 'nation of prophets', eager for knowledge and naturally disputatious: 'where there is much desire to learn, there of necessity will be much arguing, much writing, many opinions; for opinion in good men is but knowledge in the making.' He threw back in Parliament's teeth the objects for which they claimed to be fighting:

> Ye cannot make us now less capable, less knowing, less eagerly pursuing of the truth, unless ye first make yourselves, that made us so, less the lovers, less the founders of our true liberty. We can grow ignorant again, brutish, formal and slavish, as ye found us; but you then must first become that which ye cannot be, oppressive, arbitrary and tyrannic, as they were from whom ye have freed us.

So Milton, with just foreboding, looked ahead to the reinstatement of censorship. Although he tried flatteringly to pre-empt reaction by telling his Parliamentary audience that they could not so renege, one may guess that he realised quite well authority's antipathy to a free Press, and constant temptation to bring it under control. Milton's case against control was not, like the Levellers', a consciously democratic one; Milton, indeed, was no democrat. But he insisted, not only on the absurdity of leaving the decision, to print or not to print, 'to a few illiterate and illiberal individuals, who refuse their sanction to any work which contained views or sentiments at all above the level of the vulgar superstition', but on the need to trust the vulgar themselves in 'the general and brotherly search after Truth'. Difference, including what the orthodox call schism, is necessary: 'the perfection consists in this, that, out of many moderate varieties and brotherly dissimilitudes that are not vastly disproportional, arises the goodly and the graceful symmetry that commends the whole pile and structure.'[59]

The *Areopagitica* remained, and remains the most eloquent of all similar statements of principle, born out of a time of unprecedented and still scarcely paralleled use of print as the means of social self-questioning, but surviving into ages less urgent in inquiry and the need to speak. It was by no means alone, or even original in stating the case, as we have seen; but probably more than any other utterance it helped to fix in men's minds, for good or ill, the view that freedom of printing is a fundamental underpinning of all other rights in a free society. Samuel Hartlib, Milton's mentor and friend, had foreseen how 'the art of printing will so spread knowledge that the common people, knowing their own rights and liberties, will not be governed by way of oppression'.[60] Milton himself made it the supreme claim of the individual: 'Give me the liberty to know, to utter, and to argue freely according to conscience, above all liberties.'

III
WORDS ON THE MARKET

THE printed word emerges in the course of the seventeenth century, and especially in England, as the means above all others of generalised public discussion and the free exchange of ideas. The art of printing as such may have made more advances on the Continent, particularly in France, but its application, under strictly centralised royal control, was circumscribed. In England, both during and after the Civil Wars, in Scotland on a much smaller scale, and also throughout the century in the newly established Dutch Republic, printing and political freedom were very closely linked; the unrestricted use of print was firmly associated with 'democracy', a word coming into use at the same time, if in most cases with extreme abhorrence. At the same time the multiplication of print was bringing about another and quite different effect which was, perhaps, no less of an innovation, namely the transformation of writing—of 'literature in its most general sense'—into a commodity.

Books, of course, had been bought and sold before ever they were printed. They were often objects of great value, prized as much for the handiwork embodied in them—the long and exquisite labour of scribes and illuminators—as for their content. It may be thought that the same is sometimes true today, yet even the most sumptuous of coffee-table books, designed to be looked at rather than read, can scarcely excite the same feeling in its possessor as did once a fine Book of Hours. Whatever may be achieved and claimed by typographers and illustrators, if books are valued now as 'works of art', they are so in a different way; the artificial price-inflations of rarity apart, their marketable value is attached to writing itself, and only as a very subordinate consideration to how it is reproduced.

It is amusing and instructive to be told how the aristocratic connoisseur of books looked down his nose, to begin with, on the crude products of 'artificial writing'. The Duke of Urbino in 1490, we are told, took a special pride in his library in which 'all books were superlatively good and written with the pen; had there been one printed book, it would have been ashamed in such company'. A little earlier, in 1479, the future Pope Julius II went so far as to have a classical text copied by a scribe from a recently printed source; in fidelity to his master-copy the copyist even reproduced the printer's colophon, only changing the new-fangled term 'impressit' to 'scripsit'.[61] There could hardly be a more striking instance of the superstitious reverence attached to form rather than use.

It can be said that in overcoming such attitudes print raised the dignity of letters: the eccentricities of bibliophiles apart, books have been freed from their quasi-magical status as material objects. It is what is in them that matters, and print, by eliminating any adventitious human agency between the reader and the spoken word, has made this immaterial essence—the verbalised thought of the writer, neutrally recorded—absolutely general and clear. It has been maintained, indeed, that the idea of authorship in its modern sense and with the present prestige attached to it, is itself the creation of printing: 'the author, in medieval times, was little accounted of',[62] and the development of 'style' and personal originality was, it is argued, impossible when books were handwritten, to be read aloud, and when much poetry in particular was never written down at all.

The notion that an author had, in his own work, a saleable commodity was new and strange, for 'the production of literature was largely dependent on patronage' and not on any market. 'The ideas that we associate with such terms as "plagiarism", "copyright", or "author's rights" simply did not exist and were not likely to exist until the invention of Printing.'

The word 'style', derived from 'stylus', belongs in origin to handwriting, and in transference to printed literature has altered its meaning. Just because the reproduction of men's words[63] became standardised and uniform in print, all individuality was concentrated in their content, which was fixed once for all: 'The more standardised the type . . . the more compelling the sense of an idiosyncratic personal self.'[64] What was in print, though it might be changed deliberately in successive editions, was no longer subject to the subtle and continuous change of oral-scribal transmission. If writers at all times seek immortality through their words, the drive takes a different direction: 'The wish to see one's work in print (fixed forever with one's name in card files and anthologies) is different from the desire to pen lines that would never get fixed in permanent form, might be lost forever, altered by copying, or—if truly memorable—be carried by oral transmission, and assigned ultimately to "anon".'[65] Writing, or 'making' of any sort with words, thus underwent change which was at once diffusive and narrowing, both tending towards greater abstraction from personal communication and becoming reified, turned into a 'thing' which an individual might call his own, and which, furthermore, could be bought and sold.

Print, bringing words into the market-place as never before, created a new interest in them, the interest of property; it became increasingly important to know whose property they were. The use of words was progressively altered and eventually transformed thereby; it has also been claimed that the market itself was set on a new course. With the advent of printing, it is said, supply for sale took a decisive new step, marked—even while printing was still a craft, carried on by highly skilled individuals on a small scale—by the application of repetitive mechanised processes and the potentiality, if not yet the fact, of mass-production. Printing very rapidly became a trade, and followed trade in its spread: that is, the new presses which proliferated with such extraordinary rapidity in fifteenth-century Europe were concentrated for the most part in centres of already flourishing trade and commerce.

A notable example was the Imperial city of Nuremberg, described as the commercial hub of central Europe, a centre of banking and merchandise and also of many well-organised craft industries. The first printer's shop was established there in 1470, set up by one Anton Koberger (1445–1513) and developed by him into a large-scale enterprise almost of modern proportions: he combined (as did many of the early printers) publishing and bookselling with printing itself, and at one time in his career is recorded as running 24 presses, with more than 100 compositors and other workers in his employment. He was also—an indication of social links connecting art, craftsmanship, commerce and religion—the godfather of Albrecht Dürer. He acquired interests elsewhere, in partnership or business association with other printer-publishers or by setting up agents of his own; the catalogue of his firm, covering output over thirty years, lists more than 200 titles, most of them substantial volumes.[66] Though it did not survive Koberger himself, it was clearly a very considerable business, with many of the marks of a thrusting international capitalism; books enjoyed, and for long continued to enjoy, a seller's market.

The mere novelty of printed books produced what has been called an 'infatuation' of the public not, perhaps, unlike that with which television was taken up 500 years later; like TV, print proved to be no passing fashion but an innovation very soon to become indispensable; and like TV an attractive source of profit for those supplying it. In the early years of printing books were certainly not cheap in relation to other goods; but it was now possible to make the comparison, of one marketable commodity against others, which was scarcely possible for their handwritten predecessors. Grandees both temporal and ecclesiastic might still prize these most and continue for a short period to commission them, but such tastes were already an aristocratic eccentricity. Printed books—which were, according to contemporary account, among the chief goods on offer at fairs—found ready buyers among people of lesser means; not yet the poor, of course, though artisans and tradesmen, as well as the rising burghers of the towns, might be among them; scholars, previously almost bound to confine their studies to the contents of (usually monastic) libraries, might now aspire to own many books of their own.

To supply this market the trade of bookseller sprang up, to begin with and indeed for long thereafter combined or interchangeable with the business of printing. A printer might be the owner of little more than his skill and a set of type, ready to move wherever his craft was in demand—a mobility which undoubtedly accelerated the spread of printing in its earliest years. But increasingly he became a man of capital, his investment being both in machinery and trained employees and in a stock of books, the products of his own and other presses. Koberger of Nuremberg began as printer and bookseller but in later years he left printing and book manufacture and concentrated on the commission and marketing of books: the rivalry and pressure of the guilds, forcing him into one trade only, thus produced the first general publisher.

At the other end of the scale, an example may be taken from Scotland, where James IV was anxious in this as in other respects to catch up with the Continent. It was a bookseller and publisher, Andrew Myllar, to whom he turned in 1508 to set up, with Walter Chepman, the first Scottish press. The royal monopoly granted to Chepman and Myllar was in the first place for a particular piece of work, the production of a new Latin breviary; the press was to serve the purposes of government, secular and ecclesiastic. It is remarkable nevertheless—and has often been cited as evidence of Scotland's true taste in literature—that though Chepman and Myllar were granted their privilege by James for 'imprenting within our Realme of the bukes of our Lawis, acts of parliament, cronicles, mess bukes', the earliest surviving products of their original Southgait press are ballads and other pieces of poetry, including contemporary work by Henryson and Dunbar. Myllar was the technician, a dealer in books who had also learned printing (in France). Chepman was the man who put up the money, a merchant-burgess of Edinburgh—'a man of capital and property, a speculative, money-making man'[67]—who dealt in a variety of merchandise, from timber to textiles; from his point of view no doubt the opportunity to share in the production of state and church papers and (to quote the royal patent again) 'al utheris bukis that salbe sene necessar, and to sel the sammyn for competent prices', was a matter of business.

Some examples may be given of book-prices in England during the first hundred years of printing: the *Canterbury Tales* was sold at 5s. bound or 3s. unbound, with no change in price, from 1492 to 1545 (when debasement of the coinage and consequent inflation began to take effect); Roger Ascham's *Scholemaster* sold at 6d. a copy in 1573; Hakluyt's *Voyages*, 11s. 11d. in 1589; Holinshed's *Chronicles*, 26s. in 1577; Hooker's *Ecclesiasticall Politie*, 6s. 6d., unbound, in 1597; Lyly's *Euphues*, 2s., unbound, in 1581; North's rendering of *Plutarch's Lives*, 14s. in 1579; Shakespeare's *Venus and Adonis*, 1s. in 1573.[68]

Returning again to Scotland, more of the economics, including the hazards of early printing enterprise, may be learned from the post-Reformation years when, so far as surviving books and records show, the trade greatly expanded. Robert Lekpruik, who for a time was virtually official printer to the Reformed Church—one of his first productions being the *Confession of Faith* in 1561—seems to have been a man without capital of his own, largely dependent on patronage. In 1562 the General Assembly is recorded as having voted him £200 to buy 'irns' (i.e. type), ink and paper and to hire craftsmen 'for printing of the Psalms', and although appointed King's Printer five years later he evidently carried on his business hand to mouth, petitioning the Assembly for help or complaining of poverty on different occasions.

After 1570 the politics of the time overtook him: as a supporter of the 'King's Men' and printer of George Buchanan's satires he was forced to flee Edinburgh on the temporary rise of the 'Queen's Men', and set up shop successively in Stirling and St Andrews. Subsequently, like so many others, he fell foul of authority by printing without a license—a Licensing Act having been in force, at least nominally, since 1551—and deprived of property and privileges. His successor Thomas Bassandyne made a contrary movement, having earlier been a partisan of the Queen and denounced as a rebel, but established by 1574 as associate with a fellow-burgess of Edinburgh, Alexander Arbuthnet, for the large enterprise of printing the Bible (a reprint of the Geneva Bible), the first to be produced in Scotland. The proposals before the General Assembly set the price in advance as £4. 13s. 4d. (Scots); the clergy and other officers of the church ('Bishops, superintendents and Commissioners') were charged with the task of collecting orders from every parish and burgh, advance payments to be made over to 'the said Alexander and Thomas'. A little later, when the Privy Council took a hand in the arrangements, estimated costs had risen to £5 a copy, with the expectation that 'the charge and hasard will be great and sumptouse'. In fact it was not until 1579 that the Bibles were delivered, by which time Bassandyne himself was dead.

His will is an interesting indication not only of his general standing—he died a rich man by the standards of the time—but of the value of his assets as printer and bookseller. Nearly ¾ of his 'free geir' were in books and printing material, amounting to a total of £1415. 10s. 8d. The inventory of his stock of books, including copies of 350 different works, itemises the prices of each title, bound and unbound. Thus there are listed 505 copies of the works of Sir David Lyndsay, 3s. each unbound or 4s. bound; a Greek New Testament at 10s.; a book of Psalms ('of littel volume') 5s.; large numbers of Latin classic texts varying in price from 5s. to 10s.; a great variety of Humanist and Reformed works, from the *Colloquies* of Erasmus at 6d. to a Testament of Beza at 8s. unbound; a Greek alphabet, 4d. and an Italian grammar, 2s. 6d.; an *Art of Logic*, 6s.; Stow's *Chronicles*, 22s.; an *Imitation of Christ*, 6s.; *The hundreth myrrie taillis*, 16d.; a *Piers Plowman*, 6s.; *The Buke of Witchcraft*, 3s.; a Lute-book, 4s.; Skelton's *Tales*, 8d.; the English *Book of Common Prayer*, 6s; the *Institutions* of Calvin, 'in Frensche', 13s. Paper stocks are also listed, 'fyne litill paper' at 13s. a ream, 'fyne lumbard paper', 4s. a quire, 'fyne braid paper' 30s. a ream, 'lang paper' at the same price; together with £10 worth of printing ink and turpentine, material and apparatus for bookbinding, and the stock of type itself, 'thrie scour stane wecht of prenting irnes' valued at 240 marks.[69]

Similar testamentory inventories at the end of the century add further detail of contemporary prices, and also of the size, often surprisingly large, of imprints not only of Bibles, catechisms, and other books connected with the rule of the newly-established Church, but of secular and even profane works. Among the stock-in-trade left by John Ross, printer in Edinburgh 1574-80 were 200 copies of John Rolland's *Seven Sages* and 280 of Gavin Douglas's *Palace of Honour*. Ross's successor Henry Charteris, bookseller and printer, had on his hands when he died in 1599 122 copies of the epic of *Wallace*, 788 of Lyndsay's *Poems*, recently published in a new edition, and 554 of Henryson's *Cresseid*; the prices of single copies were 10s., 8s. and 4d. respectively. Robert Charteris, Henry's son, who carried on the business from his father's death to his own in 1610, had in stock at one time (itemised in an inventory of 1603) 500 copies of Lyndsay's *Satyre of the Thrie Estaitis*, 4s. each.[70]

There was money in the early book trade, though not very much for authors, whose rewards were of course entirely unprotected by copyright. Mere authorship in itself paid little, nor was even the contemporary fame of a writer—though print greatly enhanced such individualised celebrity, as has been mentioned—likely to bring wealth of itself. If Shakespeare died quite a wealthy man, who had bought his way into property and the status of a gentleman, that was thanks to his shareholding in theatrical enterprise and not because he was esteemed as a poet. Milton, in a famous instance a little later, showed the often inverse proportion between literary eminence and financial gain: booksellers and publishers have not been allowed to forget the £10 (with a further £8 for his widow after his death) that he received for *Paradise Lost* in 1667. (Twenty-two years earlier his publisher Henry Moseley had remarked in a prefatory note to the *Poems Upon Several Occasions*—which he had brought out, he said, for the love of literature alone, and not from 'any respect of gain'—how 'the slightest Pamphlet is nowadays more remarkable than the Works of learnedst men'. It is doubtful whether, despite this sour observation, the great outburst of pamphleteering at the time made anyone's fortune, though some printers may have done well enough out of it, especially if they could keep clear of political entanglement in what they were putting out; it is recorded of at least one long-lived and adaptable entrepreneur, Henry Hills, that he was successively printer to the Parliamentary Army, the Anabaptists, the Rump Parliament, to Cromwell as Lord Protector, and after the Restoration to Charles II and James II.[71] But many of the tracts and pamphlets which have proved of greatest interest to posterity were printed by men who were partisans of the cause; many were distributed free.

Beside pamphleteering, however, and even more copious in output, there was other work for printers during this period which may truly be called popular, and which certainly was produced for the market. Together with the Bible, the broadsides or broadsheets (i.e. printed on one side only of a single sheet) provided probably the chief reading-matter of the bulk of a semi-literate population throughout the sixteenth and seventeenth centuries; their number, indeed, is part of the evidence for the spread of literacy, though their content (again, like the Bible) reached many who could not read. Usually in verse, in the form of the so-called broadside ballad, they gave 'the common people' both in town and country something very different from what was to be had in books, colloquial, racy, frequently sensational, and as a rule either genuinely topical in subject-matter or purporting to be so. The earliest example of such a ballad in print—for, of course, there were certainly plenty of topical songs in circulation by word of mouth before printing arrived—is *A Ballade of the Scottyshe Kinge*, a triumphant not to say scurrilous English account of the Battle of Flodden, printed in 1513, and very many of the 'great events' of the succeeding 200 years were used in the same way.

During Elizabeth's reign, when broadside balladry in England probably reached its peak—'as characteristic a production of the Elizabethan age as the court lyric and the drama'[72]—there were in the single year of 1569–70 no fewer than 100 ballads registered at Stationers' Hall, the greater part of them dealing with the Northern Earls' Rising in 1569; and other years were not wanting in similarly rousing matter for balladry. Battles, massacres, royal occasions from the accessions of Mary Tudor (greeted from the Roman Catholic point of view) and of her half-sister five years later (from the Protestant) to the restoration of Charles II were regularly celebrated in ballads. Private scandal and crime, especially the more notorious murder-cases, provided further material; together with much else—pathetic tales of true and false love, ghost and fairy-stories, drinking songs and (a large category) bawdry—that might be classed as fiction, if such categorisation were not wholly alien to the mode.

Ballads were used, like pamphlets, for political and religious propaganda, official and otherwise. Edifying examples and pious homily occur largely in surviving collections, including, again, historical incident—the profession of the Protestant martyr Anne Askew on the one hand, or the execution and witness of the Jesuit martyr Thewlis on the other—as well as what would now be thought of simply as hymns: many of *The Gude and Godlie Ballatis* published as a book in Scotland in 1567 are likely to have circulated earlier in broadcasting form. Ballads, like pamphlets, might be reckoned seditious; the familiar attempts to impose control extended to 'printed ballads, rhymes, and songs' in the England of Henry VIII; towards the end of the century men were from time to time (two in 1579) hanged for publishing satirical balladry; ballad-sellers as well as printers turn up regularly in the judicial record of the seventeenth century as being set in the stocks or whipped or suffering other punishment.

Nor must it be supposed that such measures were mere arbitrary tyranny; a topical ballad with a catchy tune could and on some occasions undoubtedly did spread a political idea more rapidly than any more formal communication. That James II was sung out of his kingdom by *Lilliburlero* is doubtless an exaggeration; but about the same time Fletcher of Saltoun was in earnest when he said that if a man might write the ballads of a nation he need not trouble about writing the laws.

Authorship was almost as varied as content. Many ballads were by identifiable writers, including some, such as the Elizabethan Thomas Deloney, chiefly known for work of this kind; Deloney (who also wrote what would now be called novels) is believed to have been the author of some 50 ballads printed between 1586 and 1596. Others were by men ordinarily thought of as catering for more sophisticated readers, from Henry VIII's court poet John Skelton, who wrote the ballad of Flodden already mentioned, to

Marlowe and, in the next century, Marvell. In the absence of copyright there was nothing to prevent a promising poem being lifted for broadsheet use, as happened in the case of Marlowe's 'Come live with me and be my love', which was combined with Raleigh's sceptical reply to make a single broadside.

But the greater part of this street literature was and remains anonymous; and of this perhaps the most interesting is the considerable number in surviving collections which are versions of a much older popular poetry, handed on formerly in oral tradition. Many of the Robin Hood ballads, songs sung to this day such as 'The Golden Vanitie', or the immeasurably old and magical like the riddling duologue of 'The Elfin Knight', with its roots in the furthest reaches of European mythology, found their way into print from the sixteenth century down to the nineteenth, when Dickens recorded, and Cruikshank illustrated, as 'The Loving Ballad of Young Bateman', the story of Young Beichan, a legend of the Crusades harking back at least to the thirteenth century. In many cases the broadsheet version is the earliest written record of a ballad which there is every reason to believe is much older; such examples can usually be shown (by comparison with other versions verbally handed down) as in one way or another corrupt. Print became, in a word, a means of preserving and redistributing a very ancient popular art-form, and usually, it seems, the art suffered in the process, but it did not end there, for a broadside might in itself become a 'traditional' song which in turn would pass back into print.

Broadsheet literature occupies, therefore, a curious and ambiguous position in the story of print, with at least half of its foundations in a popular culture quite removed from 'book-learning'. Ballads were bought by men and women who never read a book, unless it was the Bible, and were passed on by recitation to others who could not read at all. By means of print a new ballad could become known rapidly to a large number of people, and its novelty was an important selling point; that it was newly made, 'an excellent new ballad', a record of some event 'but lately' occurred, with the assurance of a frequently most improbable veracity, ' 'tis very true and also new', was the usual claim. Yet what was thereby transmitted, whether in the circumstantial account of 'a most sad and dreadful frost and snow, which happened on the 23rd of December, 1684' or 'The Londoner's Lamentation' for the Great Fire of 1666, or 'a proper new ballad intituled The Wand'ring Prince of Troy'[73] can hardly have been news in the absolute sense of something hitherto unheard of.

Word of mouth must still easily have outstripped print; and what was in print was taken up and spread further by word of mouth. Though certainly

a form of communication, and it would probably not be stretching the term
too much to call it mass-communication, the printed ballads stand so doubt-
fully between an old mode and a new that it is by no means clear what was
being communicated. The ballads were not meant to be read, but sung.
They were frequently highly moralistic in tone, but they were bought for
pleasure—'pleasant' is the most common quality, along with newness,
claimed in ballad-titles—and not, like a pamphlet, for instruction. They
provided, in a word, entertainment. They were sold along with fairground
gew-gaws, ribbons and laces, small items of personal finery, the cheap
luxuries of the poor. Their sale was an organised business, whether
directly from bookshops (commonly at a penny a sheet) or by itinerant
ballad-mongers, both men and women. These street sellers were themselves performers or entertainers, and regarded by authority as such. After
the Restoration they were, along with every other outlet for print, subject
to licensing, and the issue of licences was in itself a source of profit: it is
recorded that a Master of the Revels in Charles II's reign, Sir Charles
Killigrew, farmed out his licensing privilege to London Booksellers.

Some sixty years earlier Shakespeare's Autolycus provided a vivid picture
of the ballad-monger at work among rustic customers, with some interesting sidelights on popular attitudes. (It is naturally assumed that ballad-
sellers are rogues). The ballads in Autolycus's pack, when he comes to the
shearing-fair, are more sought after than all his ribbons and gloves ('We'll
buy the other things anon,' says the Clown), and samples are quickly forth-
coming: one 'to a very doleful tune, how a usurer's wife was brought to bed
of 20 money-bags at a burthen' and 'another ballad of a fish that appeared
on the coast on Wednesday the fourscore of April, 40,000 fathom above
water, and sang this ballad against the hard hearts of maids'. Allowing for
satirical exaggeration, both are fair examples of a common type of broadsheet tale of wonder, including the testimonials of authenticity—'Here's the
midwife's name to 't', 'Five justices' hands at it, and witnesses more than my
pack will hold'—with which Autolycus answers the shepherdess's inquiry,
'Is it true, think you?' They were easily convinced, being persuaded in
advance that print was in itself reliable: 'Pray now, buy some,' says Mopsa
to her swain. 'I love a ballad in print o' life, for then we are sure they are
true.'

Incredible stories were true because they were in print, and they were
saleable because they were true. These two factors were to work together
to bring about extraordinary transformations: in many obvious respects
the ballad-sheets of the sixteenth and seventeenth centuries fore-shadowed
the popular newspapers of the nineteenth and twentieth. The line of

descent was not direct, however; the broadsheet ballads were an early demonstration of printing's potentialities which was not taken up for 200 years. In many ways their links were stronger with the past of oral tradition than with the mass-prints of the future, and they were in more than one sense strongly conservative. They preserved ancient forms (while at the same time altering and corrupting them); and in a political sense, though they could, as has been noted, be seditious, they were rarely revolutionary in implication in the way many pamphlets were at the same time. (It is true that the Diggers and other revolutionary groups in the mid-seventeenth century had their own special songs, but these were not ballads properly speaking.)

The ballads were indeed a quite inappropriate medium for political discussion, or for conveying 'serious' ideas of any kind; for these—a consequence in part of the whole evolution of printed communication—prose was, increasingly, the only possible mode. The age of the broadsheet ballads was also the age, admittedly, of much of the greatest English poetry, from Shakespeare to Milton, and culminating in what may be allowed as the supreme verse-epic of the English language; and no one, probably, will say that *Paradise Lost* is not 'serious'. But it is so in a way quite different from that of, say, Hobbes's *Leviathan* or Locke's *Of Human Understanding*; or, even, such of Milton's own prose writing as *Areopagitica*. Verse was suitable for conveying feeling, especially that which was beginning to be categorised as 'the sublime'; but prose alone could deal with *facts*. Thus crudely stated, the division of function seems crass, and doubtless calls for qualification; but it was certainly a very general assumption by the end of the seventeenth century, and may parenthetically be advanced as one of the reasons why Milton's most exalted poetry has seemed to many too lofty by half, elevated quite above the level of 'real life'.

The connection of this assumption with popular communication is something to return to later. In the meantime, and before considering the growth of newspapers themselves, it may be useful to look briefly at another manifestation of the same verse-prose division, referring to one exemplar in particular.

Towards the end of the seventeenth century the word 'novel' begins to be used in the modern sense, as describing a work of prose fiction; Dryden, who seems to have been the first to speak of fictitious narratives as novels, attached it indifferently to both prose and verse.[74] At the same time it still meant something 'new', or more simply news; and the meanings were confused or combined in early examples of the genre. The 'origins of the novel' are highly debatable, and can be taken back almost as far as you like, according to taste; but for present purposes it may be assumed at least that a novel was almost always in prose, and that it reached its public as a printed book. The two things were connected: whatever prodigious feats of memory were possible in the case of verse romance, it is scarcely possible that lengthy works of prose can be so committed and transmitted, and it was precisely the advent of print that made their widespread communication feasible. (It is true that under special circumstances human memory appears to have no limits: for instance, in the thirteenth century the Waldensian heretics were accused of knowing the whole Bible by heart.[75] But that was under peculiar stress; a novel will rarely be taken into the mind with such extreme urgency.)

Such early 'novels' as *The Unfortunate Traveller* of Thomas Nashe or the prose stories already mentioned by the Elizabethan balladeer Thomas Deloney are 'news' in the sense of describing surprising events, presented as actualities, and they are also entertainments. The two qualities are much more strikingly combined a little more than 100 years later in the works of a writer who for more than one reason occupies a key position in the entire development under examination, Daniel Defoe. Whether or not Defoe is, as he has often been called, 'the father of the English novel', or whether he is thought of chiefly as a journalist, his place in the story is of great importance, and by reason of his enormous output and the protean variety of his talents, might almost be called unique. In mere volume he wrote most, probably, as a journalist, bringing out his weekly *Review* continuously for nearly ten years and engaging besides in many other shorter-lived enterprises, sometimes in disguise. He was at different times, and often simultaneously, pamphleteer, descriptive writer, and economist; his activity as novelist, the chief foundation of his subsequent fame, was during a comparatively short period—from 1719 to 1724—of more than forty years of writing. But his fictions are not readily to be distinguished from his other writing: all was presented as fact, the transmission of practical knowledge and the record of actual events, and his success in carrying this out was such that to this day it is not clear to his readers (as a modern commentator puts it) 'how much he really knew and how much he simply made up'.[76] Very much of his work would today be classed as 'faction', a mixture of report and invention; long before *Robinson Crusoe*, in *The Apparition of Mrs. Veal* (1706) he set a puzzle which still provokes dispute, whether this apparently sober true relation, as 'factual' as ever was set down by a member of the Society for Psychical Research, was written in good faith by a sincere believer in ghosts or by a man who knew what would catch the public eye, and who had already mastered the art of circumstantial tale-telling.

Defoe was, to put it bluntly, a consummate liar, in print and also perhaps (as undercover agent for government, notably during the murky approaches to the Union of 1707) in other ways. He was an expert in disguise; so much so, and so persistently, covering the origins of his fiction and presenting every kind of writing as other than what it was, that it not only got him into trouble—when his ironic imitation of extreme High Toryism was taken for genuine opinion—but might be termed an obsession. Its roots were doubtless personal and need not concern us, except perhaps to remark that the urge towards masquerade and deception, to spy upon the world, seems to have a permanent share in what may be called the psychology of journalism; the more so, maybe, when combined with just such a plain, downright, 'matter-of-fact' manner of reporting the results as Defoe used with such effortless skill.

When in 1718, having suffered a setback as a political journalist, Defoe turned to large-scale invention, his success was immediate and enormous. The early publishing history of *The Life and Strange Surprising Adventures of Robinson Crusoe* is very much like that of a modern best-selling novel, including serialisation before appearance as a book, in a daily newspaper, the *London Post*. Within five years, Defoe had produced among other books six more which today are considered novels, although the distinction would not have meant much to him nor immediately to most of his readers. His 'histories' and fictitious 'journals', 'lives', and 'memoirs' of men and women who never existed deceived many at the time and in some cases for years to come; only quite recently has one of his last fabrications, *The Military Memoirs of Captain George Carleton* (which quite took in Samual Johnson, among others) been firmly identified as unaided work, an extremely plausible account of what might have happened to a soldier of fortune but did not.

All the time, drawing upon his very extensive knowledge of men and affairs, and moving smoothly from a slightly altered or adapted fact to pure fancy, he was or claimed to be conveying information and moral instruction. Probably it did not matter greatly to him if a particular deception was detected; 'unabash'd De Foe', as Pope called him, survived worse than mere exposure as a liar. For a writer of such unceasing productivity the immediate effect was what mattered, with the combined reward of gaining attention, propagating certain ideas (though this often with the most remarkable, self-defeating ambiguity) and making money.

To make money was for Defoe not only desirable but a matter of principle. As a fervent partisan of commercial society, of which trade was the operative mechanism and desire for profit the driving force—the spring of 'the whole machine call'd man' (*The Commentator*, 1720)—he believed in money as 'the general dominating article in the world', to be sought before all else: a man's most precious assets were 'money, friends, and health', in that order. The point is not that Defoe was abnormally avaricious nor, of course, that he was alone in writing for money, but rather that he was more completely conscious of it than others; he was perhaps the first author to think of his work unequivocally in such terms. For him writing was 'a very considerable branch of English commerce'; writers were primary producers of a saleable article. With this formulation the history of printing (upon which, needless to say, the transformation of writing into merchandise was wholly dependent) took a decisive turn.

No doubt there were other and perhaps stronger motives for the writing of *Robinson Crusoe*, conscious and unconscious. Defoe himself claimed for it (afterwards) the purpose of moral instruction; it seems at some points even to embody criticism of the money-system. 'Money, O Drug!' exclaims Crusoe when it is no use to him on his island; he ends up, however, like most of Defoe's heroes and heroines, very comfortably off. The book can be seen as many things, as an allegory of Protestant individualism, as a path-finder of colonialism, as a study in the operations of self-isolation, fear and guilt. It is certainly not a simple commercial success-story, but equally certainly it shows the author's conviction, which he expects his readers to share, that getting money, by any means, is the most interesting thing in the world.

The approved means, in this and other stories, are usually by having something to sell, including oneself. Defoe does not of course commend Moll Flanders or Roxana for making their way and their fortunes by pros-titution, but he exhibits it in a curiously neutral light which has been noted as a sign of 'modern' toleration and understanding. It may be so; but what strikes one about these transactions, and what does indeed remove from them any suspicion of pornography, is that when Moll or Roxana 'falls' again, or is taken up by a new protector, interest is concentrated almost entirely on what she gets by it (i.e. the monetary reward) and not on what she gives. In this respect it may not be unfair to claim that such a 'fortunate Mistress' was Defoe's true Muse.

There are many ways of writing for the market, to be sure. It is not surprising, in Defoe's world and bearing in mind his assumptions about it, to find him emphasising the solid usefulness of his wares: information, practical instruction, facts, and all in the most plain unpretentious style. In his Preface to *Roxana* he claims a difference in her narrative from others of the kind 'in this Great and Essential Article, Namely, that the Foundation of

This is laid in Truth of Fact; and so the Work is not a Story, but a History'. Elsewhere, in *The Compleat English Gentleman*, he expatiates upon the attractions of travel writings, by which a reader 'may make the tour of the world in books', and which are 'not profitable only and improving, but delightful and pleasant too, to the last degree. No romances, plays, or diverting stories can be equally entertaining to a man of sense.' He did not find it necessary to say how convincingly a romance or diverting story might imitate the genuine article. It is taken for granted that the gentleman-reader, who is also a man of sense, wants facts; yet in practice—and more easily, perhaps, by someone of Defoe's particular talents—he could well be satisfied with fiction. And though in this instance Defoe was thinking of a particular sort of reader, for whom books might, so to speak, be custom-built, it was the unlimited scope of books of all sorts that struck him more. He liked to think of himself speaking, in his books, in plain terms, as man to man, and in a manner accessible to all, and more effectively than the most eloquent of orators: 'Preaching of sermons,' he said, 'is speaking to a few of mankind: printing of books is talking to the whole world' (*The Storm*, 1704). He had a vision, even before the huge success of *Robinson Crusoe*, of the mass-market.

It may be instructive at this point to compare *Robinson Crusoe* with another immediately and lastingly popular work which shares in many ways the same background of social assumptions and nonconformist or dissenting affiliations, *The Pilgrim's Progress*. The two are separated by forty years and (in a time of rapid change) important political/social developments: Defoe was born in the year of Charles II's restoration, and lived into the reign of George II; Bunyan, born under Charles I, fought as a youth in the Civil Wars, was imprisoned under the second Charles, and died in the year of the 'Glorious Revolution', 1688. Both men suffered (if scarcely in like degree) as dissenters; both shared, at least superficially, the same general views of this world and the next—the first as a place of trial and effort, the other one of eternal reward or punishment. Each wrote a book incorporating his world-view, which—together with others, but supremely—became, and has remained, a 'household word', a lasting component of popular culture. Together these must be among the most widely read of all books in English during the past three centuries and, having been translated into many other languages, are known all over the world; both must be known by their titles at least to millions who have never read them. They may both be read in much the same way, as adventure-stories, and perhaps by children—among the most enthusiastic of their readers from the beginning—they usually are. Yet if they now seem

to belong on equal terms to a stage in the history of prose fiction, their
origins and significance in that history are very different. They embody
assumptions about communication which point in divergent directions.

Robinson Crusoe is a fake 'real-life story', its principal object, for all the
moralisings incorporated in it, being simply to communicate itself. The
expectation is that 'strange surprising adventures', if they actually have
taken place, are in themselves a pleasure to read as vicarious experience. Its
ancestry is not only in the more of less factual traval-books on which Defoe
drew and which he imitated, but in the street literature already briefly
noticed, which drew attention by relating astonishing anecdotes, testifying
however implausibly to their truth. Between Autolycus assuring his rustic
audience that his preposterous ballad-histories are 'very pitiful and as true',
and Defoe, with vastly greater sophistication, supplying his tales with
convincing touches of verisimilitude, there is a direct link.

The Pilgrim's Progress is also linked, even more directly and closely, with
the anonymous literature of broadsides, chapbooks—those rudely printed
collections of old tales and wonders which were also part of a pedlar's
stock-in-trade from the sixteenth century on—and the 'emblem books'
which displayed pictorical symbols of virtues and vices. Bunyan's own
grandfather, a travelling tradesman like himself, must have carried such in
his pedlar's pack. The story of Christian's trials on his pilgrim's way clearly
owes much to this repertory of printed folk-lore and also, surely, to sources
much older than print: not only were the tales themselves, of giants and
hobgoblins and supernatural helpers, still current in oral tradition, but the
whole allegorical scheme harks back to older modes of religious
exhortation and homily, well used before the Reformation. (The opening of
the *Progress*, 'As I walked through the wilderness of this world I lighted on
a certain place where was a den, and laid me down in that place to sleep;
and, as I slept; I dreamed a dream' is very near to that of the fourteenth-
century poem of *Piers Plowman*, whose author tells how, walking 'wide in
the world/wonders to hear', he lies down to sleep and 'Then began I to
dream/a marvellous dream, That I was in a wilderness/wist I not where'. It
is tempting to suppose that Bunyan knew something of this poem; yet he
cannot have read it, for it was not printed till the nineteenth century.)

Bunyan looked back consciously to the tradition of parable and allegory,
and his attitude to 'true report' is quite different from Defoe's, at once more
primitive—that is to say rooted in response to types of story-telling much
older than print—and more refined. Much of his prefatory 'Apology' for the
Progress is an answer to objections that he is not telling a factual story, that
'metaphors make us blind' and lack the proper 'solidity' of a responsible

writer dealing with serious matters. Bunyan answers not only that he has precedent and example in Scripture, including that of Christ himself; he offers a view of religious (or poetic) truth and its mode of operation which for subtlety and penetration has hardly been bettered by later philosophers of art.

> Truth, though in swaddling clouts [i.e. in the form of a parable] I find
> Informs the judgment, rectifies the mind;
> Pleases the understanding, makes the will
> Submit; the memory too it doth fill
> With what doth our imaginations please:
> Likewise it tends our troubles to appease. . . .

And he sums up this verse prologue with an exact account of the way that literary art works upon the mind just because it is known not to be the literal truth:

> . . . wouldst thou see
> A man i' the clouds, and hear him speak to thee?
> Wouldst thou be in a dream and yet not sleep?
> Or wouldst thou in a moment laugh and weep?
> Wouldest thou lose thyself and catch no harm,
> And find thyself again without a charm?
> Wouldst read thyself, and read thou knowest not what,
> And yet know whether thou are blest or not,
> By reading the same lines? . . .

That is the way, he says, that true meanings can be conveyed, to 'head and heart', which merely factual narrative cannot encompass. Still less can it be done, of course, by a narrative which merely masquerades as fact. His remark about 'lies in silver shrines' might very well be applied to Defoe.

Both Bunyan and Defoe were immensely popular writers, in their own lifetimes as after their deaths. Both were able to use the opportunities provided by a changing society, the spread of literacy, the increasing privacy of at least middle-class life, circumstances favourable to development of the novel. Both contributed to that development; the best known works of both might very well be found side by side on the shelves of a new reading public for whom a 'story', whether supposedly factual or avowed invention, was not something told publicly to a group of persons but read by individuals on their own. Yet though they stand close together, and may be read by the same person with something of the same pleasure, they look in different directions.

Not ideologically, since both Bunyan and Defoe shared most of the ideas and assumptions of Puritanism; it was rather in their attitude to what they were doing. Bunyan wrote in the first place, he said, to please himself:

> . . . I only thought to make
> I knew not what: nor did I undertake
> Merely to please my neighbour; no, not I;
> I did it my own self to gratify.

Defoe undoubtedly wrote 'to please his neighbour', or at any rate to catch his eye with a saleable commodity. If the public liked marvels and had an appetite for tales of travel and surprising adventures, they should have them; if he shared these tastes, as doubtless he did, the stories were easier to write (no successful author ever wrote strongly against inclination), but that was secondary. To the reader of these two books now the aims of their authors may not make much difference. But, looking back, it can be seen that Defoe, much more fundamentally an innovator than Bunyan, was near the beginning of a development which shifted further and further away from tradition and which, with the aid of print and itself modifying the uses of print, was to transform a whole area of communication.

IV

NEWS AND NEWSBOOKS

DANIEL DEFOE has been proposed as symbolic pioneer of new regions for the use of print in popular communication. Of course, he was not alone, but his is a famous name, and landmark in any view of the literary landscape. His character, his interests, his multiple activities mark him out, at the end of the seventeenth and beginning of the eighteenth centuries, as a 'man of the present age', as much as the Leveller Overton proudly claimed to be half-a-century earlier. Defoe was no Leveller, in politics more inclined to authoritarian oligarchic rule than democracy; but such men, conscious of rapidly changing times, turning their backs on the past, can share the description of being men also of the future. We can think of Defoe, the busy journalist, party-hack, literary impersonator, master-mixer of fact and fiction, as a signpost pointing to one of the great developments of the next 250 years, the growth of newspapers. But it must not be forgotten that most of these new forms which he seems so singularly to have foreshadowed had their origins well before his time. It is convenient now to look at these—parts of a continuous process in the spread of printed communication, but distinguishable from some that have been touched on already—in more detail.

Newspapers were in existance long before Defoe was born, though the word itself seems to have acquired its modern sense about the time of his birth. The earliest recorded usage in the *Oxford English Dictionary* is 1670, 'I wanted ye newes paper for Monday last past,' quoted from the official *Gazette*. But printed news-books, news-sheets, or newsletters had been in circulation by then for more than a century, and themselves had ancestors before print in the handwritten letters, summaries mainly of commercial and political information, supplied regularly by and for the European trading community. (The great banking house of Fugger was a notable exemplar, keeping its own agents and others informed in this way throughout much of sixteenth-century Europe.) From early in the same century is commonly dated 'the first printed newspaper' in an English pamphlet describing soon after the event the 'Trewe encounter' of the Battle of Flodden. It is remarkable, and not perhaps wholly accidental, that

53

the earliest prose news-story and the earliest topical ballad in print (Skelton's *Ballade of the Scottyshe Kinge* already referred to) dealt with the same happening. Even more than commerce, warfare has provided a potent stimulus to news-mongering, though one often included the other, since military vicissitudes vitally affected trade. A difference in kind may thus early be seen between market news that some persons needed to know and news of victories and defeats that everyone wanted to know.

It is also notable that from the beginning rulers have often thought everyone should not know such news, even when it was good. The progress of Henry VIII's later Scottish wars (the 'Rough Wooing') was charted by more pamphlets, which came under ban from Henry himself: a proclamation of 1544 condemned 'certain books printed of newes of the prosperous successes of the King's Ma'ties arms in Scotland', and ordered them to be brought in and burned.[77]

Printed newsbooks—they were books or pamphlets rather than sheets—became common in the latter part of the sixteenth century and began to appear, not merely attached to single happenings but with at least intended regularity. On the Continent sequentially numbered prints occurred as early as 1566, and at the end of the century an example is found in Augsburg of the general coverage which was to become characteristic of newspapers—a monthly publication which promised the 'Historical Relation or Narrative of the most important and noteworthy actions and events which took place here and there almost in the whole of Europe'.[78] Other enterprises followed, performing, on however small a scale, some of the principal functions of later newspapers as sources of current information and as what came later to be called 'organs of opinion'. Information on political affairs was provided in such as the *Avisa-Relation oder Zeitung*, printed in the north German city of Wolfenbüttel, which began publication in 1609, or the *Relation* and *Gedenckwurdige Zeitung* in the Rhineland (1609 and 1613 respectively).[79] The early occurrence of the label 'Zeitung', or 'Times', is noteworthy: the essence of a true newspaper is its attachment to the most fragile of abstractions, the present time. The first of these narratives of 'the times', the *Avisa-Relation*, was founded and run very largely to further the policies of the then Duke of Brunswick, Heinrich Julius, in the political-religious manoeuvres leading up, after his death, to the outbreak of the Thirty Years' War; it may count as the starting-point of a long line in which printed news has served the ends of diplomacy.

With the outbreak of war in 1618, the market for news immediately expanded, a demand to be supplied in the first place chiefly by the Dutch. Amsterdam, already a centre of printing, was the source of a series of 'corantos', or digests of current news collected by a well-organised network of correspondents in many different countries from Italy to the warring states of Germany and Bohemia. It was not long before versions of these were printed in London. An entry in the Stationers' Company Register for 18 May 1622 records *A Currant of Generall Newes*, printed by Thomas Archer and Nicholas Bourne[80] which may be taken as marking the inauguration of British journalism. No copy of this first issue has survived, but one of a week later offers, in translation from the Dutch, 'Weekely Newes from Italy, Germanie, Hungaria, Bohemia, the Palatinate, France, and the Low Countries'. The example was soon imitated, with other stationers joining in; in particular one Nathaniel Butter who, replacing Archer as Bourne's partner, carried on the series of 'corantos' or 'relations', more of less unbroken, for the next ten years. These had as yet no general title—what was later to be known as a newspaper's 'masthead'—but carried week by week a conspectus of contents, of which an early example (for August 21 1623) may be taken as typical; 'What hath last hapned in the Empire betweene the Emperor and the Princes. The state of Tillies and Brunswicks Armies since the last encounter. The King of Denmarks Preparations. Count Mansfields fastnesse. Together with other businesse of the Low Countries and the Grisons. The Election of the new Pope. The Turkish Pyracies. And certaine prodigies seene in the Empire.'[81]

That the reader was offered exclusively foreign news—in effect, war news—was not entirely a reflection of public taste, great though the interest in the fighting in Europe was at the time. The newsbooks were tightly controlled, and it was clear to authority that the dissemination of news was, or ought to be, a royal monopoly. News from abroad might be published, but toleration did not extend to telling of domestic affairs; for private persons to report—let alone comment upon—doings within the kingdom was for Stuart kings, as it had been for Henry VIII, out of the question. Even foreign affairs could come too near home; in 1632 the Imperial representatives in London, outraged by the Protestant partisanship of the newsbooks, protested to Charles I, and news-printing of any kind was suppressed by decree of the Star Chamber. The decree was lifted six years later, but again permission was to print foreign news only, with a monopoly of the right to do so granted to Butter and Bourne for a period of twenty-one years. But by that time the underlying conflicts of the period were about to issue in direct challenge to royal authority and civil war. Within three years the royal attempt to control the press had collapsed, and with the abolition of the Star Chamber in 1641, there began a new stage in the uses of printed news, now involved in the unprecedented and spectacular outpouring of controversy which has already been touched on.

Something of the appetite for news in the years leading up to 'the Great Rebellion' may be gathered from contemporary comment, especially from the dramatists competing to expose the fashions and follies of the age. Most references are hostile; though Robert Burton, in the comprehensive tolerance of *The Anatomy of Melancholy*, allows news to have attractions and even therapeutic value for the great and learned as well as for 'the rascal multitude' addicted to 'scurrile pamphlets'. For a great man stricken by depression (a 'famous general of Ferdinand and Isabella') 'the only comfort . . . he had to ease his melancholy was to hear news, and to listen after those ordinary occurrents which were brought to him *cum primis*, by letter or otherwise, out of the remotest parts of Europe'; and for himself Burton owned the delights of novelty: 'I hear new news every day, and those ordinary rumours of war, plagues, fires, inundations, thefts, murders, massacres, meteors, comets, spectrums, prodigies, apparitions, of towns taken, cities besieged in France, Germany, Turkey, Persia, Poland, etc. . . . New books every day, pamphlets, currantoes, stories . . . new paradoxes, schisms, heresies, controversies in philosophy, religion etc. . . . tidings of weddings, maskings, entertainments . . . treasons, cheating tricks, robberies, enormous villainies of all kinds, funerals, burials, deaths of Princes, new discoveries, expeditions; now comical, then tragical matters.'[82]

Burton, with his insatiable appetite for the odds and ends of life, would clearly have enjoyed today's Sunday papers. But the view of news-gathering and news-spreading held by most writers of the time was condescending, even contemptuous. The poet-satirist Abraham Holland, in the general denunciation of *Paper Persecutors* (1626), picked on Nathaniel Butter (whose name was an open invitation to jibing puns) and especially on the bill-posters with which he seems to have advertised his newsbooks:

> . . . But to behold the walls
> Butter'd with weekly news, composed in Parts . . .
>
> To see such Butter every week besmear
> Each public post and church door, and to hear
> These shameful lies would make a man in spite
> Of nature, turn satirist and write
> Revenging lines against these shameless men
> Who thus torment both paper press and pen.[83]

The general charge was that such 'news' was the invention of any traveller with a ready tongue, especially of soldiers back from the Continental wars. A character in James Shirley's play *The School of Complement* (1624) ascribes the happy absence of news to the fact that 'the news-maker, master Money-lack, is sick of a consumption of the wit', but goes on to tell his companion how 'It has been a great profession; marry, most commonly they are soldiers; a peace concluded is a great plague unto them, and if the wars hold, we shall have store of them; oh, they are men worthy of commendation; they speak in print . . . these will write you a battle in any part of Europe at an hour's warning, and yet never set foot out of a tavern.'[84] The pamphleteer, James Howell, himself a traveller, described Amsterdam, thronged with such informants, as 'the great staple of news'; and the phrase itself—'staple' meaning the principal mart or exchange-place of a particular commodity—was used by Ben Jonson for the title of one of the last of his plays, which is also most extensive and devastating of these satirical commentaries on the news trade.

Jonson had already attacked one aspect of the business in a bitter epigram on 'Captain Hungry' or 'Captain Pamphlet', supposed to earn a meagre livelihood by retailing invented reports of the wars:

> Do what you can for, Captain, with your news,
> That's sit and eat; do not my ears abuse.
> I oft look on false coin, to know't from true:
> Not that I love it more than I will you.
> Tell the gross Dutch those grosser tales of yours,
> How great you were with their two emperors,
> And yet are with their princes: fill them full
> Of your Moravian horse, Venetian bull.[85]

In a masque of 1620, *The World Discovered in the Moon*, one of Jonson's wheeling-dealing characters, Factor, explains how 'I have hope to erect a Staple for news ere long'; and in 1626 *The Staple of News*, a full-length play, was first performed. The first part of it is an elaborate burlesque of news-collecting and distribution, exhibiting so much of received opinion on the subject, both of Jonson's and of later ages, that it is worth quoting in some detail.

In an address to the reader the author makes his intention clear, to satirise the news-vending methods of the time, 'a weekly cheat to draw money' which 'could not be fitter reprehended than in raising this ridiculous office of the Staple, wherein the age sees her own folly, or hunger and thirst after published pamphlets of news, set out every Saturday, but made all at home, and no syllable of truth in them; than

which there cannot be a greater disease in nature, or a fouler scorn upon
the time'. The Prologue expresses his contempt for writers of such
pamphlets: '. . . all that dabble in ink/ And defile quills, are not those few
can think'; and in the first scene the hero, Pennyboy, learns of

> An office, sir, a brave young office set up . . .
> To enter all the news, sir, o' the time
> And vent it as occasion serves. A place
> Of huge commerce it will be . . .
> Where all the news of all sorts shall be brought
> And there be examin'd and then register'd
> And so be issued under the seal of Office
> As Staple News, no other news be current.

News, it is heavily underlined, is a 'commodity', collected 'From all
regions/ Where the best news are made/ Or vented forth/ By way of
exchange or trade'; and the Staple evidently has a monopoly in this very
profitable item of commerce—one of the trade monopolies which James
and Charles I were so ready to sell to favoured persons. The monopolist
news-monger Cymbal and his underlings describe the organisation of the
Staple, with the various categories of news arranged 'by alphabet'—

> . . . authentical or apocryphal—
> Or news of doubtful credit: as, barbers' news—
> And tailors' news, porters' and watermen's news.
> Whereto, beside the *coranti* and *gazetti*—
> I have news of the season—As vacation news,
> Term news, and Christmas news—And news o' the faction—
> As the Reformed news, Protestant news,
> And Pontifical news, of all which several,
> The day-books, characters, and precedents are kept.

Customers enter, and are supplied with whatever they want, mostly
extravagant in nature. A countrywoman asking for 'a groatsworth of any
news, I care not what' is told, 'Oh you are a butter-woman. Ask Nathaniel
the clerk there', but others are sold such items as 'the King of Spain chosen
for Pope on February 30th'; a perpetual motion machine 'discovered by an
alewife'; 'a burning glass found in Galileo's study to fire any fleet by
moonshine'; news of an 'invisible eel' invented by the Dutch to sink shipping
at sea, or of amphibious artillery, 'ordnance with bladders instead of
wheels'. It seems that, like warfare itself, development of weaponry has
always been good for a sensation.

The Office where all this stuff is handled is 'the house of Fame' (i.e. Rumour)

> Where both the curious and the negligent,
> The scrupulous and careless, wild and staid,
> The idle and laborious, all do meet,
> To Taste the *cornu copiae* of her rumours
> Which she, the mother of sport, pleaseth to scatter
> Among the vulgar. Baits, sir, for the people!
> And they will bite like fishes.

Because the 'Staple' is supposed to be a monopoly and because, for purposes of the satire, it is a news-agency rather than a newspaper, 'news' being sold directly, without the mediation of print, Jonson is involved in some ambiguous, but interesting comment on the actualities of news-publishing in his day. Pennyboy makes explicit reference to Butter's *Mercurius Britannicus* newsletter and asks in effect why it should be done out of business, and why

> ... if the honest common people
> Will be abus'd, why should they not ha' their pleasure
> In the believing lies are made for them,
> As you i' the Office, making them yourselves?

To this one of the Staple's emissaries, Fitton (whose name simply means 'a lie') replies, 'Oh sir, it is the printing we oppose,' and he and his master Cymbal explain:

> We not forbid that any news be made
> But that't be printed, for when news is printed
> It leaves, sir, to be news. While 'tis but written
> Though it be ne'er so false, it runs news still.

Pannyboy's further comment is:

> See divers men's opinions! Unto some
> The very printing of them makes them news
> That ha' not the heart to believe anything
> But what they see in print. . . .[86]

It is perhaps unnecessary to point out how familiar to a twentieth century reader all these jibes must be, from the assumption (at least until very recently) that journalists are indigent hacks and cadgers who will tell any lie for the price of a square meal, to the still more general argument that if the public—especially the less-educated public, the 'honest common people'—like to be told lies, why should they not be given what they want? The whole play, with its characteristic Jonsonian setting in 'all that nether world' governed by money and deceit, is remarkable for revealing a complex of beliefs and prejudices about news and its dissemination by different means which persist to this day, especially among 'intellectuals'. It may, like other of Jonson's social satires, be thought of as backward-looking, deploring new fashions and customs. But it is also prophetic.

Jonson's 'Staple' is an imaginary rival of the news-print, in particular the *Mercurius Britannicus* which, though it does not seem to have appeared with any great regularity, is cited as the first British newsbook with a 'running title', i.e. one that identified if from issue to issue as a serial publication. This and others came to an abrupt end in 1632; but the publishers, Butter and Bourne, were only waiting for the ban to be lifted—when, at the end of 1638, they celebrated with a 96-page issue.[87] Within three years the abolition of the Star Chamber and of all licensing restrictions released the flood of 'promiscuous prints' of all kinds which has already been glanced at.

The Civil War and Commonwealth years saw, in addition to the huge number of individual pamphlets, a number equally large—at least if successive issues be counted separately—of newsbooks and sheets, official and unofficial. In the turmoil of war and with the country gripped by rumour, these publications were clearly seen by the contending sides as weapons in the struggle. Among those who took immediate advantage of the freedom to print were Members of Parliament themselves, whose speeches were published in a series of *Diurnal Occurrences* from the end of 1641 onwards. These, backdating the record by at least a year, were the main source, verbal rumour apart, for those who wanted to know what was, and had been, going on; they were, for example, the means, during the rebellion of November, 1641, by which the country in general learned the inflammatory news of the 'Irish massacres'.

In such publication may be seen at work the idea of the press as a kind of extension of Parliament, a substitute in itself for the physical assembly of the whole nation: by means of regular Parliamentary reports the nation is brought back, if only as audience, into the process of representative government. It must not be forgotten, of course, that 'the nation' supposed, except by the Levellers, to be properly concerned—made up of those with an 'interest' and votes to show for it—was at that time and for long afterwards no more than a small minority. It should also be borne in mind that the principle was strenuously disputed for a further century and a half, with continual efforts of the part of authority, temporarily successful on several occasions, to forbid Parliamentary reporting. But for the time being accounts of the Proceedings, variously accurate, were generally available, the first truly domestic news in print; and to these were shortly added news of the war that Charles I brought to England in 1642.

The first regular war news-pamphlet, the *Mercurius Aulicus*, was launched by Charles from his Oxford headquarters early in 1643, and continued publication more or less regularly, till the final defeat of the Royal party and Charles's surrender to the Scots three years later. (*Aulicus* = royal, or courtly: the full title of the paper was 'A Diurnal Communicating the Intelligence and Affaires of the Court to the Rest of the Kingdome', and merely in acknowledging 'the rest of the Kingdome's' right to know of the affairs of the Court it was an interesting concession by arbitrary government.) The *Aulicus* was soon countered on the Parliamentary side by *The Kingdome's Weekly Intelligencer*; a *Mercurius Civicus* followed soon after, published on a different day of the week and dealing especially with City news, and towards the end of the same year another Parliamentary organ, *Mercurius Britanicus* (*sic*) was begun with the specific purpose of answering what was said in the *Aulicus*. Multiplication continued on both sides, and to describe in detail its complexities as newsbooks appeared and disappeared, were suppressed and revived, contradicted and duplicated each other's titles, is probably not necessary. A list of some of the titles, by no means exhaustive, may give some idea of the range: *Mercurius* qualified by other *Mercuriuses, Academicus, Diutinus, Melancholicus, Pragmaticus,* and *Elencticus* (all Royalist), *Mercurius Medicus,* and *Mordicus, Anti-Pragmaticus, Militaris, Anti-Mercurius* (for Parliament and the Army); the *Spie,* the *Scotish Dove* (which purported to carry news to and from the Parliament's Scottish allies) and the *Scottish Mercury,* the *Moderate,* which for a time was the Levellers' paper, and the *Moderate Intelligencer* in rivalry with it; the *Flying Post* and *London Post,* 'communicating the High Counsels of both Parliaments in England and Scotland, and all other remarkable passages, both Civill and Martial . . . through the three kingdoms'; *Mercurius Politicus,* launched after the establishment of the Commonwealth, and believed to have been edited for a time by Milton.

A catalogue of periodicals published in England from 1641 up to and beyond the Restoration[88] shows a rapid rise from two in 1641 to a peak of

65 and 54 in the crucial years of 1648 and 1649; dropping during the Commonwealth to between 20 and 30 and then to no more than five for the two years, 1656–8, of the most vigorous Cromwellian represssion, and rising again immediately before the Restoration to 18 and 28 in 1659 and early 1660 respectively. Thereafter the number was drastically reduced to fewer than half-a-dozen in the early years of Charles II and, after the establishment of the official *London Gazette*, to one.

These newsbooks were, or for the most part aimed to be, weekly, and the most regular of them shared out the days of the week in a more or less orderly fashion, so that in the peak year of 1648, for example, *A Perfect Diurnall* (Parliamentary) and *Mercurius Aulicus* (Royalist) appeared on Mondays; *The Kingdome's Weekly Intelligencer* (Parliamentary), *Mercurius Pragmaticus* (Royalist), and *Mercurius Anti-Pragmaticus* (Parliamentary) on Tuesdays; *The Perfect Weekly Account* (Anabaptist Parliamentary) on Wednesdays; *Le Mercure Anglois* (for foreigners in England) and *The Moderate Intelligencer* (Leveller) on Thursdays; *Perfect Occurrences* (Parliamentary) and *Mercurius Elencticus* (Royalist) on Fridays; with more than forty others, some surviving in no more than one or two issues, jostling irregularly for a share in the week. There was thus, if not a daily newspaper, some printed news for every day of the week—for at different times Saturday was also used, and even Sunday, originally chosen for publication day by the Royalist *Aulicus*, no doubt as a deliberate affront to Puritan sabbatarianism. Over a whole year the number of separate issues was very large indeed; one calculation for 1645 (not a peak year) is of a total of 722.[89]

The newsbooks were nearly all fiercely and unashamedly partisan, produced very often directly in reply to one another, as some of the titles indicate. All accused one another very freely of lying; indeed 'liar' was probably the most used epithet in all their very rich language of abuse. In this can in part be seen the stereotype already visible in Ben Jonson's contempt for newsmongering of all kinds, reinforced not only by political hostility but, on the Royalist side, by a feeling of outrage that any but courtiers should pretend to know anything about affairs of state. The rascal multitude and those who wrote for them could not have knowledge or understanding of their betters' doings, so the reports were bound to be lies.

This attitude is well represented by the Cavalier poet John Cleveland (or Clieveland), himself for a time editor of *Mercurius Pragmaticus*, who loftily described 'a Diurnal maker' as 'the sub-almoner of history . . . to call him an historian is to knight a mandrake . . . to give the reputation of an engineer to a maker of mousetraps'. Referring to Dillingham, editor of the Levellers' *Moderate Intelligencer*, Cleveland said: 'He is the citizen's harginger and saveth him the labour of walking on the 'change to hear the news . . . and though he tells lies by the gross, yet he would have the bookturners of this isle believe that he useth moderation.' To edit the *Mercurius Britanicus* for Parliament was, according to another Royalist, to have 'a patent to lie, and whatsoever thou printest in thy weekly corrantoes, though never so grossly absurd and palpably false, after thou hast got M. White's [the printer's] hand to it no man can say "Black in thine eye" '. On the Parliamentary side there was a similar condemnation, repeated in successive Ordinances, of 'false, scandalous publications, poisonous writings of evil men sent abroad daily to abuse and deceive the people'.

Of the Royalist *Aulicus* a Parliamentarian pamphlet observed that 'the greatest, and main part of the Law which the new Oxford Doctors do teach is, That it is lawful to devise what lies they can, and to publish them even in print for the advancing of their cause'. From a possibly more neutral point of view John Aubrey described Birkenhead, editor of the *Aulicus*, as one who 'would lie damnably'. The Puritan poet and pamphleteer George Wither, introducing his own contribution to the cross-fire of newsbooks (with a Parliamentary *Mercurius Rusticus*, not to be confused with the Royalist newsbook of the same title) confessed that 'all Mercuries, having the planet Mercury predominant at their nativities, cannot but retain a twang of lying'. A *Mercurius Militaris*, or *Time's only Truth-Teller* (edited by John Hackluyt, a divine who seems to have changed his allegiance several times and might be thought therefore to be impartial) advertised itself as 'faithfully undeceiving the expectation of the vulgar (who are daily abused by a Crew of brainless and brazen-faced News-Scribblers, whether Royal, Martial, of Parliamental)'. The *Mercurius Anti-Mercurius* announced its sole surviving number, of 1648, as 'communicating all Humours, Conditions, Forgeries, and Lies of Midas-eared newsmongers'. It may be supposed that the public to whom all these claims and counter-claims to attention were addressed must have developed a certain scepticism, and may even to have come to enjoy the mutual flytings of editors. Especially towards the end of the period some frankly humorous variations began to appear, such as *Mercurius Jocosus* of 1654, which promised 'the most refined fancies as well ancient as modern, choice, various, and delightful, comprising Merry tales, witty jests, quaint questions, quick answers, and overgrown bulls . . . together with the heads of all the remarkable news'—a table of contents not much different from those offered in *Tit-Bits* or any modern tabloid.[90]

But something else may be learned from the proliferation of the

newsbooks, and from their very titles. Their readership was not, probably, ever
very large—the copies of any one issue are unlikely to have exceeded one or
two hundred—and their readers as well as their editor-writers and printers
were mainly concentrated in London. Most even of the Royalist examples
were printed, not only in Oxford, but also—clandestinely—in the great
urban stronghold of the Parliamentary party. But the idea at least, and to
some extent the fact of their nationwide importance was clearly implied in
the common claim to communicate 'advertisements [i.e. news] from the
three kingdoms', and in a two-way passage of information. The *London
Post*, which appeared weekly for two sustained periods between 1644 and
1647, carried on its title-page a lively engraving of the 'Post-man' himself,
galloping and blowing his horn between London, Newcastle, Scarborough,
Berwick and Edinburgh; use of the word 'Post' in this and other newsbook
titles reflected the establishment and growth of a Post Office as a national
institution, for private as well as public use. Regular postal services—once a
week from London 'to the country' in 1641—were doubled from 1647 or
1648 onwards, and were reasonably prompt; by 1656 it is recorded that
letters from London were delivered in Winchester the next day.[91]

Some of the capacities, and more of the expectations of newspapers
which laid hold of people's minds in these years may be deduced from the
way the newsbooks spoke about themselves, and the claims they made.
Their editor-writers called one another liars, but claimed themselves to
speak the truth. The very accusation, just or not—and modern research
suggests that much of newsbook information was accurate enough—shows
up the assumption that they ought to have been telling the truth, and that
their readers had the right to expect it. Their titles, the 'true informations',
'true and perfect occurrences', the 'perfect weekly accounts', the 'exact
journals', demonstrate their collective claim, with however little justification, to let readers know 'the facts', and all the important facts, of public life
from day to day. The idea that citizens might, and should, have at least a
general notion of everything happening in the country was beginning to
take root; a connection was establishing itself between information and the
very idea of citizenship. Such an idea is taken so much for granted in the
modern world that it may be difficult to see how momentous it was; but in
the seventeenth century it was new.

Like much else new that emerged during the twenty years of civil wars
and republic, it was suppressed, or at any rate determined efforts were
made to suppress it, at the Restoration. The immediate effect of the turn-
about in 1660 was a drastic reduction in the number of newsbooks and a
swift change of the men in charge of them. (Marchamont Nedham, the

industrious and flexible journalist who had successfully changed sides several times in the preceding years, and was issuing two weekly newsbooks for the Parliament early in 1660, failed to survive Monck's coup and the return of Charles, and was replaced by Monck's own protégé, Henry Muddiman, of whose subsequent career, marking a curious detour in early newspaper history, more will be said presently.)

For a brief period immediately before the Restoration Parliamentary proceedings were, indeed, more fully reported than ever and even, for the three weeks that it lasted, given every day in *The Perfect Diurnal*, which thus became the first daily newspaper in English. But one of the first acts of Charles II's new and obedient Parliament was to forbid the printing of any Parliamentary reports whatever 'without special leave and order', and thus at a stroke deprive newsbooks of their principal material and most of their function as a source of public political information. Two years later the Licensing Act was passed which, in order to repair 'the general licentiousness of the late times', reimposed many of the restrictions exercised by the Star Chamber, though these were now vested in a licensing office, soon to be held by the powerful and sinister figure of Roger L'Estrange.

Sir Roger L'Estrange (knighted by Charles for services rendered before and after the Restoration) is an interesting actor in the involved politics of the time and may be recognised, indeed, as a character recurrent in history: an intelligent, gifted, and conscious reactionary who sincerely hated 'the rascal multitude' and considered that ideally they should do as they were told without being given any reason whatever; but that, failing that, the next best thing was for reason and information to be properly manipulated. L'Estrange had solicited for the post of Licenser in a pamphlet in which he argued that the new Act was insufficiently rigorous and should be reinforced with the most severe penalties, including not only 'death, mutilation, imprisonment, banishment, corporal pains, disgrace, pecuniary mulcts', but some special and shameful way of distinguishing so dangerous a trade as newsmonger: the 'mercury women' and others concerned in distributing and selling newsbooks should be 'condemned to wear some visible badge or mark of ignominy, as a halter instead of a hatband'.[92]

On the strength of this demonstration of zeal he was duly appointed 'Surveyor of the Press', and vigorously set about hunting down all the unlicensed and clandestine presses which survived, using a full apparatus of spies and informers for the purpose. He thus earned an extreme unpopularity, which surfaced later, during the Popish Plot, with opprobrious songs about 'the Dog Towzer'. His most celebrated victim was John Twyn, hanged, drawn and quartered in 1664 for printing a pamphlet justifying regicide.

At the same time he established himself as the sole publisher of news, with two weekly newsbooks, *The Intelligencer* and *The News*, published on Mondays and Thursdays and linked together, so that readers had to buy both; his aim was quite openly to make money out of whatever news he himself thought fit to print. How restricted this was may be judged by the prospectus printed in the first issue of *The Intelligencer*, already referred to, but worth quoting more fully as a candid and complete statement of the view of newspapers as channels of official propaganda:

As to the point of intelligence, I do declare myself . . . that, supposing the press in order, the people in their right wits, and news or no news to be the question, a public mercury should never have my vote; because I think it makes the multitude too familiar with the action and counsels of their superiors, too prag-matical and censorious, and gives them not only an itch, but a kind of colourable right and licence, to be meddling with the government. All which . . . does not yet hinder but that in this juncture a paper of that quality may be both safe and expedient—truly if I should say necessary perhaps the case would bear it, for certainly there is not anything which at this instance more imports his majesty's service and the public than to redeem the vulgar from their former mistakes and delusions, and to preserve from the like for the time to come; to both which purposes the prudent management of a gazette may contribute in a very high degree. For, besides that it is everybody's money [i.e. of common interest] and in truth a great part of most men's study and business, it is none of the worst ways of address to the genius and humour of the common people, whose affections are much more capable of being tuned and wrought upon by convenient touches in the shape and air of a pamphlet than by the strongest reason and best notions imaginable under any other and more sober form whatsoever. To which advantages of being popular and grateful must be added, as none of the least, that it is likewise reasonable and worth the while, were there no other use for it than only to detect and disappoint the malice of those scandalous and false reports which are daily contrived and bruited against the government.[93]

After such a declaration it may seem unfair that L'Estrange did not enjoy the status of, in effect, Minister of Propaganda for long. The intrigue of rivals and the outbreak of the Great Plague of 1665—which drove the Court from town and made newsbooks from London suspect as bearers of infec-tion—led to the publication, first, of *The Oxford Gazette* and subsequently, when the Court returned to the capital in 1666, of *The London Gazette*, an official news-sheet which has, indeed, continued ever since. Until the Revolution of 1688, and with some intermissions, the *Gazette* remained the only printed source of news readily available; though the demand for something more than its controlled and slender reportage resulted not only in the sporadic appearance of unlicensed sheets but in two developments, officially permitted, which illustrate divergent functions of news-publishing.

One was the renewal of manuscript news-letters, of which Muddiman, the first publisher of the *Gazette*, was the principal organiser and source. The intrigues and counter-intrigues by which Muddiman lost the *Gazette* monopoly and contrived to set up another of his own are too complicated to be described here, though it may be noted how much power and profit must have been attached to these positions to make them worth intriguing for; and also that when the news allowed into official print was both meagre and trivial, its dissemination by pre-printing methods almost, for a time, replaced it. Muddiman's highly-organised news-letter service seems to have outsold official print at all points; when his letters were issued the *Gazette* 'was never asked for', according to contemporary comment. The *Gazettes* were 'slighted', it was said, because they contained nothing of Parliamentary proceedings, whereas the news-letters, circumventing the ban on printed reports, wrote of these 'at large'.[94] The news-letters were, however, costly and necessarily of very limited circulation—a yearly subscription was as much as £5, a large sum in the late seventeenth century—and it may be supposed that their consequent restriction to an upper-class readership was a reason for their being tolerated.

The importance of a news-letter service continued after 1688, and produced a striking anomaly in the story of print. During the reign of William III a news-letter service was started by one Ichabod Dawks, member of a family of printers, which was in fact printed but used a cursive fount that imitated handwriting. Dawks's *News-Letter* continued publication for twenty years, supplying subscribers of Williamite and Queen Anne times, for 20s. a year, with the illusion of intimacy and immediacy associated with an actual letter. It had a high reputation for supplying 'inside' news and also for being up-to-date with 'the latest'. A representative issue in 1699 contains a medley of news-items which may seem familiar in range: war news from abroad; at home, news of smuggling, of highwaymen taken, a search of 'musick-houses' by the constables, with the arrest of 'idle baggages and felons'; a distillery fire, complaints against witches, the launch of a new man o' war and the execution of nine persons at Tyburn, 'most young Men but old offenders'. A contemporary description of the *News-Letter's* reception is provided by Richard Steele, who noted how it was read by 'such as were not born to have thoughts of their own, and consequently lay a weight upon everything which they read in print'.[95] The curiosity lies in such a publication's double claim upon attention, both as being in print, and therefore reliable, and as being apparently hand-written, and therefore a personal communication. Such seemingly self-contradictory ways of wooing the reader will be encountered again; but evidently they were early effective.

Another consequence of the *Gazette's* monopoly during the years when it was virtually the only newspaper was the appearance of advertising sheets. The *Gazette* carried no commercial advertisements—a word that continued to mean 'announcement' of any kind, but was beginning to acquire its specialised meaning for trade—and L'Estrange himself, deprived of the official news-editorship but still Licenser of the Press, started a *City Mercury, or Advertisements concerning Trade*, with an office attached. Offices for exchange of commercial information were not new—attempts at least to set them up go back to the time of James VI and I, when a 'Publique Register for general Commerce' was opened, with Letters Patent, but failed. The desirability of having some clearing-house of information between those 'that would (if they knew whereof) as willingly buy as the others would gladly sell' remained, and such an office was in fact in operation during the Commonwealth. In addition, commercial advertisements began to appear in the news-books of that time, and these 'advices' inserted at the high rate of 6d. a time, were mentioned with scorn by rivals as 'bumbasting out' the news-content. The supreme importance of trade must, in the years after the Restoration, have generated much pressure for the expansion of such methods, and the absence of an advertising medium was doubtless keenly felt. L'Estrange's *City Mercury* could only partially have met the demand; it was not until the general release of newspapers from restriction after 1688 that publication of news and trade advertising could begin the intimate symbiosis which has continued ever since.

The accession of William III and the triumph of 'Whig' politics produced an immediate resurgence of press activity, with six new papers started within a month of James II's flight. William's own feelings about the press may have been influenced by the fact that, reduced as it had been in late Stuart times, it could not produce a printer to strike off his first proclamation on landing in Devon in 1688.[96] The office of Licenser continued for another six years, but pressure for its removal, supported notably by the arguments of John Locke, brought abolition early in 1695. Williamite England—and also Scotland, still for another dozen years with separate legislative identity—now entered into the same freedom of the press that William's Holland had enjoyed for a long time past. There followed an expansion which, if not entirely steady, being subject to effects of the unresolved to and fro between governmental desire for control and newspapers' efforts to escape from it, can be seen as continuous throughout the eighteenth century. Newspapers multiplied and, more significantly, spread their readership.

The first new publication to take advantage of the abolition of the Licensing Act was *The Flying Post*, issued in London but attempting a wider coverage of domestic news, and in particular giving news from Scotland (its editor, George Ridpath, was a Scot). The first Scottish newspaper (not counting short-lived *Diurnals* and *Mercurius Scoticus* during the Civil Wars), printed and published in the country, was the *Edinburgh Gazette* (1699); and the Edinburgh *Courant* (1705), *Flying Post* (1708), *Evening Courant* (1718), and *Caledonian Mercury* (1720) followed during the next two decades; by the middle of the century there were seven periodicals coming out in Edinburgh, Glasgow and Aberdeen.[97] The English provinces had by this time produced a number of independent journals, the *Norwich Post* (1701) and *The Bristol Post-Boy* (1702) being the earliest.[98] To begin with these were filled largely with reprints of London news, more or less delayed, but by degrees and in increasing proportion they began to carry items of their own; together, of course, with advertising aimed at local readers. In the metropolis the first sustained daily issue, the *Daily Courant*, began in 1702; initially supplying no more than a single page of extracts of foreign news (mostly military) but soon adding other matter, including advertisements, on the reverse side. Other dailies followed, all so describing themselves in their titles, and emphasising the presumed freshness of their content; the chief of these, the *Daily Advertiser*, which continued from 1730 to 1807, has been described as 'The Times' of the eighteenth century'[99]; it supplied a varied news-service, political, commercial, and general, and a high proportion of advertising.

A list of papers to be had in London in 1709 shows a total of 19, offering a choice—for several of these came out more than once a week, the *Courant* on six days—of six different publications on Mondays, 12 on Tuesdays, six on Wednesdays, 12 on Thursdays, six on Fridays, and 13 on Saturdays. As the number of journals increased, newspapers proper were joined by a number of what are now known as periodicals, the most famous being the *Tatler* and *Spectator* produced by Addison and Steele. These two productions, breaking new ground in English journalism, had quite short original lives (1709–11 and 1711–14 respectively) and very small circulations, but an influence, far beyond their immediate readership, which has resulted in them being detached, like Johnson's *Rambler* a little later, from the history of journalism and incorporated in 'English Literature'. Whether such a distinction has any real meaning for us now is a question to return to; in the meantime it is worth remembering that their editor-writers, and probably most of their readers at the time, were keenly aware of a difference in status between their productions and those of 'Grub Street'. The idea of a periodical providing other than news, even detached philosophical discourse, goes back to the late seventeenth century, but it was not until the eighteenth that it caught on, especially in providing miscellaneous cultivated entertainment. The *Gentleman's Magazine* started publication in 1731 and lasted nearly 200 years (to 1907); the *London Magazine* and the Edinburgh-produced *Scots Magazine* (1739–1817, continuing as the *Edinburgh Magazine* to 1826) were highly successful imitators.

Development in other countries at the same time reflected different political conditions: in Holland, where the press was largely unrestricted, independent newspapers flourished and were among the chief sources of foreign news quoted elsewhere; in France on the other hand the official *Gazette* was virtually on its own, and there was no daily newspaper until the *Journal de Paris* began publication in 1777.

In America the first newspaper—the *Publick Occurrences* published in Boston in September, 1690 by an exiled English printer, Benjamin Harris—was immediately suppressed by the Governor, and got no further than this one and only issue. It was resented by colonial authority as being, among other causes of offence, unlicensed, and it is noteworthy that licensing continued in force in the American Colonies for more than a quarter of a century after it had been abolished in Britain. Among the royal instructions with which successive colonial governors were equipped from 1686 to 1730 was the paragraph:

> And forasmuch as great inconvenience may arise by liberty of printing within our said territory under your government you are to provide by all necessary orders that no person keep any printing-press for printing, nor that any book pamphlet or other matter whatsoever be printed without your especial leave and licence first obtained.[100]

Duly licensed, a second and more successful attempt at newspaper-production was made in 1704, with the *Boston News-Letter*, which, indeed, continued for another seventy-two years. Others followed, notably the *New-England Courant* brought out in Boston by James Franklin, elder brother of Benjamin. But with this venture, consciously in opposition to the colonial government, American journalism abruptly entered the renewed fight for 'liberty of the press' as an essential adjunct of general political liberties. It will be convenient to sketch the course of this struggle in the next chapter.

V
LIES, LIBELS, AND LIBERTY

In the course of the eighteenth century, and through the huge changes of nascent industrialisation and population growth in Britain, the attitudes of authority and of the public towards what was now commonly spoken of as 'the liberty of the press' remained what they had been earlier, but modified by opinion concerning liberty in general.

Restoration of licensing in Britain was out of the question, but government soon found another way of controlling or at least of hampering the press in the stamp duty imposed on all newspapers, with an additional heavy tax on advertisements, in 1712. The Stamp Acts, regularly renewed and enforced for nearly a century and a half, were in origin avowedly intended to curb the press and suppress 'false and scandalous libels, such as are a reproach to any government'. They were initially so effective that they caused the virtual disappearance of all the cheaper newspapers (those which at the time sold for 1d.) and, before long, of the more select and selective journals like the *Spectator* which in this first, short phase of its life came to an end in 1714. But the persistence of the printers, the wish of opposition politicians to make use of newspapers to advance their interests, and the demand of a public willing and able to pay more for their papers soon restored their number. The stamp duties continued to be bitterly resented and denounced by champions of press freedom—and in the American colonies, where an attempt was made to introduce them in mid-century, were frustrated outright by the increasingly disaffected colonists. In Britain they remained a hindrance rather than a gag; it is likely their effect was generally restricted to limiting the size and circulations of newspapers, which were in any case not large.

Opinion on such restrictions remained very much a matter of partisanship. Thus Addison, the Whig, deplored the first Stamp Act, as one imposed purely 'for the support of government' which he opposed. Swift, on the other hand, wrote gloatingly to Stella, 'Do you know that all Grub Street is dead and gone last week? No more ghosts or murders now for love or money.' 'Grub Street' in fact survived, and with it the extreme and frequently scurrilous support of one faction or another with which journalists of the day earned patronage and support. Addison again is a witness: 'every dirty scribbler is countenanced by great names, whose interest he propagates by such vile and infamous methods. I have never yet heard of a Ministry who have inflicted an exemplary punishment on an author that has supplied their cause with falsehood and scandal.'[101] (The press, in a word, was too useful to be done away with; but politicians naturally wished it to be a tool, not a critic of their own actions. Out of office in 1714 Robert Walpole defended the rights of the press, under the law, to criticise an administration without fear of Parliamentary interference; 'The liberty of the press is unrestrained; how then shall a part of the legislature dare to punish that as a crime which is not declared to be so by any law passed by the whole?' In office, as chief manager of British affairs under George I and II, Walpole took a different view; but though there were some prosecutions and imprisonments for libel, his preferred instrument of control was plain bribery, with most of the newspapers kept in proper state of subservience by regular payments, and some bought outright. One editor, of a paper inappropriately called The Free Briton, is said to have boasted of getting more than £10,000 out of the Treasury in four years.[102] When Walpole's transactions were investigated by Parliament after his downfall in 1742, it was reported that between 1731 and 1741 he had paid to authors and printers of newspapers at least £50,000 of public money.

Such treatment of the press implies contempt, and Walpole seems indeed to have had the lowest opinion of the journalists he bought, as well as of their opponents: he claimed that he seldom read the papers of either party himself, 'except when I am informed by some who have more inclination to such studies than myself that they have risen by some accident above the common level.'[103]

'Public opinion' at the same time—the opinion, that is to say, of the upper and middle classes, who read newspapers—was undecided, even among journalists themselves. Addison and Steele, though they valued liberty of expression for themselves, looked down on 'Grub Street' with a disdain only more good-humoured than Swift's. Political journalism aimed at the well-disposed and well-endowed was one thing: introducing the first number of the Tatler, Steele wrote, 'It is both a charitable and necessary work to offer something whereby worthy and well-affected members of the community may be instructed, after their reading, what to think.' Yet one remembers his mockery of just such persons who read Dawks's News-Letter; and when it was a question of news offered to less reliable, or less well-educated readers the case was different. Addison repeated the ironies of earlier satirists on the lies told by 'the news-writers of Great Britain', especially in war reports—'They have been upon parties and skirmishes where our armies have lain still, and given the general assault to many a place when the besiegers were quiet in their trenches. They have made us master of several strong towns many weeks before our generals could do it, and completed victories when our greatest captains have been content to come off with a drawn battle.' While regretting the Stamp Act, he affected a lofty amusement at its probable effect on the news-writers—'I am afraid that few of our weekly historians, who are men that above all others delight in war, will be unable to subsist under the weight of a stamp and an approaching peace.'[104]

Perhaps the most industrious of all these journalists was Defoe, not only perfecting the art of presenting fiction as fact but—one pursuit shading imperceptibly into the other—writing indefatigably on and about the news of the day. During much of this period he was engaged with his *Review* (1706–13), a journal very different from the *Tatler* or *Spectator*, being quite without literary pretensions—Defoe indeed despised 'literature'—and undeviatingly serious in tone; but no doubt for this reason, no less disparaging of 'Grub Street' in condemning scandal and irresponsibility. It is curious to see Defoe, whose conception of truth and accuracy was so malleable, writing in the same vein as Addison of 'our street scribblers, who daily and monthly abuse mankind with stories of great victories when we are beaten, miracles when we conquer, and a multitude of unaccountable and inconsistent stories which have at least this effect, that people are possessed with wrong notions of things, and nations wheedled to believe nonsense and contradiction'.[105]

In part, of course, he was simply repeating a received idea, for everyone, including most of its own denizens, joined in jibes at 'Grub Street'; that war-reporting in particular was unreliable, turning defeat into victory with shameless regularity, was obvious (after the event) to generation on generation. It may still appear odd, however, to find Defoe, himself so skilful a practitioner, speaking ill of the 'wheedling' of journalists. The passage is interesting as an example of the way that journalists (on the principle of poacher-yearning-after-gamekeeping) from time to time remind themselves of what they ought to be doing, while continuing, usually, not to do it. Defoe had high standards of journalism, however far he was from observing them; he wrote for money, but thought of writing as essentially a 'service'. The aim was to provide people with 'right notions of things', and the writer had both to hold his reader and be honest with him. 'The character of a good writer, wherever he is found, is this, that he writes so as to please and serve at the same time. If he writes to please, and not to serve, he is a flatterer and a hypocrite; if to serve and not to please, he turns cynic and satirist. . . . But the writer that strives to be useful writes to serve you, and at the same time, by an imperceptible art, draws you on to be pleased also.'[106]

Concerning press freedom Defoe was more cautious than many of his contemporaries: 'the liberty of the press may be the most needful liberty, but it is the most abused liberty in the world.'[107] With this may be contrasted the view to be found about the same time in the 'Cato Letters', a polemical series by two Whig journalists, John Trenchard and Thomas Gordon, which appeared in the London Journal between 1720 and 1723. Commenting on a renewed proposal for censorship and suppression of 'libels' Letter No. 32 said, 'As long as there are such things as printing and writing, there will be libels; it is an evil arising out of a much greater good. . . . I would rather many libels should escape than the liberty of the press should be infringed.'[108] At first sight this appears to be an application of the principle, that private vice produces public good, which lies at the back of much social thinking at the time: carried to satirical extreme in Mandeville's Fable of the Bees and emerging into the full respectability of political economy in Adam Smith. But on closer examination it is seen to be the other way about: 'Cato' is saying that freedom to publish is a good thing in itself, and so good and necessary for society that its occasional by-products in the way of scandal and lies are unimportant by comparison. A whole group of assumptions about human society and communication within it can be seen at work here: a great division which must be discussed in due course.

Throughout the eighteenth century newspapers were involved in political manoeuvre, as partisans or sometimes the mere paid hacks of particular politicians and factions. But they were also excluded from political life in a way not easy nowadays to understand. A particular journal's party allegiance was sufficiently important for the administration of the day (in 1724) to compile a list of newspaper-printers 'well-affected to King George', with the intention of bringing pressure to bear on the others.[109] On the other hand, though able to retail every kind of political gossip and rumour, newspapers were not permitted to report directly the proceedings of Parliament; and this restriction, and efforts to overcome it, was the chief issue between press and government during most of the period.

The struggles reflected faithfully enough the ambiguous assumptions of British society about representative government at a time when 'constitutional' rights were prized but the extension of all of them to more than a small minority was unthinkable except by outsiders. Democrat, it should be remembered, was a term of abhorrence and abuse, such as 'Bolshevik' and 'Trotskyite' have been in other times. That newspapers should report fully the acts, votes, and debates of Parliament was a proposal as outrageous as a broadening of the franchise. When the *Gentleman's Magazine* and the *London Magazine* started printing extensive Parliamentary reports in the 1730s the House of Commons took action to stop it: if the practice were permitted, one MP pointed out, 'you will have every word that is spoken here by gentlemen misrepresented by fellows who thrust themselves into the gallery. You will have the speeches of this House printed every day, and we shall be looked upon as the most contemptible assembly on the face of the earth'.[110] (It is amusing to see how persistent is the idea that Parliamentary affairs are sacrosanct, but also inherently ridiculous: exactly the same arguments have been repeated in opposition to the broadcasting of Parliament and, in the case of TV, have so far been successful.)

The ban was circumvented in various ways. The famous instance of Samuel Johnson, who, though he could not directly report Parliamentary proceedings, invented them—constructing whole debates upon the barest hints for the columns of the *Gentleman's Magazine*—marks perhaps the oddest phase in relations between Parliament and public and the role of journalist as mediator. Much more dangerously from authority's point of view, writers such as Wilkes and the pseudonymous author of the 'Junius Letters' used the press to comment with inside knowledge and without restraint on the politics of Parliament and Court. The notorious No. 45 of Wilkes's *North Briton* in 1763 offended doubly in being both a report of and attack upon the King's Speech in the Commons—with Wilkes's arrest, trial, imprisonment, and the long-running affair of 'the Middlesex Election' following.

The letters of 'Junius' to the *Public Advertiser* at the same time set a new standard in freedom of debate in print—or new at any rate since the seventeenth century. Under the greatly altered circumstances of Hanoverian Britain, political journalism showed itself as a force in a new way: 'Junius' could drive a prime minister (Grafton) out of office, Wilkes could provoke government into actions which led eventually to his personal triumph. The boast of the first number of the *North Briton*—'The liberty of the press is the birthright of a Briton, and is justly esteemed the firmest bulwark of the liberties of this country. It has been the terror of all bad ministers; for their dark and dangerous designs, or their weakness, inability, and duplicity, have thus been detected, and shown to the public generally in too strong colours for them long to bear up against the odium of mankind'[111]—was more than mere rhetoric. At the same time it should not be forgotten that, in so far as 'the public' meant newspaper readers, its numbers were very small. When 'Junius' was writing his letters to the *Advertiser* its daily circulation rose by more than 50 per cent; but even then, it did not go above 3200.

The editor of the *Advertiser*, Henry Woodfall, was prosecuted for publishing the boldest of the 'Junius' letters, addressed to the king himself; he was acquitted by an independent-minded jury in defiance of the judge, Lord Mansfield; the powers of juries, and the scope of their decisions in libel cases, were soon to become closely involved in the efforts of government to control the press and stifle 'sedition'. At the same time Woodfall's brother William was working to establish press rights in a parallel direction by reporting for his paper, the *Morning Chronicle*, the debates of Parliament. This he did without notes, solely by an 'uncommonly retentive' memory, and he was thus difficult to stop. He and other editors and printers were under intermittent harrassment, including prosecution, by both Houses—the Peers being particularly resentful of reports in the press—but were becoming increasingly defiant, on many occasions simply ignoring summons to appear before one or other House.

The struggle, which had elements of shadow-boxing, if not farce, came to a head in 1771 when, with Wilkes, 'Junius', and the City of London supporting the printers, those who had been arrested (including the Lord Mayor, confined in comfort in the Tower) were released; and thereafter the right to report fully the proceedings of Parliament was tacitly conceded. No doubt one of the reasons was that when Parliamentary reporters were excluded or prosecuted, newspapers fell back on guesswork and fabrication: in 1778 Fox urged, against complaints by a fellow MP of 'misrepresentation', that 'the true and only method of preventing misrepresentation was by throwing open the gallery and making the debates and decisions of the House as public as possible'.[112]

Prosecutions for seditious libel continued, following until 1792 the Mansfield judgment already mentioned, which left the jury in such cases with nothing to decide on but the bare fact of publication. Resistance to this ruling was part of the agitation of the time, resulting eventually in an Act which—in March 1792, as Britain was newly embarked on war with revolutionary France—in a number of ways reinforced governmental powers in dealing with newspaper sedition; but it also gave writers and printers the right of full trial by jury on the points at issue. It is of some interest that this Act was promoted by Fox, who had changed his ground since 1771, when he had supported powers to suppress 'infamous lampoons and satires'. At that time he urged: 'If we (i.e. Members of Parliament) are not to judge for ourselves, but to be ever at the command of the vulgar, and their capricious shouts and hisses, I cannot see what advantage the nation can reap from a representative body which they might not have reaped from a tumultuous assembly of themselves, collected at random on Salisbury Plain or Runnymede.'[113]

Here again—though viewed from the other side—appears the idea which was put forward at the beginning of the century, of the press as an extension of Parliament: the whole nation, though unable 'to assemble in one room', might through an unfettered press join in debating national affairs. The notion of the press as 'the fourth estate of the realm' had been growing for some time before Macaulay formulated it (in 1828), and it was a conception wider in meaning than his, referring simply to Parliamentary reports. By means of newspapers 'the nation' might not only know what was being debated in Parliament but might conduct a parallel, and possibly opposed, debate of its own; the press could function not only as auxiliary of Parliament but as alternative.

At the end of the eighteenth century, newspapers were restricted in many ways, some newly imposed: by increases in the stamp and advertisement duties, with prohibition of any attempt to pass the cost on to the public by increased prices; by requiring the registration of all journals, their proprietors and printers; by making it an offence to 'let out', rather than sell newspapers so that one copy might be read by many persons. This last restraint (by an enactment of 1789) is emphatic evidence of public demand; and in general these regulations acknowledged the power of the press and its widely accepted status: a status which authority did not like any more than governments in the past, and which had continually to be defended, but which could not be abolished.

In the same year of 1789 the Revolution in France produced even more striking evidence of public demand for newspapers. The abolition of absolutist censorship resulted in an explosion of print not unlike that in the 'English Revolution' of the previous century, but now reinforced by greater technical resources and the example of 100 years' development in Britain itself. (This was specifically acknowledged in Mirabeau's pamphlet *Sur la liberté de la press: imité de l'Anglais*—the English being that of Milton.) From a single daily newspaper, itself only established for the past dozen years, the Paris papers jumped in the first Revolutionary year to 350; to be cut down again to 13 under the Consulate, and to no more than four when Napoleon made himself Emperor, but—like other legacies of the Revolution—leaving a memory of briefly unrestricted communication behind it.[114]

The eleventh clause of the Rights of Man declared on 26 August 1789 was of 'libre communication des pensées et des opinions . . . tout citoyens peut donc parler, écrire, imprimer librement', and the declaration has usually been written into every liberal constitution since, including that of the United Nations.

In America the political struggles of the eighteenth century were reflected in the growth of a partisan journalism only less explosive—because, doubtless, it was less confined—than in Revolutionary France. James Franklin's *New-England Courant* had been embroiled in domestic controversy throughout its brief career, and the voicing of local discontents soon assumed a more far-reaching character; in the *Pennsylvania Gazette* James's more famous younger brother Benjamin was by mid-century more or less openly advocating change in the status of the colonies. The celebrated print of a snake cut into pieces, with the slogan for the different colonial states to 'Join or Die', which Benjamin Franklin printed in the *Gazette* in 1754, is counted as the first of a long line of American political cartoons.[115] Before that, the trial for sedition of the New York journalist John Zenger in 1734–5 anticipated many of the arguments and counter-arguments provoked on the other side of the Atlantic by John Wilkes and the *North Briton*; the acquittal of Zenger (who had been charged with 'Scandalous, Virulent, and Seditious Reflections' on the governor of the State) was indeed a clearer victory of principles of press freedom, and the rights of trial by jury on charges of sedition, than was achieved in Britain for a full generation.[116] In 1765 a Stamp Act was introduced to the American Colonies, similar to that which had been in force in Britain since 1712; but in America it served merely as the first focus of the campaign for 'No taxation without representation', and raised such a storm of opposition—being openly defied by various newspapers—that it was repealed a year later.

The agitations leading up to the Declaration and War of Independence were fought out by 'Patriot' and 'Loyalist' papers with much of the bitterness of the news-books in the English Civil Wars, and with much the same multiplication of journals on both sides. The most powerful of all polemics of the time, Thomas Paine's *Common Sense* (which sold 120,000 copies within three months of publication in 1776)[117] was, it is true, published as a pamphlet and not in a newspaper; but Paine was, of course, an indefatigable journalist, whose writings both before and after the Declaration of Independence had enormous influence, and are reckoned to have had a decisive effect (in stiffening Colonial morale) in the early course of the war itself.

After the Colonists' victory, the constitutional debates that ensued were carried on by the contending leaders, 'Federalist' and 'Republican', largely in letters and essays contributed to newspapers. These arguments included that over press freedom in itself. On the one hand the Federalist Alexander Hamilton held that 'the liberty of the press' was impossible to define with legal precision, and that an attempt to write it into the Constitution would be futile: press freedom 'must altogether depend on public opinion and on the general spirit of the People and of the Government'. The Republican Thomas Jefferson put the other side in a letter of 1787, expressing in classic terms the connection between democratic government and liberty to print:

> The people are the only censors of their governors; and even their errors will tend to keep these to the true principles of their institution. To punish these errors too severely would be to suppress the only safeguard of the public liberty. The way to prevent these irregular interpositions of the people is to give them full information of their affairs thro' the channel of the public papers, and to contrive that those papers should penetrate the whole mass of the people. The basis of our government being the opinion of the people, the very first object should be to keep that right; and were it left to me to decide whether we should have a government without newspapers or newspapers without a government, I should not hesitate a moment to prefer the latter. But I should mean that every man should receive those papers, and be capable of reading them.[118]

Jefferson's arguments prevailed, and press freedom, as part of general 'freedom of speech', was explicitly guaranteed in the First Amendment to the Constitution.

Such a brief sketch of newspaper evolution to the beginning of the nineteenth century—or from the English revolution to the French, and its immediate aftermath—should not be concluded without a reminder that the whole development was on a very small scale. The circulation of all the journals mentioned, and of their numerous (and generally short-lived) contemporaries was, by twentieth-century standards, minute, and might be thought insignificant. The circulation of the *Spectator* at the beginning of the century was seldom above 3000 (Johnson calculated it at 1680 in 1712); during publication of the 'Junius' letters in the 1760s, that of the *Daily Advertiser* rose from less than 2000 to a little above 3000 at the peak—a very small fraction even of that larger fraction of the population able to read newspapers.

In the new United States of America, as we have seen, the idea of newspapers as guardians of public liberty was directly linked to the need for universal literacy; if newspapers could be a kind of government, as Jefferson suggested, when no other government existed, that would only work when every man could read them. (Slaves and women, needless to say, were not included in this requirement.) Of how many that was true at the time is impossible to say, though it may perhaps reasonably be supposed that not many voluntary emigrants to the former colonies and the newly independent States—who numbered among them a fair proportion of political exiles and refugees—will have been illiterate.

In Britain itself the number of literate persons is as difficult to guess at for the eighteenth as for previous centuries, but it must be assumed to have been steadily growing. In Scotland, thanks to something approaching general education (in the Lowlands at least) it was doubtless more widespread than in the South. Throughout Britain, but patchily, influences promoting literacy were at work, from the spread of Methodism, which encouraged converts to read the Bible for themselves, to the later Sunday School movement, and even the idea (rare, but spreading) that an employee's ability to read and write was an advantage to the employer. On the other hand, the disruptions of community brought about by industrial change must have operated the other way; there were probably fewer readers among the new industrial poor at the end of the century than among their parents who had worked in a more settled poverty.

'Junius' did not write for these, but for the middle and upper classes whose members had some stake or 'interest' in government; all that was expected to filter down were slogans, 'Wilkes and Liberty', 'No Popery'. 'The mob', assumed to be illiterate, was also without 'interest' in public affairs; when it took a hand in them it was thought of as an instrument, albeit an unreliable and dangerous one. Those who wrote for and published newspapers might themselves be the tools of politicians in the most direct way, and regarded as such with more or less contempt; but in such case they were writing up and not down, for their 'betters' and in terms these were educated to use.

It was common, as has been noted, for authors now little associated with journalism to write for newspapers—Johnson, Fielding as an anti-Jacobite partisan in 1745, Smollett as, for a time, the hired advocate of Bute. Their attitude to such work was ambivalent: Johnson, who lived for many years by journalism—and almost literally hand to mouth—is a good example. He was not without some pride in having virtually fabricated whole sessions of Parliament for the *Gentlemen's Magazine*; in between the weekly (and sometimes twice-weekly) essays he turned out as *Rambler* and *Idler* he was willing to promote other enterprises, such as the *London Chronicle* for the first issue of which, in 1757, he wrote a 'preliminary discourse' judiciously summing up what an educated person might expect of a newspaper:

The first demand made by the reader of a journal is, that he should find an accurate account of foreign transactions and domestick incidents. This is always expected; but this is very rarely performed. Of those writers who have taken upon themselves the task of intelligence, some have given, and others have sold their abilities, whether small or great, to one or other of the parties that divide us; and without a wish for truth, or thought of decency, without care of any other reputation than that of a stubborn adherence to their abettors, carry on the same tenour of representation through all the vicissitudes of right and wrong, neither depressed by detection, nor abashed by confutation; proud of the hourly encrease of infamy, and ready to boast of all the contumelies that falsehood and slander may bring upon them, as new proofs of their zeal and fidelity.

With these heroes we have no ambition to be numbered. . . . That all our facts will be authentick, or all our remarks just, we dare not venture to promise. We can relate but what we hear, we can point out but what we see. Of remote transactions the first accounts are always confused, and commonly exaggerated; and in domestick affairs, if the power to conceal is less, the interest to misrepresent is often greater; and what is sufficiently vexatious, truth seems to fly from curiosity; and as many enquirers produce many narratives, whatever engages the public attention is immediately disguised by the embellishments of fiction. We pretend to no peculiar power of disentangling contradiction, or denuding forgery. We have no settled correspondence with the antipodes, nor maintain any spies in the cabinets of princes. But as we shall always be conscious that our mistakes are involuntary, we shall watch the gradual discoveries of time, and retract whatever we have hastily and erroneously advanced.

. . . as life is very uniform, the affairs of one week are so like those of another, that by any attempt after variety of expression, invention would soon be wearied, and language exhausted. Some improvements however we hope to make; and for the rest we think, that when we commit only common faults, we shall not be excluded from common indulgence.[119]

At other times he had nothing but scorn for news-writers, who needed 'neither genius nor knowledge, neither industry nor spriteliness, but contempt of shame and indifference to truth', especially in times of war: 'Scarcely anything awakens attention like a tale of cruelty. The writer of news never fails in the intermission of action to tell how the enemies murdered children and ravished virgins.' In general, he had low expectations of journalism, even while engaged in it: 'The compilation of newspapers is often committed to narrow and mercenary minds, not qualified for the task of delighting and instructing, who are content to fill their paper with whatever matter is at hand, without industry to gather or discernment to neglect.'[120] But even from his own elevated view of literature, he was ready to own that 'Grub Street' writers had their uses:

... surely, though they cannot aspire to honour, they may be exempted from ignominy, and adopted in that order of men which deserves our kindness though not our reverence. These papers of the day, the ephemerae of learning, have uses more adequate to the purposes of common life than more pompous and durable volumes. If it is necessary for every man to be more acquainted with his contemporaries than with past generations, and rather to know the events which may immediately affect his fortune or quiet than the revolutions of ancient kingdoms in which he has neither possessions nor expectations; if it be pleasing to hear of the preferment and dismission of statesmen, the birth of heirs, and the marriage of beauties, the humble author of journals and gazettes must be considered as a liberal dispenser of beneficial knowledge.[121]

Fielding, less charitable, openly sneered at 'Grub Street' and, allowing that newspaper-reading was the ruling fashion, declared that those on offer had 'scarce a syllable of truth in them', 'no sense in them', and indeed 'in reality nothing at all in them'.[122]

These are the opinions of men (none of them, of course, a democrat) with a settled idea of society, in which newspapers were accepted as an institution, and even recognised as useful; Johnson at least was willing to allow them a place in the commerce of 'common life'. But that they might seriously affect its course was very far from the thoughts of these author-journalists; the Jeffersonian notion that a newspaper-reading public could in some way be not only a necessary auxiliary but even a replacement of government would have been wholly repugnant to them. Steele might at the beginning of the century think that a journal like the *Tatler* should teach people 'what to think', but educated persons were certainly not supposed to take their views from 'Grub Street'. The 'humble author of journals and gazettes' was low in the social scale, and writing for those above him. Samuel Johnson, to be sure, knew very well that he was the intellectual superior of most of his readers, but even then he wrote with the assumption that they would understand and probably agree with him.

A 'popular' press did not and probably could not exist. The prices of papers alone (kept up by government, quite consciously, for that reason) must have prevented any considerable circulation among the poor. But towards the end of the period at least some of the prerequisites were present, the most important being unquestionably the spread of democratic aspirations, stimulated by the American and French Revolutions. Between 1789 and the Reform Bill, through the vicissitudes of the French wars and their economic consequences, newspapers were, along with pamphlets and broadsides, a bugbear to government; the most telling evidence of their influence is in the strenuous efforts at repression, as well as in such counter-propaganda to democratic agitation as *The Anti-Jacobin*.

Pitt's Newspaper Act of 1798, directed against 'the mischief arising from newspapers being printed and published by persons unknown', testifies to the effect of the new Radical prints; prosecutions under this and other statutes multiply continually. Between 1808 and 1811, for example, 42 prosecutions for libel were instituted, though not all of them were brought to court, and some resulted in acquittal. The circulations of the offending journals was not large, but their influence was wider—and enhanced, needless to say, by the prosecutions themselves. Such a periodical as Cobbett's *Political Register* flourished under persecution; *The Examiner* published by the Hunt brothers boasted of the 'flattering' attacks of authority and of consequent increases in circulation. As before, such journals were addressed to a minority—the disaffected members of the educated classes—but they certainly reached many who did not enjoy similar privileges, including literacy itself. It is recorded that illiterate labourers would go every week to a pub to hear Cobbett's editorial letter read and discussed.[123]

The stamp duties were evaded in various ways or occasionally openly defied: in the last years before the Reform Bill a number of unstamped (and therefore illegal) papers were brought out, of which perhaps the most notable was *The Poor Man's Guardian*, published by a printing worker, Henry Hetherington. Hetherington displayed the emblem of a handpress on his masthead with the motto 'Knowledge is Power' and the declaration that the paper was 'published contrary to "Law", to try the power of "Might" against "Right"'. In the first number, 9 July 1831, he said 'we will try, step by step, the power of right against might, and we will begin by upholding this grand bulwark of all our rights, this key to all our liberties, the freedom of the press—the press, too, of the ignorant and the poor'.[124] It was distributed by volunteers recruited from the same people as those to whom it was addressed: Hetherington advertised for 'some hundreds of poor men out of employ who have nothing to risk . . . to sell to the poor and ignorant'. There was at this time something like a small guerrilla army of newsvendors and hawkers, risking and frequently suffering imprisonment and other penalties, and evidently acting quite consciously, not simply as upholding 'the liberty of the press', but as agents for its wider application.

Throughout these years men were disposed to look anew at the power of the press to overcome, by mere number, the enemies of 'knowledge', whether these were the forces of oppression and censorship, or simply accident and the erosion of time. Thomas Jefferson, writing of his difficulties in tracing old legal documents, argued that print alone can safeguard legal, or any other records against 'the ravages of fire and of ferocious enemies':

> How many of the precious works of antiquity were lost while they existed only in manuscript? Has there ever been one lost since the art of printing rendered it practicable to multiply and disperse copies? This leads us then to the only means of preserving those remains of our laws now under consideration, that is, a multiplication of printed copies.[125]

In Britain one of the most irrepressible agitators of the period, Richard Carlile (bookseller, publisher and printer, prosecuted and imprisoned for re-publishing and selling Tom Paine's banned *Rights of Man*) applied the concept of mass-publication directly to political purposes, and in literal, or rather arithmetic terms:

> The Printing-press may be strictly denominated a Multiplication Table as applicable to the mind of man. The art of Printing is a multiplication of mind. . . . Pamphlet-vendors are the most important springs in the machinery of Reform.[126]

For conservative authority newspapers were 'engines of disaffection'; for their Radical opponents they were locomotives of progress. The example is given by a modern historian who points to the 'characteristic illusion of the epoch' in expecting an automatic, or mechanical result from improved technical means. It was the illusion, of course, of the utilitarians, but it was shared by a larger group who set an 'exceptionally high value upon the rights of the press, of speech, of meeting, and of personal liberty . . . In the contest between 1792 and 1836 the artisans and workers made this tradition peculiarly their own, adding to the claim for free speech and thought their own claim for the untrammeled propagation, in the cheapest possible form, of the products of this thought.'[127]

The printing press was the prime instrument, specifically so designated, of democratic aims: in the typical image or icon of the movement it appears, without anyone actually operating or in charge of it, as 'The Tyrant's Foe, the People's Friend'.

VI
MULTIPLICATION MARCHES ON

PRINTING, said Richard Carlile, is 'the multiplication of mind': for the Radicals in the early years of the nineteenth century the press was the supreme instrument in 'the march of mind', the expectation of semi-automatic intellectual and moral progress satirised by Thomas Love Peacock as the prospectus of the 'Steam Intellect Society'.[128] The press was the means of applying methods of mass-production and distribution to thought, with the advantages for society which the utilitarians looked for from application of the same methods in other branches of industry. Such advantages should, they assumed, be even greater in the case of printing than in other manufactures, since these must meet, eventually, a slackening of demand; but the demand for knowledge was without limit.

Translation of these notions into practice had certain obstacles to overcome, the most obvious being legal and governmental. Authority, fighting a dogged rearguard action against press freedom, was as anxious to restrict newspaper circulation as Radicals were to give it free scope. On the Continent, where absolutism prevailed (whether Napoleonic, Hapsburg, or Czarist) direct censorship hobbled the press; in Britain, though prosecutions for seditious libel could be, and were from time to time, resorted to, the dangers to authority offered by a much more numerous and various press were kept within bounds mainly by taxation. During the first half of the nineteenth century the argument about press freedom concentrated largely on fiscal measures, which bore heavily on all newspapers; but especially, and intentionally, on those which might aspire to be 'papers of the poor'.

From the end of the Napoleonic Wars until four years after the passing of the Reform Bill in 1832, the stamp duty on all newspapers was 4d. a copy, with an additional duty on paper and the extremely heavy advertising tax of 3s. 6d. on each advertisement (reduced to 1s. 6d. in 1833). These raised very considerable sums for the Exchequer, a point which became a strong argument for their retention; it was calculated in 1828 that the largest circulating daily, *The Times*, was on its own paying the government £1300 a week, a large sum of money at the time.[129] The price to the public was 7d. a copy, of which 5½d. was tax. At the same period the daily wage of a factory worker in full employment might be no more than 2s., and of an agricultural labourer much less. But important as these taxes were merely as a source of revenue, their main purpose was political, not economic, a function explicitly described by the Lord Chief Justice, Lord Ellenborough, in 1819. Commending the new 4d. Stamp Act, he said that it was aimed 'not against the respectable press (such as *The Times*) . . . but against a pauper press which, administering to the prejudices and passions of a mob, was converted to the basest purposes, which was an utter stranger to truth, and only sent forth a continual stream of malignity, its virulence and its mischief heightening as it proceeded. If he was asked whether he would deprive the lower classes of all political information, he would say he saw no possible good to be derived by the country from having statesmen at the loom and politicians at the spinning-jenny.'[130]

Various means of evasion continued to be found, from the use of a magazine format (only *news*papers were taxed) to the open defiance of men like Hetherington; it is interesting that one of the arguments against the Stamp Acts was that they stimulated the growth of a semi-legal, seditious, 'underground' press. Agitation for abolition of the different 'taxes on knowledge' was persistent and, by degrees, effective: the newspaper duty was reduced to 1d. in 1836 and the advertisment tax, already reduced, was the first to go altogether, in 1853. In 1855 the compulsory newspaper stamp duty was finally abolished, resistance having been at length worn down; it is remarkable that among the last-ditch opponents of the Bill in question was, again, *The Times*, which feared for its quasi-monopoly as by far the fullest medium of news, with much the largest circulation, of the day. Abolition of the tax, *The Times* said, would lead to multiplication of other, jumped-up newspapers of 'a cheap class', and these, 'in the metropolis and still more in the manufacturing districts' would purloin and reproduce the news 'which we believe to constitute our principal attraction, and to obtain which *we* spend immense sums of money'.[131] For *The Times* news was a commodity which it had, in commercial terms, cornered; as such it was a luxury article, the high price of which helped to maintain the monopoly. This jealous sense of proprietorship in news, and consequent rivalry between papers trying to get it into print *first*, is something we shall meet again in press history; what is striking about *The Times's* objections in the mid-nineteenth century is that 'ownership' of news was something to be protected not only by getting it fresh, but also by keeping it expensive.

The opposite point of view was stated in support of the abolition Bill by the Radical MP John Bright: '. . . I am quite convinced that five or six years will show that all the votes of parliament for educational purposes have been as mere trifles compared with the results which will flow from this measure, because, while the existing papers retain all their usefulness, it will call to their aid numbers of others not less useful, and, while we enjoy the advantage of having laid before us each morning a map of the events of the world, the same advantage will be extended to classes of society at present shut out from it.'[132]

In such a view multiplication and distribution were as important as freedom to print itself; it is noteworthy that on this occasion the new cheap postal system (the penny post, established in 1839) was directly involved in the provisions of the Bill, as an extension of the powers of print. The Bill in its original form, while making the stamp duty optional, gave newspapers which chose to retain the stamp the continued privilege of penny postage, regardless of weight. When it was pointed out that this gave newspapers (*The Times*, especially, being larger and heavier than any others) an unfair advantage, an order was introduced to extend the cheap rate to any printed matter below a certain weight. This general advantage has of course been preserved, and can be seen as part of the concession by the government to the whole system of social inter-communication provided by print.

The compulsory stamp duty was not the last of the 'taxes of knowledge' to go. The paper duties, imposed both on imports and on home production, had helped to keep up prices, and to raise money for government throughout the period of early newspaper evolution and expansion. Again, the division of interest was not absolutely clear-cut; the tax on imported paper was supported by British paper manufacturers. Both taxes however obnoxious to Radicals, as Free Traders as well as champions of an unrestricted press.

The arguments of the 'Taxes on Knowledge Association' eventually prevailed, and in 1861, Gladstone, against considerable opposition, ended both Custom and Excise impositions on paper. All forms of printing benefited; the paper taxes had affected book-prices as well as newspapers. But it was certainly the newspaper-press that gained most, as using large quantities of paper from day to day; it is instructive to see how opponents of abolition based their arguments precisely on this. An author like Dickens (at least according to Richard Cobden, who poured scorn on him for it) certainly had no objection to cheaper paper for book-printing, but 'refused to sign a petition for the repeal of the taxes on knowledge on the express ground that he would not promote a deluge of printer's ink in England similar to what he had seen in America'. In Parliament itself Lord Robert Cecil (the later Lord Salisbury) rejected contemptuously the connection between cheap paper and 'knowledge'. That paper for school-books, as for Bibles, might be exempted from tax he allowed; but 'Could it be maintained that a person of any education could learn anything from a penny paper? It might be said that people might learn what had been said in parliament. Well, would that contribute much to their education? They might read the foreign intelligence, of which many would understand very little, and they might see the opinions of the editor of the paper. No doubt all this was very interesting, but it did not answer any true idea of education, or carry any real instruction to the mind.'[133]

Supplies of paper at this time were in any case limited, and costs comparatively high. It may be appropriate at this point briefly to consider the provision of this, the stuff on which virtually all printing depended, as it met demands which had grown steadily over the previous 400 years. During this time—and longer, for paper was used by scribes in Europe before the introduction of printing—the only source of raw material, apart from some supplementary use of straw and old rope, was rags. The rags had, moreover, to be of cotton or linen, even mixtures of these with animal fibres (wool or silk) being useless. The actual process of manufacture changed; paper-making appears from at least the seventeenth century to have been a relatively large-scale industry, capitalised both technically (with use of water-power) and financially (in joint-stock companies), but methods remained essentially the same until the end of the eighteenth century. The important advance from hand-production of separate sheets to mass-production of a continuous paper-web (with the introduction of the so-called Fourdrinier machine)[134] did not take place until the early 1800s; use of steam-power soon followed (together with those other commonplace consequences of industrial revolution, the degradation of skilled craftsmen into machine-minders, the destruction of trade unions and depression of wages).[135]

But throughout this period of technological change and expansion, dependence of the industry on rags and rag-collection remained essentially the same: perhaps the only example of a large-scale industry based on scavenging. Rag-collecting was much the same trade in the first half of the nineteenth century that it had been since the Middle Ages. The primary source was, as always, at the botton of the social heap: rags were the product, indeed the common symbol of extreme poverty, and their collection for what would now be called recycling was the lowest of occupations. Dealers in rags could become rich (in the seventeenth century it was observed that 'several there be that have got estates out of them');[136] in due course the interconnections of the paper trade resulted in amalgamation so that a wealthy entrepreneur might be a stationer, paper-manufacturer, and rag-merchant, with international interests; but rag-collecting and rag-picking was for the poorest of the poor, next door to mendicancy, despised, dirty, and dangerous. During outbreaks of plague, as in England in 1636–7, papermills might be closed down for fear of infection; and the rags which had clothed many bodies before they became fit only to be thrown away must always have been potent carriers of disease.

At the same time demand steadily grew; there were never enough rags to satisfy it. At the beginning of the eighteenth century it was claimed that '40,000 poor' were maintained by the English paper industry, most of whom must have been at its lowest level, rag-collecting; but they were not enough. Rags were collected all over Europe—Germany, Flanders, and Italy being among the chief suppliers; by the end of the eighteenth century rags were imported from Russia and other parts of Eastern Europe, and were being shipped across the Atlantic from America.[137] This was despite the efforts of all these countries, as they developed paper-industries of their own, to restrict exports of the raw material; as late as the 1850s, an argument put forward by British paper manufacturers for retaining the import duty on paper was that it would be retaliation for foreign restriction on the export of rags.

Prices of paper are not easy to calculate, there being so many types and sizes, but it may be assumed that they rose more or less steadily as demand expanded. It may also be taken that the reward of the rag-collectors did not; they were too close to beggary to share in the growing wealth of the paper industry, and of printing itself. It is curious to think that the entire edifice of printed communication was built on this base; and that for most of the first 400 years of print very few of the rag-and-bone men and women, scavengers and pariahs, who made it possible, can have been able to read at all.

Freed from legal and fiscal restrictions, therefore, newspapers as the largest consumers of paper were still subject to the absolute limitation of shortage. Attempts were continually made to overcome it by finding other sources, for long without success. In 1861, giving evidence before the Select Committee set up after the abolition of paper duties, a leading British manufacturer said that, despite all efforts then being made- 'upwards of 100 patents taken out for different materials for the manufacture of paper'—none had proved practical. *The Times* offered a prize of £1000 to anyone who found an effective substitute for rags, and a huge variety of suggestions was made, from rhubarb and nettles to leather, this last being apparently a despairing return to the material (vellum) of most books before print.[138] Some additional materials were by then in use, notably esparto grass (important especially in the Scottish paper industry) and sweepings from textile mills, but these were no more than supplementary.

The really significant development had to wait another 20 years, when experiments with wood-pulp, which had been going on for some time, reached the point of successful commercial exploitation, and very rapidly changed not only the whole process of paper-making, from raw material to finished product, and the organisation of the industry, but the very foundations of printing itself. The nature and degree of the change can be indicated by selected figures. In 1860 the output of all kinds of paper in Britain was 100,000 tons; imports, though they had risen steeply since 1800, added only a small fraction, just over 1000 tons; imports of rags, supplementing what was collected within the UK, were 16,000 tons. By 1900, after woodpulp had been in use for fifteen years or so, paper-output was more than 500,000 tons a year, and the raw material was almost entirely imported: 16,000 tons of rags were still coming into Britain from abroad, but that was against 194,000 tons of esparto grass and 448,000 tons of woodpulp.[139]

Today, although other raw materials are used, both the traditional rags and others newly developed, woodpulp remains by far the most important, and its output has enormously increased. World consumption of paper in the early 1970s is estimated at 140,000,000 tons per year, to the production of which went over 114,000,000 tons of woodpulp (the difference being made up of rags and other materials, including an increasing use of waste-paper). A large part of all paper manufactured and used throughout the world is newsprint, and the price has risen steeply since the Second World War; once again paper-costs have come to exercise some restraint on sizes and circulations of newspapers, but at a level of consumption hundreds of times higher than in Western Europe and America a century earlier, and now spread all over the world.

Sources of raw material have switched geographically from regions of dense (and poor) population, productive of quantities of rags, to those covered with softwood trees. It is reckoned that a single edition of a mass-circulation newspaper (say a 20-page issue with a circulation of 4,000,000) consumes the equivalent of nine-acres of trees. In some parts of the world whole forests have been destroyed to make paper; in others plantations of exotic conifers, grown for wood-pulp, have transformed the landscape. In the Western industrial countries at least, yearly consumption of all kinds of paper has risen from 8 lb per head (for the UK) in 1860 to something in excess of 40 lb today. Of newsprint alone consumption in Britain in 1980 was about 1,380,000 tonnes, of which the greater part—more than a million tonnes—was imported, already manufactured, from Canadian and Scandinavian sources. British manufacture of newsprint has steadily declined since the Second World War, only two mills still being in operation (in June 1981); and in the Western world generally a curious re-adjustment of economic power has taken place, not unlike that effected in the oil trade, by which a few small countries—Canada, Finland, Norway and Sweden—have obtained partial control of a commodity vital, or believed to be vital, to modern communication.[140]

'Consumption' of paper is a term, needless to say, that requires qualification. It includes, and increasingly in modern times, all those uses of paper, as packaging and in other manufacturing processes, which have apparently nothing to do with print. But it should not be forgotten that the wrapping-up of commodities for the market is seldom print-less, and that a great deal of the reading matter daily presented to our eyes is in fact 'on the packet'. If it is not an exact guide to levels of literacy, paper-consumption cannot be divorced from it. In 1834 a London publisher and printer, appearing before an official inquiry into paper-manufacture, attributed the increase in paper production directly to the growing number of people who could read. Under questioning, he insisted upon this as cause rather than effect: when the inquiry suggested to him that increased paper consumption had been brought about rather by 'the great increase in printing', he replied, 'the great increase in printing, *arising from the great increase in education*'.[141] 'Education'—still at that time in Britain forty years away from the 'universal' and compulsory—taught people to read, and what they read, it seems, more than anything else, was newspapers. Some verbal usages may be reflected upon: it was more than 100 years at that time since 'the papers', 'a paper', had been synonymous with printed news-media; it was not until woodpulp made enormous supplies of cheap paper available that the identification appeared as it were in reverse, and the rolls of paper themselves, as yet unmarked, began to be known as 'newsprint'.

In the meantime the inventions which speeded up and increased the output of paper were paralleled by others in printing technique itself. The development of the cylinder press, the application of steam power which soon followed, and the successive devices for mechanised typesetting, were all designed to the same end, to accelerate the mass-production of printed material. It was newspaper production, clearly, that provided the chief stimulus, and the competition between different newspapers: there were large rewards for whichever paper could be 'on the streets', in large numbers, ahead of its rivals.

In the self-consciousness and desire for self-advertisement which characteristically induce newspapers to give news of themselves—it being assumed that this also is of compelling interest to the public—each advance in technology was a matter of boasting, as an attraction itself. That not merely news, but news of news, its gathering and delivery, should be an allurement is a psychological curiosity, but a reflection nevertheless of genuine feelings (with poetic warrant: 'How we brought the Good News . . . '). It is evidently part of the peculiar excitement which surrounds the arrival of any news, and which rises in proportion to belief in its urgency, this in turn being connected with speed of transmission. It is natural to assume that efforts will be made to deliver important news as quickly as possible; by association it comes to be assumed that because news is carried with speed it is in the same degree important. The observation seems perhaps hardly worth making, but the urge to devise ever faster means of transmitting and distributing news, and the aura of enthusiasm with which successive means were invented, adopted, announced and greeted in the second half of the nineteenth century— telegraphy and submarine cables, the individual ingenuities of correspondents vying with one another, and the continual improvement of high-speed printing methods—are a good illustration of the kind of self-generating excitement in which journalism flourishes and its techniques change.

In the last two decades of the nineteenth century, therefore, the technical means, the material supplies, and the motives were all present for another large expansion in printed communication to take place. All conditions worked together—mechanical speed and ease of printing, availability of very cheap raw material, the removal of legal and financial restrictions, the extension of literacy, in theory to the entire population—and it is hardly possible to arrange these factors in sequential causative order. But the combined effect promised change large enough to be one of quality as well as of mere additional numbers: the 'multiplication of mind' might be expected to proceed by mathematical progression.

It should be remembered that about the middle of the century, circulation of British papers, though still probably the largest in proportion to population of anywhere in the world, was by modern standards quite small. The Times, at 65,000 in 1861, remained far ahead of all other dailies in Britain, most of which were doing well if they sold 25,000 to 30,000 copies. It was certain weekly papers that first approached what we would now consider mass-circulation, notably Lloyd's Weekly, a miscellany which began as a newspaper (therefore paying stamp duty) in 1843, and its close rival the *News of the World,* first published in the same year. Both were priced as low as possible (3d.) while still paying duty, the *News of the World* in particular being consciously launched as 'the paper of the poor'. 'The paper for the wealthy classes is high-priced' (it said editorially in its first issue). 'It is paid for by them, and it helps to lull them in the security of their prejudices. The paper for the poorer classes is, on the other hand, low-priced, and it is paid for by them; it feels bound to pander to their passions.' The latter recipe, followed if not acknowledged, brought the *News of the World* a circulation of 110,000 within a few years, with *Lloyd's* close behind. When the different tax impositions were successively lifted *Lloyd's* lowered its price, becoming a penny paper shortly before the last of them, on paper, was abolished in 1861; thereafter circulation rose rapidly to 350,000.[142] Before that it was *Lloyd's,* in 1855, which introduced to Britain the recent American invention of the rotary press; *The Times* followed with a variant of the same machine a year later. *Lloyd's* is also credited with introducing many other devices for speeding up the output of very large 'runs' of print.

But although indications were not lacking in Britain of what might be done, it was the American press, already technically advanced, that began to do it, on a scale and with methods much like those used today. As elsewhere, it was a continuous process, only artificially to be divided by date-lines, and with to-and-fro of example and imitation across the Atlantic. There had been something like a 'popular press' in the young United States from the early years of the nineteenth century, and, unhampered by tax or other restrictions, it expanded rapidly—although confined, geographically, to the eastern States. The rapidly growing city of New York was its most fertile ground. The first successful 'penny' (or one-cent) paper was the New York *Sun* (1833), which promised 'to lay before the public, at a price within the means of everyone, all the news of the day, and at the same time afford an advantageous medium for advertising'. Its particular innovation was a concentration on police investigation and criminal trials, reported with an eye to sensation and 'human interest'. (The quasi-humorous treatment of police courts was in fact borrowed from an English example.) The formula proved so popular that within two years the *Sun* was selling 15,000 copies a day, far more than any other paper in the States,[143] and it soon had imitators. In 1835, James Gordon Bennett, a Scot who had emigrated in 1820, started (with $500 capital) the New York *Morning Herald* as another 'penny' daily and, by the same methods, rapidly pushed its circualtion up to 17,000, with 19,000 of a weekly edition; by the outbreak of the American Civil War in 1861 this had risen to 100,000.

Bennett was a flamboyant man who ruthlessly exploited all sources of sensation, especially of crime, and made himself a central figure—with his opinions, plans and details of his domestic life—in the daily drama offered to readers. He seems to have been the first to use the phrase (applied to himself) of a 'Napoleon of the press', and his editorial style was a remarkable blend of buffoonery and megalomania.

> I go for a general reformation of morals—of manners. I mean to begin a new movement in the progress of civilisation and human intellect. I know and feel I shall succeed. Nothing can prevent its success but God Almighty, and he happens to be entirely on my side. . . .

> I am determined to make the *Herald* the greatest paper that ever appeared in the world. The highest order of mind has never yet been found operating through the daily press. Let it be tried. What is to prevent a daily newspaper from being made the greatest organ of social life? Books have had their day—the theatres have had their day—the temple of religion has had its day. A newspaper can be made to take the lead of all these in the great movements of human thought, and of human civilisation. . . .[144]

His methods and character were vigorously attacked, and a 'penny' paper of a different kind, Horace Greeley's New York *Tribune*, founded in 1841, and pledged explicitly to do without sensational reporting, expecially of crime, equalled the *Herald* within ten years. After a continued rivalry of some eighty years (at one point of which Greeley described Bennett's son and successor, James Gordon Jr, as 'a low-down, blatant, witless, brutal scoundrel') the papers, no longer so different from one another, were combined as the *Herald-Tribune*. Both had long since been overtaken in the furious competition of the end of the century, in which 'the Bennett type of journalism' had trimphed, though in other papers than Bennett's. Its 'secret', discovered by the father and put to further use by the son, was described retrospectively by another journalist (E. L. Godkin, editor successively of the sober weeklies, the *Nation* and New York *Evening Post*). It was, he said:

> . . . that there was far more money to be made by catering to the tastes of the uninstructed, or the slenderly instructed, masses than to those of the educated few . . . there was more journalistic money to be made in recording gossip that interested bar-rooms, workshops, race-courses, and tenement houses, than in consulting the tastes of drawing-rooms and libraries. He [J. G. Bennett Sr] introduced, too, an absolutely new feature which has had, perhaps, the greatest success of all . . . the plan of treating everything and everybody as somewhat of a

joke. . . . Even crime and punishment have received a touch of the comic. . . . By adding to his comic deportment wonderful enterprise in collecting news from all parts of the world, Bennett was able to realise a fortune in the first half of the century, besides making a deep impression on all ambitious publishers.[145]

If Bennett was the first man who 'made news into a readily saleable consumer commodity'[146] his achievement was hugely surpassed after his death in 1872. In the booming of American industry and the presentation, more than ever, of all social exchange in terms of commodity, three men in particular were associated with selling the commodity of news, Joseph Pulitzer, Edward Wyllis Scripps, and William Randolph Hearst. All three, in fierce rivalry, made huge fortunes out of the newspapers which, in the last decade and a half of the nineteenth century, they pushed to circulations of unprecedented size. Pulitzer's New York *World* (which he bought in 1883, when it had a circulation of 15,000) was the first to pass half a million, and reached a million during the Cuban War of 1898. Hearst's New York *Morning Journal*, taken over by him in 1885, was selling 1,250,000 copies by the end of the century. Scripps in the meantime built up 'chains' of newspapers, in different cities of the US, which in aggregate circulation compared with those of the New York rivals.

The methods used by these men were much the same, Pulitzer and Hearst especially being forced by competition to imitate one another. The aim, stated by Pulitzer in the first issue of his new *World*, was to be 'not only cheap but bright, not only bright but large'; the appeal was explicitly to 'the mass of the American people', although this mass, as care was taken to point out, should include 'the millionaire and the railroad magnate, as just as good as any other man'.[147] 'Brightness' and 'breeziness'—the *World*, parodying, perhaps unconsciously, Heber's famous hymn, announced its Sunday issue as the 'Brightest and Best'—comprehended selection and brief treatment of the most sensational items of news, and direct appeal to the eye. Headlines (already on the front page) were large and clamant; illustration was lavish, although at this time technically limited to 'cuts', or engravings, satisfactory reproduction of photographs having yet to be devised. The illustrations included not only political cartoons—a kind of visual polemic at least as old as print—but something new in the form of comic strip-cartoons and picture-jokes, of which whole pages were provided in the Sunday *World*. In 1893 these began to be printed in colour, and among them was a favourite, depicting child-life in the New York streets—an early example of American society's attachment to 'cute' childhood which continues to this day. The central character of this strip,

'The Kid of Hogan's Alley', was distinguished by the bright yellow of his clothing, and soon became known as 'The Yellow Kid', and one of the chief assets of the paper. Hearst bought the cartoonist for the Journal, but Pulitzer continued in the *World* with another artist; rival 'Yellow Kids' appeared and were simultaneously advertised on New York billboards. From this bizarre contest arose the term 'yellow journalism'.[148]

The 'circulation war' was itself exploited as matter for public interest and diversion, both papers regularly printing their claims and targets; but real warfare gave more scope. The events leading to the short Spanish-American War of 1898 gave the *World* and *Journal* opportunities which, indeed, they might be said partly to have made for themselves; both Hearst and Pulitzer were accused of rousing 'war fever' for their own ends. That the outbreak of war over Cuba was actually engineered by the 'yellow press' would be difficult to prove, but its benefit to newspaper proprietors in pushing circulation is unquestionable. E. L. Godkin made the connection unequivocally at the time:

> Gross misrepresentation of the facts, deliberate invention of tales calculated to excite the public, and wanton recklessness in the construction of headlines which even outdid these inventions have combined to make of the issues of most widely circulated newspapers firebrands scattered broadcast throughout the city. . . . It is a crying shame that men should work such mischief simply to sell more papers.

> The reason why such journals lie is that it pays to lie, or in other words, this is the very reason for which they are silly and scandalous and indecent. They supply a want of a demoralised public. Moreover, such journals are almost always in favour of war, because war affords unusual opportunities for lying and sensation.[149]

A moderate modern comment sums up the characteristics of the Pulitzer and Hearst papers, and their imitators, as 'flamboyance, activism, primitivism, and a sometimes spurious air of excitement'.[150] The 'activism' was a quality especially prized by Hearst, who boasted in the Journal's headlines of a 'Journalism that Acts':

> Action—that is the distinguishing mark of the new journalism. It represents the final stage in the evolution of the modern newspaper of a century ago—the 'new journals' of their day told the news and some of them made great efforts to get it first. The new journalism of today prints the news too, but it does more. It does not wait for things to turn up. It turns them up.[151]

The implications of this programme will be looked at later. Hearst, a younger man than Pulitzer, lived to see it widely adopted, and not only in America. But it was Pulitzer, perhaps, who expressed most succinctly the principle which animated both in their 'campaigns' and which, in its combination of evangelical fervour with exhibitionism, defined the functions of a paper 'made for millions'. In advice to his editors (publicly announced, of course) in 1895 he told them:

> Always tell the truth, always take the humane and moral side, always remember that right feeling is the vital spark of strong writing, and that publicity, *publicity*, PUBLICITY is the greatest moral factor and force in our public life.[152]

Though Hearst and Pulitzer thought in American terms, these precepts had already been taken up, if not as yet quite so vigorously, in Britain. The 'new journalism' as a label had indeed originated in Matthew Arnold's cool welcome to a moderate example in the *Pall Mall Gazette*, edited by W. T. Stead:

> We have had opportunity of observing a new journalism which a clever and energetic man has invented. It has much to recommend it; it has ability, novelty, variety, sensation, sympathy, generous instinct: its one great fault is that it is feather-brained.[153]

This may be set beside the self-description of a British contemporary, the *Star*, launched by T. P. O'Connor as a halfpenny daily in 1888, the year after Arnold was writing. The new paper, O'Connor said in his 'Confession of Faith' in the first issue, would have 'no place for verbose or prolix articles', but would offer:

> . . . plenty of entirely unpolitical literature—sometimes humorous, sometimes pathetic; anecdotal, statistical, the craze of fashions and the arts of housekeeping—now and then a short, dramatic and picturesque tale. . . . Men and women who figure in the forum or the pulpit or the law court shall be presented as they are—living, breathing, in blushes or in tears—and not merely by the dead words they utter. . . . Our ideal is to leave no event unrecorded; to be earliest in the field with every item of news; to be thorough and unmistakeable in our meaning;. to be animated, readable, and stirring.[154]

How the new paper was to combine all these qualities, and in particular where the line was to be drawn between the reporting of events and 'picturesque' invention, readers were left to find out; but by these promises

O'Connor drew enough of them to be able to boast in the headlines of his second issue, 'An epoch in journalism/The world's record beaten/ 142,000 copies sold.'[155]

The *Star* may be taken as typical of the 'new journalism' as it operated in Britain at the turn of the century, when it was joined by several others, notably the *Daily Mail* (1896) and *Daily Express* (1900), all selling at a halfpenny, and distinguished from the more expensive and more 'serious' papers by highly condensed or fragmentary treatment of news, short 'stories' of all kinds being scattered throughout the paper under brief headlines, not so large nor so sensational as American models, but already composed with an eye to attracting attention in themselves rather than simply as announcing a subject. 'Curious Church Raid', 'Tested in Suffering', 'The Drama at Westminster' (*Daily Mail*); 'A Royal Surprise', 'With a Hole in His Head', 'Sensation in Pretoria' (*Evening News*); 'Chasing a Rebellion', 'Converts Burnt Alive', 'Kruger Bends the Knee' (*Daily Express*) are examples taken from a single day, 14 March 1900; the news of the day ranged from the final stages of the Boer War to the exploits of a zealot investigating 'popery' in the Anglican Church. Few of the items took up more than half a column, and many were single paragraphs; in the *Star* of the same date one of the longest items was fiction, an extract from a romantic novel being serialised at the time. There were entirely miscellaneous columns of 'Gossip', 'Chat', 'Interesting Items'. There were many illustrations, still in the form of engravings, and mostly consisting of portrait-sketches of persons in the news. Of these, only the *Express* as yet carried main news on the front page; the *Daily Graphic*, in the format later to be known as 'tabloid', had news and pictures on the front, but in appearance as rather more of a magazine than a daily newspaper. The idea of 'the news in pictures' could hardly be realised, however, until the inventions of photogravure and half-tone printing made rapid reproduction of photographs possible. These techniques, already in use in America, were soon adopted in Britain, and fully exploited in the first place by the new *Daily Mirror*, unsuccessfully launched as a woman's paper in 1903, but taken up by Northcliffe and rapidly transformed into a 'picture paper' not unlike its form today. The *Mirror* may be reckoned as the first complete transference to Britain of methods pioneered by American journalism, and rapidly gained circulation, rivalling the *Mail*, at that time well ahead of other British papers; in 1910 a special 'Memorial Edition' for the death of Edward VII sold over 2,000,000 copies.

In different degree, the entire press was changing at the same time, and in the same direction. The most conservative of British newspapers, *The*

Times, was bought by Northcliffe in 1907 and its equipment and, to some extent, its style were 'modernised'; by the outbreak of the First World War its appearance and presentation of news, with headlines carefully graded according to the adjudged importance of the subject, photographs, and lengthy special 'features', were much as today, except that the front page was still reserved for advertising only. Printing of news on the front page was indeed the last concession to the 'new journalism' made by such papers as *The Times*, which clung to this distinction until some years after the Second World War. *The Times*, consciously a journal for the well-to-do, and considered—even when editorially opposed to government policy—as representing the views of the ruling groups of British society, was also engaged in the circulation struggle, and twice reduced its price shortly before the First World War: from 3d. to 2d. in 1913, and in March 1914 to 1d. Joining the ranks of 'penny papers' so much despised during the nineteenth century, it increased its circulation more than twofold, pushing it up to 150,000 by the outbreak of war.

The forces behind this general trend may be thought of as chiefly economic. The production of newspapers in the Western world—and they hardly existed elsewhere except in imitation of the West—was a 'business', that is a commercial enterprise, run by private individuals or limited companies, closely linked with the rest of 'business' in which industrial society was engaged, conducted for and dependent upon profit. It is interesting to look at a summary of the consequences by a historian of British newspapers (to whom this outline is much indebted), writing at a time, in the late 1880s, when these transformations were beginning to be felt:

> Newspapers, if they are meant to prosper and to be really useful to the public, are and must be business concerns almost before anything else. Proprietors, editors, and writers alike may be philanthropists and enthusiasts, and if they have not somewhat more than the average amount of philanthropy or enthusiasm, they are hardly likely to pursue any of these callings of their own accord, though they may be driven into them by force of circumstances. It is by no means rare, moreover, for philanthropy, genuine or spurious, strong political partisanship or zealous propagandism of some sort, to be the dominating motive for the taking up of newspaper business of one kind or another. . . . But these are the complements, if not the exceptions, of newspaper enterprise, which, if it is to fare well and be of lasting benefit, must be entered upon and carried through in the ordinary way of business. It may be thought, indeed, that in some newspaper enterprise of the present day there is too much, rather than too little, of the prosaic commercial spirit. The community suffers, though the individuals

connected with it may gain, when a paper is 'worked' for money-making purposes alone, like a shop, or a factory, or a patent medicine. But this need not and does not very often happen. . . . [156]

The many ambiguities in this passage will be apparent, very much more painfully now than when the writer, Fox Bourne, was recording, with some unease, the tendencies of his day. There are doubtful meanings in the word 'enthusiasm', and the writer himself is aware of the slipperiness of 'philanthropy', which may be genuine or not, and, when it is spurious, presumably conceals some other motive. These psychological matters are, perhaps, the fundamental questions to be considered in examining the aims and performances of newspapers. But the more obvious conflict is that between 'business', or money-making, and 'usefulness to the pulbic'. A 'business' is one that is 'worked' for making money, and though that may not be its sole object, it is the indispensable one; it can only be abandoned at the cost of the business itself. Under pressure, money-making tends inexorably to edge out other considerations, and in the newspaper business, as in others, the pressure may be both negative and positive. If for some reason, but especially because it is falling behind in competition with others, a newspaper is losing money, there is the strongest pressure to change in one or another way its mode of production or its nature, as product, or both. But there is also pressure,[1] as impossible to resist under 'the laws of the market', to make more money when and wherever that is possible, with the same implications for change, or 'development'.

Both these sorts of pressure on newspaper-businesses were beginning to be exerted with new force when Fox Bourne was writing: there was fierce competition, and it was competition for very large rewards. The methods by which a Hearst or a Pulitzer could become a multi-millionaire soon crossed the Atlantic. Business became big business, on a scale and involving investment hitherto unthought of, carried on competitively but by a smaller number of firms: although the number of individual newspapers published in Britain has fallen fairly slowly since 1900 (more rapidly after the Second World War), the reduction in number of proprietors, by amalgamation and develpment of 'chains' has been much more rapid.

In this period, with much ebb and flow, very large differences between different papers and different rates of development in different countries, the 'newspaper industry' may be said nevertheless to have moved with some steadiness in one direction, the nature of which is indicated by the term itself. Publishing newspapers has come to be thought of as an industry like any other, turning out printed material in the same way as the distilling industry turns out liquor or the motor industry cars, and subject to the same pressures and vagaries of the market. These include, through competition itself, the compulsion upon one producer to imitate another, both in production methods—tending always towards greater speed and quantity of output with less labour—and in the form or fashion of product. Considered purely in 'business' or economic terms, the movement appears automatic, towards obtaining the largest possible circulations and, as the means of attaining them, progressive uniformity of product. In the second half of the twentieth century especially, just as industry generally has created and become dependent on the largest possible markets, newspaper production has obeyed the same drive to giantism. 'Consumption' is reckoned in bulk totals. In the late 1880s in America the combined circulation of daily newspapers for the first time surpassed the total of urban households in the US.[157] Today, combining 60,000,000 daily newspapers and 40,000,000 magazines and other periodicals, there is approximately one for every person, adult or child, in the country[158] In Britain the circulations of newspapers and periodicals together amount (1976) to more than 78,000,000 for a population of 55,000,000.[159]

Such figures convey nothing but an idea of market size and, very roughly, of levels of literacy. The assumption is that in these countries, where some kind of newspaper or periodical is seen at least once a week by virtually all men and women, the entire adult population is able to read. (In many other countries, of course, ·it is not yet the case, but educational policies aim at it nearly everywhere.) Where there is universal literacy, reading becomes, it seems, a universal need: it is not an essential natural function like breathing or eating, but much discussion of the subject assumes that it is. Charles E. Scripps, a descendant of E. W. Scripps, is quoted as saying that 'mass communications have become a staple of consumption in our society, much like food, clothing and shelter'.[160]—i.e. accepted as a necessity of life. Although it may appear to be true, supported by the kind of crude statistics just cited, the statement, even as a picturesque exaggeration pardonable in a magnate of the industry, should be looked at more closely. To what extent are newspapers and other means of mass communication actually necessary to life today?

It is difficult (though not impossible) to imagine the extremely complex inter-relations of present society—of government, of manufacture and commerce, of different social groups and interests—working without constant interchange of information, much of it likely to be in print. It is a commonplace, indeed, to blame all sorts of social breakdown on short-comings in the interchange, 'failure of communication'. So much seems clear and undeniable. It is not so clear, however, that what is referred to, the 'staple of consumption', is the same thing as the flow of information, from all to all, without which, we assume, modern society would cease to function. The metaphor of 'consumption' must not lead us astray; words in print are not consumed in the same way as food is digested. Newspapers may be produced much as is another characteristic 'staple' of Western industrial society, the motor-car, and in both cases there is a strong suggestion, promoted by advertising, that the product is bought for itself, a self-sufficient object, almost as work of art. But of course that is not so: cars are bought for what they do, namely carry people more or less rapidly about, newspapers are bought for what they convey. It is their content, the 'information' in them, that is the article of consumption.

When we try to see more clearly *what* they convey the notion of necessary function may seem less obvious (in much the same way, perhaps, as the idea of the indispensable motor-car loses force when the actual journeys are examined which people make by its means). It is difficult to separate a commodity from its function; the difficulty is created by commerce, in the assumption which it cannot help implanting in both parties—sellers and purchasers—to every commercial transaction. A commodity, to a trader, is simply what is sold, the fact that it is saleable makes it a commodity; and *what* is sold, its nature and the nature of the needs it is expected to satisfy, are more and more lost sight of. We may now try to examine the 'what' of printed mass-commmunication today, bearing always in mind that, as commodity, it is a special case, since it is among the most important means—the 'media'—which most affect the judgement of men and women, and have therefore an influence on what they think about all commodities.

VII
SERVANTS OF SOCIETY?

SINCE the Second World War three Royal Commissions have been appointed to deliberate on the workings of the Press—evidence in itself of continuing and unresolved doubts about the function of newspapers in contemporary society. From 1947–9, from 1961–2, and again for nearly three years, 1974–7, these Commissions looked at different aspects of the organisation and performance of the British Press. Each in turn had a particular remit, reflecting the current anxieties which had caused it to be set up: the first, initiated through the House of Commons by the National Union of Journalists, was concerned especially with concentration of newspaper ownership and the effects of a trend towards monopoly; the second, set up after the closure of various newspapers, including the national daily *News Chronicle,* was to inquire only into the financial side of newspaper production; the third, instituted by the Labour Government of 1974–9, was to examine the alleged political bias of the Press, specifically a bias against 'the left', and also 'invasion of privacy' by newspapers. Both the first and third, however, ranged over a much wider field than is suggested by these subjects, and their Reports provide much information not only of a factual kind but also reflecting current opinion about newspapers, what was held to be their proper purpose, and the degree to which different papers fulfilled it. Neither Report, however, offered any fundamental criticism of the Press as institution, taking it for granted—though with a different emphasis from that of C. E. Scripps—that newspapers and 'the newspaper industry' were an essential part of the modern world.

The 1949 Report summed up the function of the Press in social-political terms:

> The development of the Press into a great industry coincided with an increase in the demands made upon the Press by the character of society. The extension of the franchise and the increasing complexity of public affairs have thrust upon the Press the responsibility of conveying and interpreting to the public a mass of information on subjects as complicated as they are important.[161]

In 1977, the third Commission opened its Report with a more detailed and inclusive definition:

Newspapers and periodicals serve society in diverse ways. They inform their readers about the world and interpret it to them. They act both as watchdogs for citizens, by scrutinising concentrations of power, and as a means of communication among groups within the community, thus promoting social cohesion and social change. Of course, the Press seeks to entertain as well as to instruct and we do not dismiss this aim as trivial, but it is the performance of the serious functions which justifies the high importance which democracies attach to a free Press.[162]

The question of 'freedom of the Press' was not discussed by the earlier Commission, since 'it was assumed that the value of a free Press was not in question'.[163] The 1977 Report, however, took it a step further:

We define freedom of the Press as that degree of freedom from restraint which is essential to enable proprietors, editors, and journalists to advance the public interest by publishing facts and figures without which a democratic society cannot make responsible judgements.[164]

In view of both Commissions, therefore, the function of the Press was, mainly, political. To this end the earlier Commission considered, 'industrialisation' had been advantageous, though certain drawbacks were also noted: 'to the extent that it [the evolution of newspaper production into an industry] has facilitated the collection of news and the sale of newspapers at a low price it has enabled the Press to report and interpret more fully', but on the other hand 'to the extent that is has given added importance to the commercial aspects of newspaper production, it has tended to divert the attention of newspapers to ends other than those to which the interests of society require them to attend'.[165]

The 1949 *Report* did not inquire what the 'interests of society' might be which were different from the commercial interests of newspapers; but the 1977 *Report*, recognising that 'freedom of the Press carries different meanings for different people', pointed out that 'the public interest does not reside in whatever the public may happen to find interesting, and the Press must be careful not to perpetrate abuses and call them freedom'.[166]

This observation, though not given particular emphasis by the Commission, may be taken as a succinct statement of the problem with which all three inquiries were trying to grapple, namely the divergence of 'interests' and the social effects of interpreting the word 'interest' in different ways. Before turning to this question, however, it may be useful to refer to the findings. Circulations and day-to-day contents of newspapers were analysed in both *Reports*. The first had to deal with the situation in 1947, when newspaper sizes were restricted by an acute shortage of newsprint, which was rationed, and when for a time circulations themselves were also limited, or 'pegged', by agreement. Nevertheless many were very large, and in aggregate much larger than at any previous period of British newspaper history; indeed considerably higher than thirty years later. The total of all morning, evening, and Sunday papers, 'national' and 'provincial', was 33,444,000 in 1937, 57,731,000 in 1947, and had fallen to 55,339,000 in 1976. Several of the largest individual circulations fell between 1947 and 1976.—the *Daily Express* from 3,855,000 to 2,594,000 (2,325,000 in 1980); the *Daily Mail* from 2,076,000 to 1,755,000 (up again to 1,984,000 in 1980); the *News of the World*, with the largest circulation of any newspaper in Britain, from 7,890,000 to 5,138,000 (4,472,000 in 1980). At the same time certain of the so-called 'quality' newspapers, such as *The Times* and *Daily Telegraph*, increased their readership; in these cases from 268,000 to 310,000 (315,724 in 1980) and from 1,015,000 to 1,308,000 (1,445,000 in 1980) respectively.

No doubt these figures represent some real, if small, changes in reading habits, the decline in popular and evening papers especially being commonly attributed to the rivalry of TV. Its effect, if any, on the content of newspapers is harder to show. Some examples may be taken from the tables in which the 1949 *Report* attempted to analyse content in terms of space allotted to different categories.

Breakdown of total space in 1947

	news	'features'	'other' editorial matter	advertisements
	%	%	%	%
Daily Mail	49	15	15	21
Daily Express	50	16	13	21
Daily Mirror	40	15	29	16
The Times	41	7	12	40

A further breakdown of total editorial space in the same papers showed the following:

	news	'features'	leading articles	correspondence	cartoons, puzzles, 'miscellaneous'	pictures
	%	%	%	%	%	%
Mail	62	19	3	1	6	9
Express	63	20	3	1	9	8
Mirror	48	17	3	6	15	12
The Times	68	12	6	5	3	5

Of total space given to news the same papers gave the following proportions:

	Home news %	external %	other %
Mail	80	16	4
Express	76	19	5
Mirror	86	14	none
The Times	51	28	21

A further division of 'home news' within the general total noted space given
shows the following proportions:

	political, social, economic %	law, police, accident %	personalities, Court news, etc. %	sport %	finance and commercial %	'other' %
Mail	23	11	4	33	4	9
Express	23	13	2	32	4	6
Mirror	21	23	3	24	none	15
The Times	23	3	7	16	9	2

Of the total political news proportion of space given to Parliamentary
reports was *Mail* 5 per cent, *Express* 6 per cent, *Mirror* 2 per cent, *The
Times* 11 per cent. The proportion of total editoral space occupied by
headlines was: *Mail:* 19 per cent; *Express* 22 per cent; *Mirror* 17 per cent;
The Times 11 per cent.[167]

The *Report* of the third Royal Commission noted little change in this
general allocation of space by different newspapers. More space was given
to sport in 1975 than in 1947, and also to pictures, but otherwise there was
'a very high degree of stability in the pattern of content'.[168] It was suggested
that this stability indicated 'a highly conservative industry, or at any rate a
widespread belief within it that success with readers can be achieved by
sticking to the same pattern'.[169] Some figures of space allotment, analysed
by the author, in the same papers in 1981 show a continuation of this belief,
though certain changes may be noted. On one day (7.9.81) the proportions
were as follows:

Daily Mail (36 pp. tabloid): editorial 63 per cent, advertising 37 per cent.
Of total editorial space, news and commercial 17 per cent, crime 4 per cent,

sport 30 per cent, gossip 15 per cent, women's topics 10 per cent, entertainment 17 per cent, comment 5 per cent, cartoon, puzzles, astrology, etc. 2 per cent. The proportion of editorial space occupied by pictures, either on their own or as illustration of other items was 18 per cent.

Daily Express (36 pp. tabloid): editorial 61 per cent, advertising 39 per cent. Of total editorial space, news and commercial 23 per cent, crime 2 per cent, sport 30 per cent, gossip 9 per cent, women's topics 6 per cent, entertainment 18 per cent, comment 5 per cent, cartoons, puzzles, astrology, etc. 7 per cent. Proportion of editorial as pictures 19 per cent.

Daily Mirror (32 pp. tabloid): editorial 64 per cent, advertising 36 per cent. Of total editorial space, news and commercial, 9 per cent, crime 12 per cent, sport 28 per cent, gossip 14 per cent, women's topics 9 per cent, entertainment 15 per cent, comment 3 per cent, cartoons, puzzles astrology, etc. 10 per cent. Proportion of editorial as pictures 22 per cent.

The Times (24 pp.): editorial 76 per cent, advertising 24 per cent. Of total editorial space, news and commercial 48 per cent, crime 1 per cent, sport 16 per cent, gossip 9 per cent, entertainment 13 per cent, comment 4 per cent, cartoons, puzzles, letters 9 per cent. Proportion of editorial as pictures 9.5 per cent.

(To the small amount of space given to commercial news in the tabloids should be added special weekly supplements in the *Mail* and *Express*, the total size of the paper on these days going up in proportion. It should also be noted that *The Times* carries many regular features on particular subjects, such as science and religion, together with weekly book reviews, which the others only touch at irregular intervals. *The Times* does not have a 'woman's page', but carries regular lengthy features on fashion and other matters presented elsewhere specifically to women—e.g. in the *Mail's* 'Femail' pages.)

The overall distribution of space is not very different from that in 1947 when, because of shortage of newsprint and the consequent small size of papers, competition between different editorial categories was at its keenest. The most noticeable change is in space given to pictures, which has roughly doubled. The very large amount of space given to sport, around 30 per cent, remains much the same, if anything having slightly dropped since 1947. 'Entertainment', on the other hand, was not given as a separate category in 1947; now, comprising anything related to TV and radio, the cinema and the theatre, it has certainly increased its share of space.

These figures, though they are some guide to the more mechanical aspects of editorial policies in deciding allotment of space, give no idea of actual content. Something may be gathered from the selection of subject-matter—the choice of news and aspects of news which a paper makes from day to day. But the same subject can be treated in so many different ways, and so many variable factors contribute to its presentation—including length, terminology, size of headline, position on the page and in the paper as a whole—that little is to be learnt from this alone. On the day chosen as example (7.9.81), the current news included a development in the IRA hunger strikes in Northern Ireland: this was given as a front page 'lead' in the *Mail*, with inch-and-a-half headlines, 'New Blow to Hunger Strike', and with a report that spread onto the succeeding page; in the *Express* it was also on the front page, but only in a 'box' at the bottom, and with half-inch headlines, 'Crack in Maze Hunger Strike'; *The Times* carried a report half-way down its front page under a half-inch headline, 'Blow to Maze protest as fifth man ends fast', the report itself being twice as long as that in the *Mail*; the *Mirror* did not carry the story at all.

Other front page items in the *Mail* on the same day concerned the annual conference on the TUC, 'No pay curbs, warns Kitson', and the Princess of Wales, 'The Queen gives Diana a black look'; in the *Express*, a statement by a chief constable, 'My Fear, by Police Boss', given as an 'exclusive' lead story, the Princess of Wales, in a photograph and reference to story inside, and the illness of a British athlete, 'Tummy bug beats Wells'. The main story in *The Times* was an industrial-political item '5000 jobs hang on decision over British or American torpedo', with four others, 'Solidarity "will lead revolution"', together with other news concerning Poland, 'EEC foreign ministers optimistic on Namibia', and TUC news, 'Healey gets Basnett union vote', 'NUPE refusal to lower sights'. The *Mirror* carried as its most prominent front page item 'Dressing Sex': Girls who dare to be different', drawing attention, with photograph, to a 'women's' feature inside; 'Villain', similarly announcing a serial account of 'the life and violent crimes of one of Britain's most ruthless robbers'; and at the foot of the page 'TUC hit-list plot' and another pictorial announcement of matter elsewhere in the paper, 'Diana, Princess under pressure'.

In *The Times* of the same date there were altogether 42 items of varying length dealing with political and economic affairs, exclusive of five full pages of 'business news'. The *Mail* had 10, mostly brief (none more than 300 words); the *Express* 11, of about the same range in length; the *Mirror* 7. There were in addition comments more or less closely attached to the political news of the day, from a leader in *The Times* dealing directly with the chosen 'lead' story, on a decision in arms-manufacture, to a facetious 'personal' column in the *Mirror* on the TUC conference. In all four papers the headings given to these stories were fairly explicit, although, as the examples given indicate, often choosing a sensational form of words ('My Fear', 'Hit-list Plot'). Other items, far more numerous in the three popular papers, had headings designed less to inform than to rouse curiosity, if not to titillate. For instance, in the *Mail*: 'Why the Secret Policeman team was left a little short-staffed' (concerning a charity performance), 'Day of the Blazing Saddles' (cyclists' speed record attempt), 'The Damage done by Dr. Blunder' (forensic medicine case). In the *Express*: 'Di's hat magic' (The Princess of Wales), 'Dustman carts off a fortune' (domestic mishap), 'Nick-nick mimic is nicked' (minor courtcase), 'Games of their life' (sporting contest for transplant surgery patients). In the *Mirror*: 'Leap Lively' (para-chute stunt-artist), 'Spiderman's bathtime blunder' (domestic mishap).

These examples are of items to be classified as news, and exclude the much larger proportion of space given to special features, preponderantly concerned with entertainment. In the *Mail*: 'Punch-drunk on success' (cinema), 'The Noble lion in waiting' (TV), 'Dead-beat Bowie' (TV), 'The ship that nearly sank Lord Lew' (cinema), 'King of Diamonds' (TV). In the *Express*: 'The new Bowie' (TV), 'Bulldog spirit comes out of the wilderness' (TV), 'Major Freya . . . in full command of Shakin' Stevens' (pop music). In the *Mirror*: 'Bowie's top of the slops!' (TV), 'They're still all wild about Harry' (band music), 'Death of an angel' (TV), 'Weighing up Wogan' (TV). The other very large category of sport produced similar headings. *Mail*: 'Wright's power show!', 'Why Greig fumes at Auld's joy', 'Ferguson agony hits Stein too', 'Wells misery!'. *Express*: 'A touch of real class', 'Didn't he do well?', 'A tepid trial', 'A trying time'. *Mirror*: '"Wipeout" real threat', 'Francis away like a dream', 'The nightmare will soon be over for Ron'.

Other examples may be given, picked at random from the popular press (in September, 1981). 'Billy is still my man' (*Daily Record*, pop-star personal item); 'Kay for Courage' (*Record*, crime report), 'Spanking Police Chief is accused' (*Mail*, court case), 'Nurse who wanted to kill' (*Mirror*, court case), 'The love slave clue' (*Express*, missing person story), 'Is sex driving you mad?' (*Mirror*, foreign news report), 'Topless model in rape trap' (*Star*, crime report), 'Kicked in the teeth' (*Record*, local government report). It should be emphasised that these headings, though the 'story' in question was in most cases very brief, all had a prominent position, in some instances as the 'lead' on the front page, in proportionately large type.

With these indications of content in mind we may turn back to the expec-tations of the Royal Commissions. The Commission of 1947–9 spent some time discussing 'the standard by which the Press should be judged', giving their own views first:

> The Press may be judged, first, as the chief agency for instructing the public on the main issues of the day. . . . The democratic form of society demands of its members an active and intelligent participation in the affairs of their community, whether local or national. It assumes that they are sufficiently well informed about the issues of the day to be able to form the broad judgments required by an election, and to maintain between elections the vigilance necessary in those whose governors are their servants and not their masters. . . .Democratic society, therefore, needs a clear and truthful account of events, of their background and their causes; a forum for discussion and informed criticism; and a means whereby individuals and groups can express a point of view or advocate a cause. The responsibility for fulfilling these needs unavoidably rests in large measure upon the Press.[170]

The opinions of newspaper proprietors invited by the Commission did not appear to oppose or diverge very far from this summing-up.

> The chief function of a newspaper is to report current events and interpret them to its readers. It is also an important and proper function of the Press to comment on matters of public interest for the guidance of the public, to inform, educate, entertain, and enlighten its readers, and to provide a forum for the expression and exchange of opinion. (Odham's Press Ltd, proprietors of the former *Daily Herald*)

> Editorial staffs freely assume . . . the following moral obligations to the public: (i) that of giving in the newspaper a correct and balanced account of what is happening; (ii) that of expressing opinions on controversial matters in such a way as to advance, by fair argument, tendencies, purposes, etc., that appear to be desirable. (London *Express* Newspapers Ltd.)

> The proper function of a newspaper is to report fairly, accurately, and objectively local and/or national and/or international news, according to its particular field; to provide, when necessary, fair, accurate and objective background information to enable the public to understand news items; to comment upon important subjects; to diagnose, express, and lead public opinion and to give expression to this in the form of letters to the editor; and to further any political opinion it may hold. (The Newspaper Society, representing provincial English newspapers)

> A newspaper's function is threefold, to publish news (serious or otherwise) of interest to its readers, to publish opinionative articles and readers' letters on current topics, to express its own opinion. (*Daily Mirror* Newspapers)

... if a newspaper desires to attain importance and stability it must tell its readers what has happened within the compass over which their interests are spread. (Kemsley Newspapers Ltd., owners in 1947 of two national Sundays and a chain of provincial newspapers)[171]

These statements beg more than one question, but the chief one, still unresolved, is what is in 'the public interest'. 'Interest' itself, in modern usage, is an ambiguous word, since it can mean either 'the fact or quality of mattering; concernment; importance', or, as a verb, no more than the direction of attention or curiosity: whence it may happen that something may be made interesting which is of no great interest. The views just quoted slide from one meaning to the other; 'matters of public interest' becomes 'news of interest to ... readers', and it may be doubted whether, though the phrases are used by different spokesmen, either of those in question would have noticed an essential difference between them.

The Commission of 1974–7 showed more awareness of this crucial matter but beyond the observation already quoted, that 'public interest' may not be the same as 'whatever the public may find interesting' was not able to take the discussion very much further. Its chief concern under this head was the conflict between a newspaper's right of inquiry and a 'general right of privacy', and also between the obligation on the Press to provide, so far as possible, impartial political information and the natural bias of what is predominantly a product of capitalist industry. Its *Report* referred on the one hand to critics for whom 'the concept of freedom of the Press is a fig leaf concealing the real interests of its capitalist owners' and on the other to such a rigorous statement of the opposite point of view as that of a writer in the *Wall Street Journal*:

A newspaper is a private enterprise owing nothing whatever to the public, which grants it no franchise. It is therefore affected with no public interest. It is emphatically the property of the owner, who is selling a manufactured product at his own risk.[172]

An intermediate point of view put to the Commission by the Newspaper Publishers' Association identified the problem but was unable to suggest a solution:

... a newspaper is still a piece of private property with public responsibilities, and the issue at the heart of the present inquiry is whether such a hybrid can survive under modern conditions. Is a press which is run on strictly commercial lines now capable of discharging its public functions?[173]

'Public responsibilities', 'public functions', are also highly elastic terms, which, indeed, define themselves in relation to issues that are constantly changing. The importance or otherwise of these issues—and the degree, therefore, to which they become matters of 'public responsibility'—is impossible to state according to an agreed scale; such a scale does not exist. It is in process of creation all the time, and as a rule one of the most powerful influences in creating and modifying it is the Press itself. A newspaper addresses itself to 'the public', to a group that is to say which excludes no one and in theory includes everyone; by consequence anything whatever that it reports becomes public property and thereby of some supposed public interest. Anything at all may be 'of interest to readers', and will be so by virtue of being made public, as 'news'.

Here we find the one quality, not too difficult to define, which all these statements agree upon. Without particular emphasis, no doubt because it is thought to be self-evident, the content of newspapers is expected to deal with issues 'of the day', 'current' events, 'what is happening'. As we have seen, the newness of news has been an essential from the start, one of the chief claims of whomsoever or whatsoever has been the news-carrier, verbal messenger, printed news-book, or 'late extra'; not things that have happened but things that are happening are expected to interest people. It is instructive to compare the phrase, 'the present conjuncture', 'in this conjuncture of time', so common as to be almost obligatory in newspaper reports of the eighteenth century, with the present, even more threadbare 'at this moment in time': both expressive of the idea not simply of something taking place now but of its being somehow a focus, of all times and circumstances conjoining to produce it. Philosophically it is a perfectly respectable proposition; as a catch-phrase it has the effect of suggesting that an event is significant simply because it is happening, or has very recently happened, and is being reported.

Such a quality of evanescence, which not only makes everything interesting that is 'new', or has only just taken place, but also relegates to absolute non-interest whatever is a little longer past, 'yesterday's news', is characteristic of gossip. Gossip—'to talk idly, mostly about other people's affairs' [OED]—is similarly attached to present events, or the very recent past; as noted before, the typical introduction of a topic in gossip-conversation is 'Have you heard the latest?', and it is the bearer of the most recent information on any subject who dominates the exchange. Gossip is 'idle', that is to say the information it deals in is not apparently purposeful or useful; it is mostly about 'other people', being notoriously an outlet for hostile feelings, but avoiding the effects of confrontation, in accusation or confession. It is a pleasurable activity or, more accurately, it is one which avoids pain. It uses the coin of human intercourse but, proverbially, its small change: exchanges of real weight or value which demand serious attention, and which may be expected to have actual consequences, are excluded. That gossip does indeed have consequences and (when malicious, which it often is) may eventually cause much damage and hurt, is well known, but these are at a remove, distanced not only by absence of the subject ('behind a person's back') but by the 'lightness' of tone. Gossip is for the moment only, and is not expected to be remembered, except as material for further gossip; of negligible value in itself, it is prized as something to be passed on while it is still 'new'—and it is new, of course, to anyone who has not heard of it. Thus gossip turns into rumour; for which, again characteristically, no one will admit responsibility.

It is obvious that very much more of the content of newspapers than is confined to the 'gossip-columns' can be described as gossip: the 'lightness' or triviality of much information, its partiality, fragmentary nature, random or arbitrary selection, its emphasis on what is 'new' and therefore surprising, and also its conscious transience; so that each day's issue can begin its 'idle talk' afresh. To describe most of what is printed in most newspapers in this way is not necessarily disparagement. Gossip has a social function: not for the exchange of useful or necessary information, nor as part of a learning process, but for confirmation of group existence. It is perhaps analogous to the continuous substratum of noise which other social animals than man make among themselves—the clucking of hens or cries of a flock of seagulls, the chatter of a troop of monkeys.

It may be conjectured that these group noises serve to remind each individual of the presence of others, and thereby to reassure; they continually signal sameness, so that a different sound, whether emitted by a group-member or an outsider, is at once distinguished and treated as alert or alarum; they reinforce rituals and habitual behaviour, and aid recognition and acceptance of the familiar. A flock or herd coheres by such means; the boundary is defined by the distance that these social noises carry, and an individual who strays out of earshot immediately becomes uneasy, and may be lost. In the human species the operation of such noise is directly normative, strengthening accepted standards and discouraging change; much gossip is therefore censorious. Adverse gossip—comment on transgressors and nonconformists—has moreover a certain social-psychological thriftiness; it can produce the effects of presumption of guilt, and consequent exclusion, but without the cost of legal process or personal liability.

Gossip is a powerful force, and if it plays a part in man's existence as social animal it is not likely to be abolished merely by disapproval. But gossip transmuted into print is different from that exchanged *viva voce*. Its power is enormously increased simply by spreading very much further and more rapidly, but also because print confers a different status upon it. Reading gossip is not the same as hearing it; it is passive for one thing, without the possibility of question and answer, expression of doubt or disagreement, or any of the subtle modifications of understanding that intonation, gesture, and other non-verbal additions to actual conversation allow for. Print is crude, and crudely apprehended: either it is true or not true. As a rule, it is expected to be true: the impersonal nature of print makes it harder for a direct charge or even a suspicion of lying to come home. Men know that other men deceive, exaggerate, and make mistakes, but print, by reason of its detachment from the writer, and also of its permanency, is somewhat protected from natural scepticism; as it is to some extent dehumanised utterance it is absolved of human frailty and error.

Newspapers both claim and disclaim this privilege, the one loudly and continually, the other *sotto voce* and only from time to time. Their public claim is to tell the truth, even (in aspiration at least) the absolute truth. The statements of standards submitted to the first Royal Commission on the Press included repeated professions of adherence to 'accuracy' and 'correctness'; the proprietors of the *Express*, in reply to the Commission's query about 'reasonable standards of accuracy', said: 'The only standard of accuracy which we find tolerable is complete accuracy.'[174]

A rather less ambitious rule is sometimes admitted. The realities of news-gathering and transmission, together with comment, were described with some candour by *The Times*, then at the height of its authority and influence, on the death of one of its most powerful editors, J. T. Delane, in 1879. An obituary apologia spoke of the day-to-day pressures on an editor: 'As it is impossible to say what a night may bring forth, and the most important intelligence is apt to be the latest, it will often find him with none to share his responsibility. . . . The editor must be on the spot till the paper is sent to press, and make decisions on which not only the approval of the British public, but great events, and even great causes, may hang. All the more serious part of his duties has to be discharged at the end of a long day's work, a day of interruptions and conversations, of letter-reading and letter-writing, when mind and body are not what they were twelve hours ago. . . . All this ought to be borne in mind by those who complain that journalism is not infallibly accurate, just and agreeable.'[175]

The excuses offered are as instructive as the admissions themselves, especially the assumption that the last item of news to arrive is likely to be the 'most important'. The overriding value placed on the newness of news is to be seen here; together, perhaps, with the expectation that news of events will in fact arrive in a certain order, either of steadily mounting climax or of alternating assertion and contradiction, the last-comer carrying naturally the most weight. It is an essentially aesthetic, specifically a dramatic formula, the prototype of which is the device of successive messengers of disaster or triumph whose skilfully graded entrances produce the maximum excitement in an audience. It has, needless to say, little connection with the disordered and inconclusive way in which a day's events actually occur. It does, however, show the further expectation that a newspaper's reports, collected and compiled in whatsoever haste and disarray, will impose a certain structure and, as record, a permanent order upon 'history'.

Here again there is some divergence between what newspapers publicly claim for themselves and what may be privately admitted. That they are in some sense an historical record is undeniable; their accumulation since they came into existence is among the chief resources of historiographers, and extended publication is a source of particular pride, an early foundation being as much valued by a paper as by any other long-lived institution. The 'daily map of events in the world' which John Bright expected newspapers to provide and their readers to educate themselves by should extend backwards to present a complete panorama of world history.

Yet a sense of human history as a continuum is not usually very marked among those who own and produce newspapers. The 1947–9 Press Commission itself observed how 'a newspaper is created afresh every day', so that 'each issue is designed as something separate and distinct from every other issue and tends inevitably to concentrate on what has occurred since the last was published'.[176] A journalist (a sub-editor on the *Express* who gave evidence to the first Commission) put it more brutally: 'We as newspapers are not concerned with what will appear important to posterity. What we have to do is to produce something which will seem, if not important, at least interesting to the man in the street, and to the man in the street the daffodils in Regent's Park are often more important . . . than a massacre in Chungking.'[177]

A catch-phrase often heard in newspaper offices, 'It's water under the bridge', expresses the same idea of discontinuity, together with the implication (since this tag is most often used when a mistake of some kind is discovered in a past issue) that no one will remember or care about events more than a day past. Or, to put it more exactly, no one is expected to remember or care about the detail or actual circumstances of past events;

he or she, the man or woman 'in the street', is however expected to have a certain feeling about the past, to carry over impressions and attitudes which the newspaper concerned preserves and fosters. This is largely produced by selection and emphasis, in which as between one journal and another there is indeed a high degree of continuity and consistency, so that the reader of a particular newspaper is likely to go on learning about the daffodils in Regent's Park and to remain ignorant of massacres in Chungking.

It may be that another paper will record what has happened in Chungking, and yet another will carry news of events not touched by the other two, and so on until the 'world map' and universal register is collectively assembled. Such is the hope of those who, like John Bright, have thought that multiplication of newspapers must lead to improvement in information. One will relate one thing, another another, and the same event will be reported from different points of view; thus a comprehensive and accurate account of affairs will be arrived at. In the same way the partisan bias of one will be modified by those of all the rest, so that among them all the judicious reader may arrive at a balanced conclusion.

That is not, however, the way that newspapers are read, except perhaps by a very few who, moreover, are usually in possession of knowledge of the matters in question from other sources. Their knowledge, moreover, is likely to show that, as all newspapers—whatever their different editorial policy or bias—suffer in some degree the same disabilities in collecting and reporting news, all are liable to mistake. Unanimity is suspect, especially in political reporting, being a strong indication of a single 'inspired' source; but on the other hand variety may simply be variety of error. Against the 'complete accuracy' set up for themselves as criterion by the proprietors of the *Express* the estimate may be set of the editor of one of the *Express* group newspapers (John Gordon, of the *Sunday Express*), who told the Commission that 'whenever we see a story in a newspaper concerning something we know about it is more often wrong than right'.[178]

The witness was speaking both as a journalist, with expert knowledge of newspaper practice, and as an ordinary member of the public: the observation, however regretfully made, was 'plain fact', 'we all know it to be true'. Common experience bears him out: indeed the Commission themselves were able to report an instance under their very noses, in a speculative newspaper account of their own discussions and proposals the greater part of which was 'not only untrue but devoid of any resemblance to the truth'.[179]

This 'inside story' was pure speculation but was presented as fact. The phrases 'it is understood' and 'it seems' are used in such cases to suggest, not that the account is mere guesswork but that it comes from a private source which cannot be divulged; their effect is rather to enhance than cast doubt on authenticity. One of the main passages of imagination in this case began with the words 'In fact . . .'.

Evidently newspapers, deliberately or not, conduct themselves by two standards, but only one is openly acknowledged, the very highest. (The very word 'standard', with its associations of rule and cynosure, has been chosen as the title of more than one newspaper.) The aspect presented to the public is of 'complete accuracy', reliability, responsibility, omniscience; admissions such as those in the tribute to Delane, quoted above, are rarely made in print, and, however bitter rivalries between newspapers may be, mutual accusation is even more uncommon. In their beginnings, as we have seen, editors frequently called one another liar, but libel laws and professional solidarity have virtually abolished this salutary practice. 'Dog doesn't eat dog': the shared interests of journalists and newspaper proprietors in presenting a favourable collective image of the Press are stronger than the drives of competition.

The public—the newspaper-reading public, reckoned to be virtually the whole adult population[180]—is not necessarily imposed upon. The Royal Commission of 1974–7 made some inquiry into 'attitudes to newspapers', among both the public at large and 'influential' citizens, and found a fairly widespread scepticism, especially of the popular press. 'Over 60 per cent of the readers of the *Daily Mirror* and the *Sun* thought that they exaggerate the more sensational aspects of the news, and between 40 per cent and 50 per cent of their readers thought that they invaded private grief and printed too many trivial stories.'[181] The 'influential' persons questioned were sceptical in much the same degree. Bearing in mind John Gordon's evidence to its predecessor, the Commission endeavoured to find out from them—as people more than ordinarily likely to have had personal knowledge of matters reported in the Press—what their views were of newspaper accuracy in such cases. Comment was 'very unfavourable' in 46 per cent of replies, and 'very favourable' in nearly as many (43 per cent),[182] a finding which does indeed bear out Gordon's expectation that Press reports, when they can be checked against first-hand knowledge, will turn out to be 'more often wrong than right'.

Such attitudes are no doubt very general. The experience of discovering even one newspaper report to be untrue, according to personal knowledge, may induce a certain scepticism about all the rest; the divergence of reporting may add to it; suspicion of partisanship or subservience to official requirements and 'reasons of State' may confirm it. Against the 500-year-old conviction, born of semi-magical belief in the power of print, that if a thing 'is down in black and white' it is true, must be set the more recent folk-wisdom that 'you can't believe everything you read in the papers'.

Nevertheless, the papers are read, enormously, and are given, perhaps, a kind of semi-credit. With variation according to subject, reportage is believed less completely, probably, than an account by a reliable friend but more than verbal hearsay or rumour. Print alone no longer guarantees credibility, but it confers a certain weight beyond spoken gossip. To the journalist who wrote or edited it, a misleading or outright mendacious report may with the lapse of 24 hours be 'water under the bridge', but nevertheless it is permanently *there*; once in print it acquires importance which survives the suspicion, even the demonstration that it is untrue. Some awareness of newspaper function as a record of 'the times' probably enters into the complex of feelings and assumptions in the minds of most newspaper-readers, and by no means only readers of *The Times*. They may suspect that much of what they read is inaccurate, ignorant, and biased; they may observe that, true or not, a large proportion of it is entirely trivial. But they read it, perhaps for want of anything better, perhaps from habit, and allow their opinions to be influenced by it. The daily 'map of events in the world' may be not much more use than the projections of medieval cartographers, inhabited by dragons and mermaids, but it is a world-picture of a sort, accepted by many; in some degree, possibly, by all.

Part of this world-picture is, paradoxically, the fact of its own triviality and unreliability, and it may be thought that this apparently mitigating feature produces the most pernicious effect. It is a misfortune to be deceived by false information, but it is far more damaging to recognise falsehood and still be guided by it. In this respect, however, newspapers are no more than part of a larger system of misinformation, to be looked at in the next chapter.

VIII
COME BUY! COME BUY!

FROM early in their history newspapers and their news-book ancestors were a vehicle of advertising. In its origins, advertising goes back to the beginnings of print, with Caxton's notice inserted in one of the early books from his press and drawing attention to others, 'If it plese ony man . . . to bye'; and this kind of advertisement, colloquially known as a 'siquis', 'if anyone', appears in handwritten form, antedating printing itself. Early printer-publishers commonly issued lists of their stock-in-trade, or attached them to newly printed works as they came out.

Similarly, the first advertisements incorporated in news-books, the Mercuries, Intelligencers and the like of the seventeenth century, were mostly inserted by the printers themselves, and listed other books, pamphlets, or other matter currently issued from the same press. Such 'house-ads', as they would now be called, might occupy a considerable proportion of available space, drawing the contemporary accusation that they were being used as padding, 'bumbasting out' a thin provision of news. It should be remembered that the word 'advertisement' formerly meant no more than information, or public announcement, and could therefore be used to describe the whole content of news-prints. It only gradually acquired its present more specialised application to commercial announcement, usually today with reference to articles for sale. In this discussion, however, it will be used in the modern sense.

The first printed advertisements did not bring in money except indirectly, although the fact that such information was of value, to buyers and sellers alike, had already occurred to various enterprising persons. The idea of an exchange-office of wants and supply, unsuccessfully set up in London early in the seventeenth century, persisted and can be found, transposed into print, towards its end, in the *Collection for Improvement of Husbandry and Trade*. The editor of this early *Exchange and Mart* thought of himself strictly as go-between, of a remarkably neutral kind, collecting commissions; an example in 1692 announced: 'I know of a peruke maker that pretends [claims] to make perukes extraordinary fashionable, and will sell good pennyworths. I can direct to him.'[183] The candour of this announcement, passing on the advertiser's boast without comment, may be taken either as the naivety of advertising copy in its infancy, or of a very subtle skill in convincing sales-talk. But in any case it is quite different from modern press advertising in keeping the most important information, the identity and whereabouts of the seller, private.

Before this, however, one of the first men to seize on the notion of advertising as a source of profit was Roger L'Estrange, whose *City Mercury*, already mentioned, was started specifically as an advertising medium. L'Estrange hoped thereby to recoup himself for loss of his news-monopoly to the *Gazette*, and a division of function, and of revenue, seems to have been arranged between his venture and the *Gazette*, which in 1666 published a notice (actually called 'An Advertisement') disclaiming all interest in commercial announcements: 'Being daily prest to the publication of Books, Medicines, and other things not properly the business of a Paper of Intelligence. This is to notifie once for all, that we will not charge the *Gazette* with Advertisements, unless they be matter of state; but that a Paper of Advertisements will be forthwith printed apart and recommended to the Publick by another hand.'[184]

The subsequent career of L'Estrange, turbulent as ever, did not allow him to maintain his exclusive rights for long, but he undoubtedly hoped to corner them, as he had for a time cornered and controlled news. It may not be without psychological interest that he, who of all men of his time had perhaps the most complete and conscious grasp of the powers of the press to manipulate thought, should also have been among the first to see the promise of commercial advertising.

When the British press, released from the restrictions of licensing, began its great expansion in the early years of the eighteenth century, its advertisement content grew at the same time. Trade was expanding not only in the great commercial cities but throughout the country; one of the main reasons, probably, for the multiplication of provincial papers was their usefulness to local trade. The news they carried was, initially at least, copied directly from the metropolitan journals, but the advertising mingled with it in their columns concerned local need and supplies. By the middle of the century, even though burdened by multiple taxes levied not only on the newspapers themselves and the paper they were printed on, but the advertisements they published, nearly all papers carried columns of advertising, of the most varied kind.

Over the next 100 years, while industry and trade transformed the social as well as the physical landscape, the advertising carried by newspapers did not alter greatly in kind, though increasing all the time in total bulk. That it should be taxed was increasingly resented, and agitation for removal of the burden was part of the general campaign against the 'taxes on knowledge' carried on during the first half of the nineteenth century. As we have seen, it was the first to be successful, and when in 1833 the advertisement tax was reduced from 3s. 6d. to 1s. 6d. the increase in press advertising was so large and immediate that within a year the Exchequer actually gained by the concession. In 1853, though resisted by Gladstone as Chancellor of the Exchequer on the grounds that he could not afford to lose the £180,000 annually raised by it, the tax was finally abolished against the votes of the government. Commercial interests and newspapers themselves, not unanimous in demanding abolition of the stamp duty, all pressed for freedom to advertise: 'Well-to-do people cared little for the prospect of having to pay only 4d instead of 5d for their papers, and many of them dreaded the prospect of a really cheap press springing up and, as they thought, flooding the country with sedition; but they could see nothing but benefit in a lowering of charges for advertisements. And some of the high-priced journals, particularly *The Times*, the *Illustrated London News*, and the *Weekly Dispatch*, encouraged them in their views.'[185]

The bulk of advertising soon increased. In 1852 *The Times* normally carried four to five pages of advertisement in an eight-page issue; these were concentrated in the front and back pages, but were also regularly brought together in a supplement which contained nothing else. By 1854 the paper had increased in size to 12 pages, of which six and occasionally seven were given to advertising, and this proportion remained fairly constant as sizes continued to grow; in 1862, after the abolition of the paper tax, 16 pages were normal, of which about half were filled with advertising. A Scottish paper of the same period—the *Glasgow Herald*, to take an example from another great centre of commercial and industrial activity—maintained the same proportion, though with a less obvious response to removal of tax-burdens: eight-page issues as the norm, with three to four pages of advertisement, over the decade 1852–62.

It must be borne in mind that newspaper advertising at this time, as throughout the previous century, changed hardly at all in form, consisting of straightforward announcements which, if by no means always truthful, were generally terse and to the point. They were printed in small type, taking up the least possible space and though following the conventions of the age in polite address—so that tradesmen would 'humbly' or 'respectfully' solicit attention—generally using the least number of words. This was of course a direct reflection of cost, as it is today in the 'small ad.' columns of newspapers; but it also showed a significantly different attitude to advertising in general.

There can be no doubt that advertisements of this sort provided a real service, both to those who inserted and those who read them; not only to traders but to their customers. Assuming actual need, they confined themselves in the main to the simple announcement that it could be satisfied; in the early case of the maker of perukes, already quoted, even the name of the supplier, the essential point of all modern advertising, was suppressed. Members of the public read advertisements not casually or inadvertently but purposefully, looking for the offer of some goods or service they already desired; and because advertisements were genuinely useful to readers they made newspapers themselves more saleable. Thus it is interesting to note that the supplements published by *The Times* in the mid-nineteenth century—four close-printed pages, 24 solid columns of miscellaneous small advertisements—were supplied 'gratis', and so labelled, as an additional, free service to readers. Perhaps it is not necessary to point to the contrast with advertising supplements today. It may be that they are not apologised for, though many readers feel they should be. But they certainly are not something to boast about.

Since advertisements were presumed to be an attraction to readers, charges (tax apart) remained comparatively low, and some categories of information that would now be classed as advertising were printed free. Until well on in the nineteenth century, indeed, theatrical announcements were actually paid for by the newspaper concerned; although the same paper would often carry paid theatre advertising at the same time. When a newspaper chose the name of 'Advertiser' as title—as many did—the older meaning of the word—signifying public as well as commercial advertisement—should be borne in mind, to be sure. But it is most unlikely that any would have called itself 'the Non-Advertiser', or would have found many buyers if it had. Advertisement, in a word, was among the kinds of desirable information a paper offered its readers; circulation, it may be said, was raised by advertising, and not the other way about.

In the 1860s and indeed for long after, in such a paper as *The Times*, advertisements of all sorts were printed as are those in the 'personal' columns today, in small type and with no attempt to catch the eye. They were not even arranged in any particular order. Certain categories—for example, the 'carriage trade', sales of horses and carriages, the conveyances of the rich; the very large traffic of domestic service, both 'situations vacant' and the 'want places' of those seeking employment—were gathered together. But a great many others were indiscriminately mixed, with a frequently amusing promiscuity: advertisements for patent medicines, household coals, food and wine, 'mourning attire', next door to personal messages, charitable appeals, and announcement of property for sale. The *Glasgow Herald* of the same period carried much the same mixture, on a smaller scale: three to four pages of six columns each filled with the same miscellany—allowing for social and economic differences between Glasgow and London—of wants and supply, in no particular, certainly no rigid order. The *Glasgow Herald* did however use the device, as did other papers in large port-towns with much shipping business, of distinguishing shipping notices by a small standard block of a sailing-ship, sometimes of a steam-vessel. By the 1860s notices of railway services were similarly furnished with a small silhouette block of a locomotive.

Generally speaking, the reader was offered only minimal assistance in finding the advertisement he was looking for; with the implication that he would indeed be looking for it, seeking information actually desired, and willing to scan columns of close type in order to find it.

In the meantime the uses of print in advertising had developed spectacularly, not in newspapers but upon walls. Billposting of some kind is older than print (Luther's were not the first Theses to be nailed to a church door), and it is reasonable to suppose that in the sixteenth and seventeenth centuries printed bills were more numerous than surviving specimens suggest, although in the later period these are already plentiful. Thereafter the production of every sort of bill, commercial and political, became a large part of the work of jobbing printers, and in the later eighteenth and early nineteenth centuries was possibly more copious, proportionately at least, than it has ever been since. Handbill advertising escaped tax; it was also technically much easier to strike off in new and startling forms. None of this outdoor advertising was as yet very large in size, but printer-designers showed progressive ingenuity in attention-seeking devices, especially in variation and outlay of type. Lettering grew in size, from the largest in an ordinary printer's repertory, 72-point, or one inch high, to specially cut founts of 'poster type' which could be of almost any size. At the same time the actual shape of lettering changed, with the design of exaggeratedly bold types such as the 'fat face' and 'egyptian' introduced in the first quarter of the nineteenth century. New printing presses, constructed of iron instead of wood, were able to handle poster lay-outs of a yard high, instead of the old broadsheet of a foot square or less. These large and clamorous announcements were in the first place chiefly commercial, but were soon used for many different purposes, including political agitation. The walls of Britain were palimpsests of posters, official and commercial, advertisement of goods for sale, auctions and roups, 'wanted' notices and other legal proclamations, announcement of every kind of sporting and social event, and electioneering and political bills which—often with deliberately satirical intent—imitated the same forms.[186]

Towards the end of the nineteenth century this kind of 'outdoor' advertising—which penetrated indoors as well, into most buildings frequented by the public—had enormously increased, so that every available urban wall was occupied, and posters spread by means of road and railwayside hoardings, into the country. These posters, often very large, used pictures as well as words, and some became famous on their own account—for instance Millais' 'Bubbles' painting used in reproduction to advertise Pears Soap. In others very large lettering was used, giving rise to jokes about travellers who mistook 'Bovril' for the name of a railway station. These were effects which newspaper advertising could hardly imitate. Nevertheless 'display', occupying a great deal more space on the page, and using some of the typographical ingenuity that had gone into bill-posters, began to be mixed, especially in the popular penny and halfpenny press, with the old close-packed columns of single small advertisements.

The means used were often no more than repetition of key-words (as 'Sale Sale Sale'), with a liberal application of exclamation marks and nothing else to catch or hold attention; an example from the *Daily Sketch* in 1900 repeated the trade name of a brand of tobacco 25 times in a single column, which could accommodate on average the same number of separate small advertisements. Other advertisers showed rather more imagination; another example from the same issue of the *Daily Sketch* took up most of a column with a discursive account of the merits of a certain 'health salts':

THE BLESSINGS OF THE POOR
NOT THE RICH!!!
HEALTH AND LONG LIFE are usually blessings
of the POOR, not of the RICH, and the FRUITS
OF TEMPERANCE rather than LUXURY AND EXCESS.
BEST PREVENTATIVE
and
CURE for BILIOUSNESS,
SICK HEADACHES, IMPURE BLOOD,
FEVERISHNESS, MENTAL DEPRESSION,
CHILL, ORDINARY COLD,
ALTERNATING CHILLS AND HEATS.

The advertisement went on to warn against false claims and imitations, concluding with a resounding climax,

THE SECRET OF SUCCESS!
STERLING HONESTY OF PURPOSE!!
WITHOUT IT
LIFE IS A SHAM!!!

The back page of the *Daily Sketch* at this time—a lavishly illustrated paper, though as yet by engravings only—was often occupied entirely by 'display' advertisements, enclosed in 'boxes' of irregular size and presenting the appearance therefore of the varied 'make-up' to be adopted by 'tabloid' newspapers later.

The methods of the 'new journalism' and new advertising techniques went together, both following American examples, and though they did not always show themselves side by side—the *Sketch* was, illustration apart, quite conventional in its news columns, and sparing of headlines—it is clear that they influenced one another. It was not uncommon for advertisements deliberately to ape news-stories, of a suitably sensational kind, with headlines and text indistinguishable at first glance from the regular news columns. But this so-called 'chameleon technique', though used occasionally to this day, appears to have been less effective than advertising which, while clearly marked off from the news of the day, may be said to have shared its spirit; especially its use of headlines to keep up an air of perpetual excitement.

A remarkable example of local enterprise in this direction may be taken from a small Scottish weekly, the *South Suburban Press*, which served one area of Glasgow, and was very largely an advertising sheet for retail business. The front page of one summer issue (16 July 1887) carried advertisements prominently displayed in 'boxes', many using the repetitions already mentioned—'Costumes! Costumes! Costumes!', 'Hams! Hams! Hams!', 'This Week! This Week! This Week!'. But an inner page has a far more elaborate layout for a milliner's advertisement which occupies two full columns and makes the front-page efforts to engage attention conventional and modest by comparison. The opening passages give the flavour:

GIGANTIC OPERATIONS!
THE PURCHASES OF MR WILSON IN
LONDON, LUTON, etc., Surpass in
MAGNITUDE
Any former Purchase of
STRAW HATS, STRAW BONNETS, LEGHORN HATS,
FANCY HATS, LACES, RIBBONS, FLOWERS, FEATHERS,
SILKS, VELVETS, STRIP, and FANCY GOODS

GREAT PURCHASE OF EIGHT ENTIRE STOCKS
OF STRAW HATS
IN ONE STOCK ALONE THERE IS (*sic*)
120,000 HATS AND BONNETS

STRAW HATS!

STRAW HATS!!

STRAW HATS!!!

TONS UPON TONS ARRIVING DAILY
THE LATEST STYLES IN STRAW HATS
AS WORN AT ASCOT
BY THE *ELITE* OF THE UNITED KINGDOM
The Popular Colours are
COQUELICOT, CARDINAL, BOREAL, NAVY
ROYAL, FAWN, BEIGE, TUSCAN, CREAM,
GREY, SLATE, VIEUX ROSE
We show *every* New Shape of STRAW HAT
or BONNET in the above Colours; also
GOBLIN, GRENAT, BROWN, LILAS, HELIOTROPE, and all Fancy Mixtures and
Combinations.
STRAW HATS—TONS

and so on for another column and a half.

The declamatory extravagance of this kind of advertising speaks for itself. In it print is used to make the loudest possible noise, as it were, much as a barker at a fair—or, more closely related, the shopkeepers of an earlier time, all crying 'Come buy! come buy!' together—would seek to be heard above the surrounding din. As those older forms often passed imperceptibly into rhyme and song, so such a printed advertisement, especially in its layout, imitated verse, a point to be returned to later. (Rhyming jingles are of course commonly used in advertising to this day, both in print and in the broadcast mass-speech in competition with it.) But a more conscious influence on the composers of advertising copy was probably the treatment of news itself, especially in headlines, although it is extremely difficult, here, to tell which was the instigator of a process carried out by journalists and advertising writers in step with and encouraging one another.

It is important to remember that the use of headlines as we know them is a quite recent innovation in newspaper practice. Headings of a kind, usually the barest minimum, sometimes helped the reader of eighteenth century papers to find his way through the closely printed columns, but often they

☞ GIGANTIC ☞OPERATIONS.

THE PURCHASES OF MR WILSON

IN

LONDON, LUTON, &c., Surpass in

☞ MAGNITUDE ☜

Any Former Purchases of
STRAW HATS, STRAW BONNETS,
LEGHORN HATS, FANCY HATS,
LACES, RIBBONS, FLOWERS,
FEATHERS, SILKS, VELVETS,
STRIP AND FANCY GOODS.

GREAT PURCHASE
OF
EIGHT ENTIRE STOCKS OF
STRAW HATS.

IN ONE STOCK ALONE THERE IS 120,000
HATS AND BONNETS.

STRAW HATS !
STRAW HATS !!
STRAW HATS !!!

TONS UPON TONS ARRIVING DAILY.

THE LATEST STYLES IN STRAW HATS
AS WORN AT ASCOT
BY THE *ELITE* OF THE UNITED KINGDOM.

The Popular Colours are
COQUELICOT, CARDINAL, BOREAL,
NAVY, ROYAL, FAWN, BEIGE,
TUSCAN, CREAM, GREY, SLATE,
VIEUX ROSE.

We show every New Shape of STRAW HAT
or BONNET in the above Colours ; also
GOBLIN, GRENAT, BROWN, LILAS,
HELIOTROPE, and all Fancy Mixtures
and Combinations.
STRAW HATS—TONS.

We give an example of the value we offer :—
OVER 100,000 NEW STYLES IN STRAW
HATS, White, Black, and all New Colours,
worth from 2s 6d to 7s 6d; all at 10½d each.
Another vast sea of HATS and BONNETS,
worth 1s to 2s 6d ; all at 5½d.
Legions of New Straw Hats in Henley, Ascot,
Oaks, New Princess of Wales, Jubilee, Prin-
cess Maud, Regatta, Sunbeam Club Hat,
Cambridge, Tennis, Myosotis, and
Twenty other New Shapes of the
same class.

LADIES' STRAW HATS !
MISSES' STRAW HATS !!
BOYS' STRAW HATS !!!

The LARGEST STOCK OF STRAW HATS &
BONNETS IN THE KINGDOM.
Every possible kind of Straw Hat that is worn
by fashionable ladies can be obtained at
the Colosseum.

STRAW HATS.   STRAW HATS.

SEE OUR WINDOWS FOR THE
MOST MARVELLOUS VALUE in STRAW
HATS EVER OFFERED.

IN THE COLOSSEUM WE HAVE in STOCK
A HAT OR BONNET FOR EVERY
PERSON IN GLASGOW.

Part of an advertisement which appeared in the *South Suburban Press,* 16 July 1887 (see page 125). Reproduced by permission of the British Library.

were absent altogether, one news-item running on to the next with no more division than a printed rule. When they were used their misleading tendency might be condemned for 'dressing the paper with an air of news when there is none'.[187] From time to time news judged to be of exceptional interest was given a heading of its own: 'Death of the King, George IV' when he died in 1830 may count as the first true headline in *The Times*. The same paper published the delayed news of Waterloo under nothing more striking than the standard 'Official Bulletin', with a supplementary 'Gazette Extraordinary'; a reticence the more remarkable since warfare more than anything else has stimulated the growth of headlines. Thirty years on the Crimean War excited *The Times* to fairly frequent special headings, including a 'three-decker' for 'The Fall/of/Sebastopol'; the Indian Mutiny produced more, but though *The Times* broke into headlines with increasing frequency they did not become a permanent feature until the Boer War at the turn of the century. In the meantime the popular papers in Britain had been using headlines freely for many years; but the real pioneering and flowering of invention, as in other departments of journalism, was in America.

Warfare, again, was the main stimulus. The New York *Herald*, already by 1860 with a circulation of 100,000, began to use single-column headings in the presidential election which was the run-up to the Civil War, and during the war these came into regular use, occupying more and more 'decks' and employing a variety of type-faces. Other newspapers followed suit; examples from the New York *Times* (a paper which set itself to avoid the sensationalism of the *Herald*) show headlines to announce three climactic events at the end of the war, the occupation of Richmond, the surrender of Lee, and Lincoln's assassination, which ran to more than 20 'decks' each. At the tops of the columns, in large and heavy type, were the legends, respectively: 'Grant/ Richmond/ and/ Victory'; 'Union/ Victory!/ Peace!'; and 'Awful Event/ President Lincoln/ Shot by an/ Assassin'.[188] These headlines exhibit not only the response, by that time an established one, to a happening of the greatest possible public interest, but in their different form the dependence of headline-language on public understanding. When the end of the war was in sight and the military position generally known it was not necessary to use more than single words, 'Grant/ Richmond', 'Union/ Victory' to make the essence of the news instantly comprehensible. The murder of Lincoln, however, was unexpected; so that, after alerting attention with the warning 'Awful Event' it was necessary actually to describe what had occurred in a coherent sentence. (It was not, however, a complete sentence according to ordinary rules of syntax, a point to be returned to presently.)

By the end of the century, and with the rise of the 'yellow press' already briefly described, every story had its headline, taking up more and more space, and using larger and heavier type-faces. During the approach to and brief course of the Cuban war (which is regarded by many historians as brought about largely by their agitation) Pulitzer's *World* and Hearst's *Journal* competed in 'banner' and 'streamer' headings (e.g. 'Declaration of War!' in inch-and-half type on the *World's* front page for 17 April 1898; 'Manila Ours!' in the *Evening Journal* for May 2, in 3¾-inch letters right across the front page) of the largest possible size. For the time being, indeed, it seemed that typographical resources were exhausted, and Pulitzer even ordered the melting down of the largest faces after the war, but rival papers continued their use, and heavy type and clamorous headings soon returned to his own.[189] The *World* had, in fact, shown particular ingenuity in headline compositions from the beginning: examples from front-page headings during the first months in 1883 include: 'Screaming for Mercy', 'Love and Cold Poison', 'Death Rides the Blast', 'Victims of His Passion', 'Baptized in Blood', 'Duke Meets his Doom', 'Little Lotta's Lovers'.[190]

Examples already given will show, perhaps, that the art of headline writing has not greatly advanced since. British newspapers have, indeed, seldom matched the invention and capacity for allusive condensation of American practice. Puns and the more obvious sorts of word-play are commoner in British headlines; such as 'Labour's Grand Slang', 'Pride Fighters', 'The Deadly Husband' may often be found among the day-to-day repetition of 'Crash Horror', 'Jobs Fury' and the like. Occasionally, a headline appears not merely to announce or add a gloss to what follows, but to be the chief reason for it: it is difficult not to think that when a popular newspaper not ordinarily concerned with chess reported at some length on the private life of a British Grandmaster, it did so not so much for the sake of the gossip as in order to head it 'Chess Ace and his Czech Mate Part'. But such creative flights are not common.

Headlines have different national styles, as do other elements of journalistic practice; but they have in common certain features, apparent through differences in usage and even of language. They constitute a specialised language of their own, with their own syntax, logically independent of conventional grammars. In terms of grammatical logic it is difficult to say what even the simplest example, 'Death of the King', actually conveys. Others are very much more obscure, and even when there are no ordinary linguistic obstacles, may be quite impenetrable, as some American headlines are to British readers: e.g. 'Wood Murder Charge Court Scene', a sequence of nouns with no other parts of speech which appears to be entirely without meaning.[191] Such headlines, of course, are readily understandable by those who 'know the background'; as in all forms of language, proper interpretation depends on knowledge of the context, as well as on familiarity with usage. And when familiar enough to be readily understood, the 'language of headlines', like all other forms of language, begins to influence thinking.

Headlines work by alerting attention and simultaneously producing an impression; both effects act together but are not in fact identical, since headlines do actually use words and not simply alarm-signals. (The difference becomes clear if one thinks of two types of road-sign, one of which, in words and/or ideogram, specifies a particular hazard or command, 'Road Narrows', or 'Slow', and the other which consists simply of an exclamation-mark, with no explanation offered. Headlines, though frequently exclamatory, are usually of the former kind.) Headlines convey information, although often of a minimal sort, usually depending for effect on some knowledge already possessed by the reader; sometimes, as already noted, they serve merely to rouse curiosity by a 'dramatic' word or words ('Showdown', 'Wanted'), when they come very close to the unsupplemented exclamation-mark. It is significant that they are often called 'captions', a term also used for the short explanatory text printed with newspaper pictures; a headline may of course be accompanied by an illustration, but it does not require one: it supplies its own picture. This is the reason for the absence of narrative, even of the most rudimentary sort, from headlines, which do not tell the reader of something that has happened but what is happening, as a description may be given of events in a picture. Verbs, if they are used at all, are nearly always in the present tense, though the action described is in the past. ('Envoy Visits Scotland', 'Kidnappers Release Millionaire'). As the caption of a picture alludes to what is present to the eye, so such a headline alludes to an image 'in the mind's eye', which it itself creates.

Much of the effect, indeed, is directly visual, in the typography used, tending steadily to larger and 'heavier' type-faces. It is a universal assumption of journalistic practice, perfectly well understood and accepted by the public, that the larger and heavier, or blacker, a headline the more important the news to which it refers. (The biggest and blackest headlines, consequently, are generally reserved for warfare, a declaration of war having on occasion taken up almost the whole of a paper's front page.) The presentation of news according to such a scale naturally makes difficulties, cumulative and aggravated by competition, both between different newspapers as rivals for public attention, and between different items in the same newspaper. As every story competes for headline-space, this occupies more and more of the total space available, most of the popular papers in Britain showing a continuous increase over the past half-century.[192] In the resultant visual cacophony, as ever larger and more prominent type is considered necessary to match every degree of 'news value', the reader may well be partially stunned by the clamour for attention.

Precisely the same is true, of course, of printed advertising, in which many of the progressive stages of magnifying of type-faces originated. As has been noted, headline-writers have borrowed from advertising techniques most of the gradations and variations of type in common use. As an historian of typography has observed, it is in advertising, where the need to attract attention exerts its strongest pressure, that most innovation has occurred: 'All advertising specialists are aware that unlimited choice of lettering is necessary to the business of setting that responds to the one and only test: its effectiveness.'[193] The same writer points out that not only size and thickness on the page but details of lettering design respond to such needs in subtle ways: for example, the sans-serif 'which began c.1820 as a by-product of a gentlemanly survey of the monuments of ancient Greece, [was] next adopted by advertisers because it was a novelty, used by engineers and draughtsmen because it was easily thickened, finally progressed to acceptance as a norm by artists and intellectuals' because it was 'believed to be "modern"', and was taken over by newspapers on the way. 'To the publisher of popular and ephemeral reading-matter the sans-serif is appropriate precisely because it has no literary accent. Its only authority is that of the most powerful of all forces of modern society, the 'mass-market".'[194]

It is unlikely that ordinary readers are aware of such nice distinctions, or indeed have any idea of the earnest discussions concerning the use of this or that type-face that commonly go on in both newspaper and advertising offices. But it must be assumed that they are affected by the decisions taken there, always with the same object of employing variety, size and form of lettering to engage visual attention regardless of the meaning of the words to be printed. The contribution of the words themselves is of course much greater, but to some extent they are used in the same way, to make 'impact' without regard to appropriateness. 'Impact', freely used to denote the effect on readers, is a significant choice of epithet: a physical-mechanical expression describes the mental operation of reading, with subject-object relationships reversed. The reader no longer actively apprehends a text but is the passive recipient of a blow.

Some words make a strong impact and are used again and again: Best,

Worst; Joy, Fury; Life, Death. Advertising, which purports to tell good news, makes most use of the first of each pair; journalism, which finds bad news more generally interesting, of the second. The word New itself is indispensable to both. Such words help to form a 'block language'[195] employed throughout the pages of a newspaper, in both advertising and editorial columns; supplementary and relatively discursive texts may be added in both cases, but the tendency is to reduce them and to rely more and more on headline or sale-slogan to do the work.

This reduction can be seen taking place both in the general development of advertising and journalism and in the 'case histories' of individual news-stories and advertising campaigns. As a particular 'story' or series of linked events unfolds from day to day less explanation is needed, more readers' understanding can be assumed, and the headlines can be permitted to carry more of each successive item on their own. Having created the context, references can be progressively condensed, until a very few words can, as the phrase goes, put the reader 'in the picture'. In just the same way an advertiser may need to put a new product on the market with comparatively lengthy accounts of it (though also with preliminary attention-rousing devices of enigmatic brevity, 'Coming!' 'Watch this Space!'); but once it is established, repetition of the simplest slogan, or representation of the 'brand-image' may be reckoned enough. The point here is not that they are doing exactly the same thing—news, however much selected and even manufactured, must be more variable and therefore require more explanation than the entirely self-determined statements of an advertiser—but that they are doing it to an increasing extent in the same way. The 'blocks' of their language tend towards simplification and familiarity, and necessarily so, for they thus become easier to receive.

The reason why a headline-language has been developed, with all the abridgement, elision, and distortion of information which accompany it, is commonly said to be a desire for speed. Newspapers are of course obsessed with the passage of time; not only are they engaged in a continual race to 'get the news out' in competition with one another, but they assume a similar attitude in their readers, scrambling to learn it. No doubt it is not pure coincidence that New York, of all modern metropolises said to be the one whose citizens are in the most unremitting hurry, saw the first growth of a journalism in which headlines, which can be taken in 'at a glance', came to dominate the presentation of news. The 'tabloids' followed, started in Britain and later taken up in America, where the first of its kind was announced as specially designed for hasty reading in the street or strap-hanging in the subway.[196] But if haste is assumed to be the original motive, and excuse, in journalist and reader alike, there is another kind of agreement, or collusion, between them. The reader in a hurry is not expected to be critical; the hasty writer has a license for carelessness, over-simplification, and error. It is just this level of communication, where attention is vociferously sought but is not, or meant to be, sustained, where the exaggerations, half-truths and untruths common to popular journalism flourish, and to which the language of headlines and summaries, at once exciting and vague, is peculiarly suited. It is communication, moreover, which in terms of the received ideas that are its stock-in-trade, suits both parties; it is easy to write in the sense that it requires little thought or care, and it is—the supreme quality usually claimed for it—'easy to read'.

The same, of course, is true of most (though not all) printed advertising. So necessary, indeed, is it for advertisers that their 'copy' should be read without effort that much of it is so designed and placed that it may be read inadvertently. This applies most to 'outdoor' advertising, but to a great deal printed in newspapers as well, and the latter is still very much the more important, in terms of expenditure, of the two.[197] The 'small' or 'classified' advertisements remain in a different category in which, as already remarked, the assumption of actual, individual need renders mass-appeal and ease of absorption unnecessary. The 'display' advertisements are meant to catch the wandering, half-attentive or even downright inattentive eye and then to suggest a need which, it may be, has not been felt before at all: thus a mass-market is created and sustained.

It is true, and not without significance, that journalistic practice is, as a rule, careful to distinguish between advertising 'copy' and 'editorial' matter: there are codes of practice insisting that a certain proportion should be kept between the space in any one issue occupied by both, and that the distinction should be made clear, if not prominently so. Perhaps the main point to be noticed here is that these rules are imposed, with varying success, by journalists on advertisers; the latter would, it seems, be content if the distinction vanished altogether. The so-called 'chameleon' technique, by which an advertisement disguises itself as news or the like, is now uncommon, though prominent and even bizarre instances still occur.[198] The tribute thus paid by advertising to journalism—that 'real' news is more likely to be read than anything else—remains effective. But the distinction becomes less clear and, perhaps, of less importance to practitioners on both sides of the line as methods approximate. For though their day-to-day purposes are different, the general aim, it may be thought, is much the same for both, or at any rate for those who employ them. They expect to have the same readership, or 'audience', and as an American observer puts it, 'The audience is the customer, and those who own and use the system [of mass-media] are salesmen.'[199] In detail, advertisers and newspaper-writers are not selling the same things: on the one hand the multifarious goods of the market, on the other simply themselves. Newspapers continually advertise themselves, explicitly and implicitly—as having a large circulation, a wide news-service, or many pictures, or some other attraction for readers; as being, no less than food, necessary to life. But they also advertise the idea of advertising, and all that goes with it; the picture of the world as one of commodities and of society as one of consumers; of the word itself, their own stock-in-trade, as merchandise along with the rest. In this activity commercial advertising joins from the other side, wooing the 'audience' with material variously attractive, even suggesting that it is to be enjoyed for itself, as part of a non-stop entertainment to which, without differentiation, all contribute.

Much of this entertainment, offered both by advertising and 'the media' which carry it, is pictorial; a large share of it today, in TV, is outwith the scope of the printed word. But an enormous amount of it takes the form of printed text, from the 'stories' in newspapers and magazines to the most rudimentary advertising slogan or single-word headline. Its volume is incalculable. Costs can give only the roughest notion: thus the total expenditure on advertising of all kinds, excluding TV, was in Britain twenty years ago (according to the *Encyclopaedia Britannica*) £385,000,000, approximately 1.5 per cent of gross national product; in the US, $9,650,000,000, approximately 1.8 per cent of g.n.p.; the figures are certainly higher now. Such sums led the historian of print already quoted to comment, 'The volume of lettering of all kinds needed to sustain the burden of this advertising . . . must be enormously greater than is required by the total . . . of biblical, liturgical, literary, educational, journalistic, periodical, official, and traditional.'[200] If, as we have been arguing, very much of what is printed in these other categories, certainly the journalistic component, is functioning in much the same way, the total is much larger. Economic calculations, again, can give only the roughest idea of its dimensions: as that (according to the third Royal Commission on the Press) newspaper and periodical publishing in Britain employs some 140,000 persons, about 0.6 per cent of the workforce of the United Kingdom, 'with a net output similar to that of the aerospace industry and larger than the brewing industry'.[201]

All these words, written, printed, and distributed by all these people—the notional totals being, of course, only a fraction of equivalent numbers for the modern world as a whole—constitute what may be called popular literature. Its different forms, its continual clamour for attention, envelope the existence of men and women, of industrial society at least, much as the air they breathe. Like air, it is taken in and absorbed without conscious effort; it is not, like air, necessary to life, but it creates its own necessity in appetites that it stimulates, expectations it fulfils, assumptions it teaches.

Much of the preceding discussion has concentrated on the content and methods of the 'mass-media', newspapers with the largest circulations and the most obvious 'popular' appeal. It may be useful, to redress the balance, and to emphasise that, much as newspapers differ one from another, they all share some of the functions described, to end this section with an example taken from the least 'popular' of British papers, *The Times*, and not recently, but more than sixty years ago.

At the end of July and in the first days of August 1914, *The Times* reported the approach of war under headlines of mounting urgency: 'Peace in the Balance', 'British Efforts for Peace', 'War Declared by Austria', 'The Arming of Europe', 'On the Brink of War'; on 1 August, a Saturday, and the beginning of the Bank Holiday weekend, the main headline was 'Europe in Arms'. Fighting had, of course, already started on many fronts. On the same day *The Times* carried on another page an advertisement for the *Daily Mirror*, prominently displayed in a 'box', with a photograph of a bathing belle:

> The Great Picture Newspaper
> Monster August Bank Holiday Number, 24 pages.
> Full of BEAUTIFUL PHOTOGRAPHS
> A splendid display of SUMMER SNAPSHOTS.
> Grand series of EXCLUSIVE WAR PICTURES. ½d

The solemnity of *The Times* and the frivolity of the *Mirror* are not thus juxtaposed to point the difference between them, though that is real enough, but rather to show, in the enterprise they were jointly engaged in, their symbiosis.

IX
THE POWER OF LANGUAGE

FIVE hundred years after Gutenberg we live in a world filled with, regulated, interconnected, and largely defined by words in print. It seems that all the languages of mankind have been set down in print, and many of them have become distinct languages only because they have been printed. There are cultures, or the fragmentary remains of cultures, which are still illiterate, but there is none[202] today which is literate without print; it is probably more difficult for us to imagine a society in which literacy is a scribal skill only than one without reading and writing altogether. We learn to speak and understand speech in early childhood much as human beings have always done, but to this accomplishment (still the most extraordinary of all, acquired by young children apparently without effort or conscious thought) we now add another, in the ability to translate the symbols of speech into the yet more abstract symbols of written language; nearly all of this written language, for nearly all readers, is in print. If the learned skill of reading is not as yet universal, its universality is assumed in all parts of the world to be needful; and this requirement, and the possibility of meeting it for virtually all of the world's inhabitants, is the creation of print.

It is true that other means of communication over distance and through time have been developed in the past three-quarters of a century, but these are as yet no more than auxiliaries of print, and seem unlikely to gain any more independent status in the foreseeable future. It is also true that, as the scope of the exact sciences has enormously enlarged, words as such have become themselves auxiliaries to another mode of record and communication, mathematics. But for most men and women words, the oldest of all human inventions (since we are disinclined to call 'human' those guessed-at ancestors who could not speak) are the means above all by which they make themselves, their thoughts, needs, wishes and intentions known to one another; and words for most of them in at least some part of their social existence mean words in print.

Once in print, words become public in a manner hardly possible otherwise: for while speech will pass into the memories of many, and may thus be preserved and transmitted, generation by generation, to many more, it is not fixed and recorded and must certainly be modified in the course of transmission; and scribal record is too limited to reach more than a minority. But print fixes words absolutely and in authoritative form: that is to say, once printed, a word cannot be changed except by re-printing; and every word in print must be traceable theoretically to an individual. At the same time print makes these words available, theoretically, to everyone. Print constitutes a network connecting all with all, and uniquely combining individuality with community, since for everything in print somebody has been responsible, and everything in print is, or may be, open to everybody. The past is open to the present through the ever-growing repository of print; but the present itself becomes a public possession.

This, the realisation of 'the multiplication of mind', had been the ideal of the champions of print since the beginning. But translation of the abstract ideal into practice has produced effects very different from those which men like Carlile, or Jefferson, or Milton looked for; precisely as multiplica-tion has spread the printed word round the globe and into every corner of modern life it seems to have contributed less and less to the enlargement of 'mind'. The products of 'mind', it is true, have not been destroyed; on the contrary, it can be said that almost everything that ever was in print is still in print somewhere, thanks to print's preservative power, and very much of it more extensively than ever. The enormous modern editions of world literature, themselves the topmost layer of previous editions, piled up as the ever wider courses of an inverted pyramid, dwarf the possible readerships of the past. Millions of copies of Shakespeare, Goethe, Pushkin, Burns, tens of millions of Bibles exist and may even be read; the library which, as Erasmus pointed out, was once confined within walls and could be burnt in one fire, now fills the world and is safe, unless the world itself is set on fire.

But this great treasure-house of print, the still-accumulating legacy of 'mind' as literature, is overwhelmed, in terms of bulk and extent, by another literature which (though much of it is also, nowadays, preserved in libraries) exists from day to day and is not expected to last longer. It is concerned with the present business of consumption, it exists to be sold and to assist in selling, itself both marketable goods and marketplace. As it is for consumption it is merely by this fact removed from the region where print is the extended communication of 'mind'. Thoughts are not consumed, or *used up* when transmitted; on the contrary, they may be expected to grow thereby. But there is a kind of mental activity and inter-change to which the idea of consumption does seem to apply: to entertain and be entertained, in current usage, seems to be of this kind. To entertain has of course had many meanings, and none of them altogether excluding the others, but 'to engage the attention of agreeably, to amuse with that which makes the time pass pleasantly' may perhaps be accepted as the dominant definition today, and one that applies to by far the largest part of printed literature in a great part of the world. What is held to be agreeable, pleasant, and amusing will vary but the point about 'the literature of entertainment', embracing a huge area of contemporary writing from novels to advertising copy, and including almost the whole of popular journalism, is that it sets itself to be entertaining as its first aim, if not always its most important one; if it has other qualities, of instruction or persuasion, and even when these are its primary purpose, they are not what is offered to the reader.

Entertainment of this kind undoubtedly *is* consumed, and in much the same way as is food or any other commodity used from day to day and replenished without cumulative effect. (Too much food, it is true, leads to obesity, and maybe the same can be said metaphorically of a copious diet of entertainment-literature; but only specialised eaters like camels or fat-tailed dormice expect to store up much of their intake.) Entertainment literature is almost by definition ephemeral: as it passes the time so it passes with time and requires to be continually renewed. It is thus perfectly suited to mass marketing and continual consumption, of a kind quite unlike that envisaged by Carlile and his like; for while they may have thought that the appetite for knowledge, the products of 'mind', would be unlimited, they did not expect it to be unchanging. The continuous absorption of something as pastime, which leaves no hunger except for more of the same, they can hardly have thought of.

Reading is often a pastime in a narrow and exclusive sense, not expected to leave anything in the mind of the reader. It may well be objected that this is impossible, and that something remains of even the slightest matter, read with the least attention: this is indeed an important principle in advertising technique. But the main object of such reading in the reader's mind is simply to fill a hole in it, and there is evidently a very large and possibly an increasing vacuity to be occupied. Thought is difficult and often impossible, but utter vacancy of mind makes the subject uneasy: rather than think or become conscious of thoughtlessness most of us, perhaps, will read anything. And as it fills vacancy without demanding thought or close attention, pastime-reading progressively vitiates mental capacities, or so it seems: if it is sought for 'relaxation' only during intervals of non-activity, it tends to enlarge these intervals at the expense of more energetic or painful occupations. The market for pastime-reading is very large, therefore, is growing, and requires little effort to maintain; or, more accurately, the efforts it requires for maintenance and expansion are those appropriate to marketing as such (business enterprise) and have little to do with the labours of authorship.

The effects are visible in all the main uses of print for an undifferentiated 'reading public'; a common characteristic is that these are more and more directed at a public thought of as a mass, or in statistical terms. Perhaps the most spectacular development has been in book-publishing, until lately generally considered in some degree removed from the requirements of mass-marketing. Especially since the Second World War this, the earliest and in many ways hitherto the least altered branch of printing, has undergone large changes, financial and in organisation. Partly as a direct consequence of these changes the kind of books published has also changed, or perhaps it would be more true to say that there has been more and more concentration on one kind of book, that deemed suitable for mass-marketing. Firms have amalgamated and, after often many generations as private or 'family' enterprises, have 'gone public', coming into the hands of managements and their accountants concerned only with gaining the largest return on the investment of shareholders. In many cases, especially in Britain and America, publishing houses have, without changing their names, become no more than one among many channels of investment controlled by large corporations. Investment has been on a proportionate scale, and with it expectation of profit; every effort has therefore been made to reduce the uncertainties of what in the past involved the hazards of individual taste and judgment. Books must be sold quickly and not by thousands or even tens of thousands, but by the million; and such sales must be not merely hoped for but guaranteed in advance. As in the case of all other goods produced for a market which is at once 'free' and, in the mass, dirigible, the result is achieved by advertising; with the special characteristic shared by goods which are not things but words—a characteristic most eminent in newspapers—that advertising and the commodity advertised become virtually indistinguishable.

The issue of these influences can be seen in the so-called 'blockbuster book', to the production of which a large share of present effort and ingenuity is devoted by publishing firms. Such books are designed to be not just 'best sellers', but to sell in millions, overwhelming their rivals in contests which are themselves turned, like gladiatorial combats, to the uses of entertainment. The process of ensuring their success begins before they are written in a concerted use of all means of publicity. A book may be 'projected' as a film or TV programme which will prepare the way for its publication later, or the process may be reversed. In effect the choice of form appears to be a matter of indifference, since the purpose of each in a concerted 'campaign' is to draw attention to the others. A recent description of the techniques used in American publishing sums it up as follows: '. . . the aim of such efforts is a multimedia merchandising program in which books, movies, and television programs based on a single work—and all associated programs—are fused into a coordinated whole, as a packaged "property"'.[203] The 'literary property', the commodity to be sold in various forms, need not actually exist, even in manuscript form, for such a property deal to be put through. The 'spontaneous generation of a literary property' 'does not have to take place in the mind of an author; it can occur around a conference table in the office of a producer or an agent, who may then add to it "elements", including the writer, who is "acquired" sooner or later in the packaging process'. 'The essence of such a system is to make the promotion in one medium feed the promotion in another to achieve a maximum marketing effect in both.'[204]

It is perhaps apparent that the work which eventually arrives in print by such processes is unlikely to have lasting value. The writer quoted above goes on to describe the crescendo of publicity and financial manoeuvre preceding the 'launch' of a new 'blockbuster' novel in the US, including the prominent reporting in the press of its different stages. The actual content of the book was 'a matter of minor interest', but when the most interesting news, of its purchase, was made public—'New . . . Novel Sold for Record-Shattering Figure'—it was also noted that the book 'is full of fabulous characters, European aristocrats, glamorous women, American television and business personalities, and a heroine . . . who appears destined to capture the imagination of the reading and movie-going public'. The point to notice is that, for all the notoriety achieved by the author, who is able as a result of the 'campaign' to boast, 'I'm the most highly paid first novelist and the most highly paid second novelist in the world',[205] authorship has become of little importance. The fame created in advance may, according to the promoter's choice, as well be gained by one person as another.

It may also be observed that where such large sums are involved ('properties' being bought for millions of dollars in the American examples described) the works chosen for treatment are likely to be few; it is essential to the 'blockbuster' method that there should be not many but few, ideally only one, on the market at the same time, which 'everyone' will buy (and perhaps read). Fewer books published by fewer firms, though sold in mounting millions of copies, will not conduce to the freedom and variety in which literary creation thrives; and though there seems to be as yet little evidence of direct political censorship exercised by the publishing 'conglomerates', it is clear that the censorship of choice, which no publisher can avoid, must in their case exclude everything that does not lend itself to mass-marketing. Choice—which in the initial stages may appear almost arbitrary, raising the object to instantaneous fame and riches much like the winner of a sweepstake or the football pools—will certainly not fall upon an author who by reason of originality or the expression of unpopular views is unlikely to have the widest possible appeal. In place of any actual individuality of authorship is substituted the singularity of 'the winner', the one in the spotlight. As in the film industry to which publishing of this kind is so closely related, such 'star-billing' produces the opposite of genuine variety, as one well-groomed star becomes more and more like every other. The concluding comment of the American observer of the process may be given at some length:

> The kind of emotional remoteness from 'the product' which one senses in the conglomerates' central management people now seems to be communicating itself to the people who are directly in charge of the publishing houses owned by the conglomerates, and more and more it seems that books are being regarded as interchangeable products somehow possessing, because of the manner of their promotion, a strange sort of uniformity. What is particularly striking to me about the frantic mass-merchandising and big-book promotions is the *undifferentiated* quality of what is being hawked once those books not singled out as potentially big money-makers have been, in effect, thrown into the discard. . . . It's all treated as 'product'. And it is so because the mass merchandising, the hype, the frenzied pursuit of Number One which the book publishing industry has turned to as a central and universal tool is in its very essence anti-art and even anti-thought.[206]

What, it may be asked, does the writer mean by these last accusations? The most remarkable thing about the whole of the transactions he describes is that all of them—even the supposedly 'secret' negotiations, the very secrecy of which is used to heighten the factitious air of excitement—are offered in themselves as public entertainment. The 'product' marketed is promoted by means, and in an atmosphere, hardly to be distinguished from that generated by itself, as a work of art. That a novel of the sort in question is a work of art would be difficult to deny without altogether too fine-drawn definitions of literary art: if such a work is one made from varied elements of invention and modified experience, then productions of this kind, even when assembled more like a motor-car than a book, cannot be excluded. However, to allow as much may not affect the conviction that the process of which it is the end-product is indeed 'anti-art'. It is art of a special kind, whose salient features are shared by the two other categories of mass literature, popular journalism and advertising.

The brief examination offered earlier of popular newspaper content is an indication of the degree to which 'news'—the reporting of actual current events—is turned to the purposes of entertainment, quite apart from the very large amount of space given to the concerns of popular entertainment in undisguised form (TV, cinema, pop-music and, of course, book publishing of the kind just described). If sport is added, then material not pretending to be concerned with anything but pastime will account, perhaps, for more than half the letter-press, with illustration, of many popular newspapers. But in any case, when 'news' is selected and treated as it is, any real distinction is lost between it and those parts of a paper designed avowedly for diversion alone.

Most printed advertisement uses the same means; if the 'small ads' are excluded (as has been argued, they constitute a category of their own, having little to do with the large-scale operations of 'the advertising industry') almost all advertising contains some element of entertainment. News presentation and advertisement alike employ less and less the language of direct communication, and more and more suggestion, oblique implication, association, non-logical connections. These are the tools of poetry; and if 'creative advertising' more obviously uses the poet's technical equipment—neologism, paradox, figurative speech, personification, puns, metonymy—a selection of any day's headlines will show most of the same devices in use. Typographical layout itself mimics the forms of *vers libre*; the extraordinary condensations of 'headlines' are a caricature of the concentration of poetry. In advertising at least these affinities are recognised, as the much-used phrase 'creative advertising' indicates (it is 'creative' in two senses, of course, in creating a demand where none existed, and in being itself a work of creation). Advertising, to quote a typical apologist, is 'an art and not a science', a 'creative process', and one concerning which 'it may be argued that it may not be a bad thing . . . to be a little removed from reality'.[207]

This creative art, whether in the form of news or direct advertisement (the two can perhaps be lumped together as 'adnews') is still predominantly a verbal one. Great though the importance of picture-images may be, especially under the influence of universal TV, in presenting the world as a continuous entertainment-spectacle, words are essential to the process. Their use is very close to the classic art of rhetoric. 'If a copywriter wished to claim ancient and noble ancestry for his profession', observes a student of advertising language, 'he might with some justification see himself in the tradition of persuasive oratory going back to . . . ancient Greece and Rome.'[208] Following this hint, it is instructive to turn to what is still the most penetrating account of the orator's art, and the claims made for it, in the Dialogues of Plato. In the *Gorgias* especially, Socrates sets out to discover in what the orator's or rhetorician's skill consists, and what it is for; and it emerges that oratory, though purely oral, produced for the ancient world exactly the same effects, and by the same means, as has the printed word in the process of becoming a commodity. Oratory also was for sale: Gorgias, the master-orator, was both ready to practise it himself and to instruct others in the art which, he claimed, could control and dominate all others, conferring 'on every one who possesses it not only freedom for himself but also the power of ruling his fellow-countrymen.'[209]

The first point that Socrates establishes is that oratory, the 'art of speech', divorces words from any particular use in conveying information and instruction and offers instead a generalised function, said to be superior, of producing 'conviction'. This conviction, he goes on to show, is different from that produced by actual information:

SOCRATES: If you were asked whether there are such things as true or false beliefs, you would say that there are.
GORGIAS: Yes.
SOCRATES: But are there such things as true and false knowledge?
GORGIAS: Certainly not.
SOCRATES: Then knowledge and belief are clearly not the same thing.
GORGIAS: True.
SOCRATES: Yet men who believe may just as properly be convinced as men who know?
GORGIAS: Yes.
SOCRATES: May we then posit the existence of two kinds of conviction, one which gives knowledge, and one which gives belief without knowledge?
GORGIAS: Certainly.[210]

This brief exchange is not only the crux of the whole Dialogue, from which inevitably follows the exposure of Gorgias and his more sophisticated fellow-Sophist Callicles, but a succinct description of the modern arts of persuasion as practised in advertising and allied forms of mass-communication. It is noteworthy that the orator, whose audience could never be numbered in more than hundreds at a time, claims nevertheless to reach and sway many more than can a teacher. As Socrates observes, 'The orator does not teach juries and other bodies about right and wrong—he merely persuades them; he could hardly teach so large a number of people matters of such importance in a short time.' If his 'popular' audience is also an 'ignorant' one, his task is so much the easier, and if he himself is ignorant of the subject in hand it is of no consequence, for, says Socrates, 'The orator need have no knowledge of the truth about things: it is enough for him to have discovered a knack of convincing the ignorant that he knows more than the experts.'

This knack, says Socrates, is *pandering:* producing 'a kind of gratification' which convinces or persuades without knowledge and which 'pays no regard to the welfare of the object but catches fools with the bait of ephemeral pleasure and tricks them into holding it in the highest esteem'. In Periclean Athens the branches of pandering instanced by Socrates were cooking, beauty-culture, and popular lecturing as well as oratory. If today the advertising industry and popular journalism are added to the list it can be seen that these between them embrace all the ancient sub-departments, with the same qualifications in their practitioners, who require no more than 'a shrewd and bold spirit together with a natural aptitude for dealing with men'. Print, it may be said, has altered nothing except in bringing an enormously larger and, perhaps, more passive audience within range.

The essence of pandering, today as ever, lies in flattery. The method of advertising, the criterion of the blockbuster-author, and the pretext of the journalist, is 'giving the public what it wants', telling the mass-audience 'what it wants to hear'. Herein lies the *art* of these different forms and their various techniques, all gaining attention and wooing consent by means, briefly described above, which are expected to give pleasure. So, it may be said, do all the arts, including those to which we grant respect: and if that is agreed, how do we reconcile such a view with the Platonic condemnation of pandering and the modern American critic's indignant repudiation of 'anti-art' and 'anti-thought'?

Plato's root objection to pandering in all its forms was its false pretences: that it pretends to be concerned with the good of its object but has quite other ends in view. Clearly this applies to advertising, which, whether 'truthful' or not in its claims about the commodity advertised, always practises deception in the discrepancy between its ostensible and actual purpose. It pretends to have the welfare, or gratification of the buyer in view, but is in fact only concerned with selling. It may well be that the goods to be sold meet the advertiser's claims, and that it suits his purposes to be 'honest'; but actually to serve the buyer and put his interests first can never be a primary motive, taking precedence over the need to sell. It is interesting to see the extent to which 'consumerism'—the idea of putting consumer interests first—is regarded as a threat by the advertising industry, which 'cannot run with the hare and hunt with the hounds', i.e. cannot protect consumers from the persuasions it itself is putting forward. 'Truth in advertising' is itself an advertising slogan, and a means to more subtle deceptions: 'if advertising has an obligation to tell the truth, that obligation is to its clients (i.e. producers and sellers of the commodity in question) and not to the consumer.'[211]

The deceptions practised by journalism are of more than one kind. There is the large-scale and continuous falsehood put about by newspapers which pretend to report affairs comprehensively, accurately, and impartially, and do not. To a great extent, certainly, they cannot, working as they do under pressure of time and space; to some extent perhaps impartiality at least is not even desirable—at any rate it is argued that partisanship in journalism is a source of vigour and interest, and that through contending points of view the truth may be arrived at, as in the adversarial notion of justice. But even when these mitigations are taken into account, it remains the case that the Press as a whole—in Britain, and also in most other countries where it is described as 'free'—pretends to provide a general picture of all that men and women require to know in the exercise of their rights and duties as citizens: 'the facts' (to quote the most recent Royal Commission on the Press) 'without which a democratic electorate cannot make responsible judgments'. Even more, it purports nowadays to present the 'daily map of the world' on which they may base their judgments and actions as members of the world community. Clearly, even if any individual could read all the newspapers published, thus arriving at the synthetic view alluded to, it does nothing of the sort; if the most widely-circulating parts of the daily and weekly Press are considered on their own, as the only ones that many millions of readers see, the pretence is grotesque.

It may be objected that such a newspaper as the *Daily Mirror* or *Express* does not make any such claim. But that is not so: a purely local paper may serve a limited view and do so openly and candidly, but the mass-circulation papers admit no boundaries to their purview. Implicit in the very fact of their mass-circulation is that are all providing 'news of the world'. Obviously, the coverage of world 'events' offered by such a newspaper is so small and selective (accuracy apart) that no reader at all capable of reflection can suppose it to be truly general in scope. But that makes no difference: what the paper does, day by day, is to persuade readers that its world-picture is, not comprehensive, not impartial, but *sufficient*. Whatever powers belong to repetition, whatever hold upon attention is

effected by clamour and the appearance of urgency, whatever authority is
carried by the bare fact of being in print, combine to this end, that the
reader should accept the paper's view as adequate; that it contains all he
needs and wants to know.

The last assumption notoriously provides motive and excuse for everything in the Press that critics deplore: newspapers are a commodity and
must therefore conform to the consumer's taste. If the public wants sensationalism, titillation and triviality, these are what must be supplied and—so
the argument runs—there is no deception in supplying them, for the consumer must know what he is asking for. This pretext is itself quite dis-
ingenuous, and constitutes the second and most damaging deception
habitually practised by newspapers. It ignores the fundamental precept of
mass-merchandising, which is the basis in turn of the whole advertising
industry, that the public does *not* know what it wants, that appetites must
be stimulated or new-invented and demands created from nothing. Newspapers sell themselves by selling their world-view; and this world-view,
which the papers create, is not chosen at random, still less one adopted for
its breadth and penetration, but precisely that view which tends to make
the public less, not more, observant, well-informed and critical; less and not
more concerned with the truth or otherwise of what it is being told.

It is the last of these effects which is the most harmful.

How much credit is given by the public to the claims of advertising is
impossible to say, but personal observation and surveys of opinion suggest
that it is not large. That is to say, very few, probably, believe in any literal
sense what advertisement says of the variously superlative qualities of
goods on sale. Few, perhaps, actually suppose that they will gain, along
with these goods, the prizes of wealth, ease, health, sexual gratification or
personal eminence freely promised by suggestion. But that they allow
themselves to be *influenced* by these claims and suggestions the mere
existence of the advertising industry is sufficient proof. Even if it be
granted that the first persons advertising agents deceive are themselves
and their clients, so that the powers of advertising to control and direct the
market are sometimes exaggerated, that 'our industrialists are far too
profit-conscious to spend the amounts they do on advertising without
expectation of return'[212] can be taken as axiomatic. The very belief that 'it
pays to advertise', is one that tends to make its predictions good: in an
atmosphere permeated by advertisement, whose importunacies it is almost
impossible to avoid, what is not advertised can hardly, in market terms, be
said to exist. In the 'ubiquitous presence' of advertising (to use again the
words of the apologist already cited) 'much as people feel that they are

ignoring it, frequently they are inadvertently reacting to it'.[213] Perhaps the most curious current example of this faith in the seductive powers of advertisement against the dictates of reason is shown by the cigarette manufacturers, who find it worthwhile to cover hoardings with alluring suggestion flatly contradicted by the 'Government health warning' at the bottom. Such advertisements are only an extreme example of the 'fact'—and whether or not it is truly a fact of mass psychology, it is apparently vindicated in practice—that people may be swayed by rhetoric which they know to be false.

Exactly the same can be said of the rhetoric used by newspapers. The press is of course intimately connected with the advertising industry, economically dependent on it, and influenced by it, through its effect on journalists as individuals, in general attitude to a world full of commodities. The commodity newspapers have to sell is their own world-view, entirely compatible as a rule with that of 'merchandising' in general and—while there are differences in detail from one journal to another—sharing certain overriding assumptions. These include 'the idea that our age is composed of sensational events'[214] and at the same time that it is one of endless triviality, in which the dimensions of a beauty queen can have the same 'news value' as an industrial dispute or the fate of a political dissident. They include the further apparent inconsistency that while 'our age' is one of continual upheavals and catastrophes, there is nothing fundamental to be questioned about its institutions; that in politics and all public affairs 'personalities' are more important than principles; that men and women, while capable of being moved by sentiment, to which frequent appeals are made, are actually and necessarily driven by desire for material possessions, power over others, and fame; that this last, most prized of mankind's treasures is to be found in the 'publicity' which newspapers themselves dispense.

The objection to such notions is not so much that they are unamiable and cynical as that they are artificial, and serve to project a fantasy world no more credible than that set up to promote the sale of beer, or motor-cars, or clothes. The fantasy is seductive in the same way and at the same level, offering quick and shallow gratifications; that slight, passing indulgences are promised is an essential part of the seduction. The feelings stimulated by the most extravagant means are not expected to be deep or lasting. Indignation roused by violent headlines, the 'Anger', 'Fury', 'Horror' which are the sub-editor's stock-in-trade, is not usually the kind that leads to action, nor is it so intended; those who use them are guilty less of wishing to incite mob violence as of indifference to their meaning. They are just noisy words, an easy way to excite a momentary flash of interest, and much of the time, probably, they are read in the same spirit. Erotic suggestion, which notoriously fills the popular papers and, more than anything else, perhaps, is believed to sell them, is seldom a provocation to urgent lust; it does not pander to actual bodily desire so much as provide unceasing slight titillation. Temptation to envy, greed, covetousness, lechery, anger, pride and sloth is presented day after day, but in no case—except perhaps the last—with overpowering force.

It is assumed by newspaper-producers that none of the appetites for which they cater, and which they help to promote, is capable of directing attention for long. Not even sport is expected to hold a very sustained interest, though it comes nearest, probably, to a subject of serious study. Most record and narrative, consequently, is brief and, while making the most energetic efforts to catch attention, does not attempt to keep it; a continual state of sub-excitement, moving rapidly from one stimulus to the next, is provided for, with tedium as result. It is tedium, however, of a particular kind, which does not lead to abandonment of the pursuit. People go on reading, or half-reading, newspapers and magazines, turning over the pages in manifest indifference to material apparently yelling for attention; there is perhaps an analogy with the habit-forming qualities alleged of 'convenience' foods, said to give small satisfaction, but difficult to give up.

Communication itself suffers, not simply in the poverty of whatever, in detail, is communicated but in implications about its very possibility. Readers of newspapers and advertising, voluntary and involuntary swallowers of the non-stop flow of words, don't believe a great deal of it, but their lives are in almost every corner affected; their outlook, their behaviour, their own language itself is moulded in this circumambient sea. Print has, perhaps, had a tendency from the start to encroach upon and destroy popular language: the formulation of syntactical rules, uniform orthographies, and the enlargement of vocabularies by word-loaning and word-coining were all disseminated by the grammars and lexicons and polyglot versions of the early years of printing; these, moreover, were only the most active agents in a general spread, with growing literacy, of 'bookish' speech. But to begin with, even if much richness and variety of language was thus flattened out, the compensation in a language of rapid growth and change, accelerated by print, was greater than the loss.

What has happened in this century seems to have been a reverse process, by which the extremely impoverished language of mass-print is robbing popular utterance not only of whatever remains of local, regional, even national variation, but of the more formal speech-patterns and vocabularies acquired from 'book-learning'. Learning—the acquisition of certain language-skills—is, indeed, required today, but it is of a different, specialised kind, in the ability to construe technical jargons or to make sense of the forms and notices of bureaucratic instruction. It is doubtful if the person who has learnt how to fill in an Income-tax form will in any way have enlarged his grasp of language as a general tool of communication. But on the other hand the consumer of mass-print, where communication is at its most general, is deprived both of the riches of language and, much more damagingly, of confidence in any language as a means of conveying truth. If the productions of mass-print are all in one way or another deceptive, and recognised, more or less, to be so, they are received or consumed as pastime alone, and the very idea of language as a means of truth-telling is replaced by the rhetorician's own definition, that it is a means of flattery and persuasion.

The standards of Gorgias, of Tisias his teacher and Callicles his pupil appear to have triumphed. By means of mass-communication (of different kinds, but primarily in print) language is an instrument of manipulation, not of instruction; thereby it is corrupted itself, and corrupts its users and its audience. When the audience accepts flattery and deception as the rule it becomes difficult if not impossible to make it accept anything else. Communication is no longer, even relatively, connected with what is the case, but is governed by what the audience is used to and finds 'probable': the rhetorician's guiding principle is 'never mind the truth, pursue probability through thick and thin', and by 'probable' he means no more than 'what the public finds acceptable'.[215] To say anything actually new or surprising is, it seems, out of the question; the communicator is as much a prisoner of the language he abuses as his audience, in fact he is the prisoner of his audience and believes, perhaps quite sincerely, that he cannot speak to it in any other way. What guide can he have? It is perfectly possible, admits Callicles, to pander not simply to individuals, but 'to the souls of a crowd, without regard to its real interest': an adequate description, it may be thought, of most of mass-communication today. If the practice is under criticism, as it might be by a Royal Commission, what defence can be made, or rule suggested, by which one sort of persuasion may be distinguished from another? 'Public interest' is the answer found both by Callicles and Royal Commissioners. But public interest is too slippery a standard even for the arch-Sophist, who is driven to admit that he has never known an orator genuinely guided by it. There is still a guideline to hold on to, which Callicles falls back on at the end of the Dialogue: pushed by Socrates into a corner, he says that the orator 'should be the State's servant'.[216]

That seems to be the last word. To turn from mass-communication in the 'Western World', where pandering to the reader-as-consumer comes—most of the time—before pandering to the State, and contrast with it the equivalent in those other contemporary societies where the State is pander to itself, is not encouraging. At first sight the newspapers of the Soviet Union, and of the different countries in the 'Eastern' or Soviet-dominated division of the world are, after a diet or western popular journalism, an enormous relief: sober in appearance, almost wholly without adventitious attention-seeking devices; filled with reports and articles of length enough to allow some adequate exposition and argument; modestly (in every sense) illustrated, and entirely without advertising. Commercial advertisement, the ubiquitous importunacy which the citizen in the West can scarcely ever escape from, is of course most conspicuously absent from the entire Eastern scene, its place being taken, but only partly, by political slogans. The newspapers of the USSR and of the 'People's Democracies' are slimmer than their Western counterparts (if indeed there are any true counterparts) but contain probably not much less reading matter, solidly set out, than such as *The Times* or *Le Monde*, if advertising were excluded. The reader is not wooed with distractions or, in the sense in which we have been using it, with much 'entertainment'; sport, though acknowledged as of much popular interest, is given little space outside the journals specialising in it—a column or so at the most in *Pravda* or *Izvestia*, only rarely with photographs. The tone of these and parallel organs outside the Soviet Union itself, which often reproduce the most important articles with great, or slavish fidelity, is serious, informative, instructive.

Yet we know, and it is not denied by the authorities concerned, that all information and instruction is of a particular kind, not the fruit of free inquiry but with certain ends in view. It is authoritative in a literal, overpowering sense as the voice of authority; almost everything said is understood not merely to have been sanctioned by the appropriate organ of the State, but to be its direct utterance. What is not so is assumed to have slipped in by accident. As we have seen, the efforts of authority to control the spread of dangerous ideas by print have always been ineffective so long as censorship was imposed only after publication. The establishment of an *imprimatur* and an Index could restrict and hamper but never eliminate the subversive tendencies of print; even the most complete system of licensing gave scope for evasion by printers and publishers independent of the licensing authority. Only control of the printing-publishing process itself, from start to finish, offered the possibility of absolute surveillance; and such control was achieved nowhere, except temporarily and patchily, until this century.

Where, nowadays, it has been established the 'multiplication of mind' has been pursued, it seems, on the largest possible scale. In part, no doubt, it has been carried out in terms which would have been approved by such libertarian printers as Richard Carlile, who would not have objected either to the imagery or the expressed aims of those who set themselves up, with the printing press as the most powerful machine available, as 'engineers of souls'. That they could do it for so many would, again, have been reckoned only an advantage. Enormous numbers can now be reached, and without the trouble of marketing; State and Party newspapers have circulations of millions, books are issued in editions even larger than those of the 'blockbuster' promotions, and all in effect by decree. The distinction between the two mass-modes is in the idea of purpose: whereas the mass-produced novel or the mass-circulation newspaper in the West has apparently no other object than to sell itself as commodity, the literature wholly controlled by the State is produced with an extraneous aim, to serve whatever interests the same State conceives to be its own. (Even if we allow that 'the State' is a mythological entity, actually divided into different functions, which may have conflicting objects, a remarkable degree of unanimity is in practice achieved, for the appearance of unanimity is the supreme common interest of divided factions.) Uniformity of culture is a necessary and acknowledged part of orthodoxy, and the uniformity is more important than any detail of form: 'The official doctrine of culture changes in dependence upon economic zigzags and administrative expediencies. But with all its changes, it retains one trait—that of being absolutely categorical.'[217]

The frivolity of journalism in the West, its sobriety in the East, the comparative and aimless variety of one beside the purposeful unanimity of the other are real distinctions. Nevertheless in lasting effect they may prove a distinction without a difference. The consequences of mass-marketing in the West are, it has been asserted, 'anti-art' and 'anti-thought', the very opposite of the enlargement of mind, but the conscious engineering of minds to produce uniformity of thought evidently has very similar results in the end. Differences certainly exist: literature that is believed to be *for* something, however obnoxious, is not so wholly degraded, or is degraded in a different way from the writing that is not for anything but sale. The rhetoric of communist journalism is not the same as that of a popular newspaper in the West composed of gossip, sensation, and quasi-pornography; it is the rhetoric of an official puritanism which seems to hold its audience in greater respect. But it may well be thought that this respect is chiefly apparent to outsiders; for those habituated to it and its unremitting exhortations it is perhaps much the same sham. The flattery of a perpetual official optimism, which cannot allow certain disagreeable truths to be told, even when they are common knowledge, is neither better nor worse than the flattery of advertising and its editorial adjuncts of trivia. Either way, we may guess, it is received with the same mixture of scepticism and acceptance which, as has been suggested, is the most corrupting effect of such misuse of language. Either way, the very possibility of truthful communication is in danger of being forgotten, whether in print or any other mode. It is interesting to be told that everyday speech has deteriorated in the Soviet Union as in the West, not only becoming more slovenly, but being marked in the same way by uniform and obsessive grossness. (It is claimed that Russian, with more variety of obscene imagery, offers more scope than the pitifully impoverished profanities of current Anglo-American, but the movement is said to be in the same direction.) Perhaps the cause is the same, that where most of printed communication is both suspected and accepted, and truth has become, in the cant phrase, 'a dirty word' colloquial utterance is reduced to mere expletives and repetitions of 'dirty words', the language of resentment and despair.

Of course, this is far too crude a picture; it does not reflect the actual state of affairs so much as the ideal objects of its opposed components: the view of the press on the one hand purely as a field of private enterprise 'owing nothing whatever to the public ... affected by no public interest ... the propety of the owner, selling a manufactured product at his own risk' (see Chapter VII); and on the other, that summed up by Zhdanov, arbiter of cultural policy under Stalin, as being simply 'a powerful instrument in the hands of the Communist Party'. Probably the official press of the Third Reich most closely approximated actual practice to the ideal of its controllers, but it should be noted that in the case of the National Socialists the ideal was rather different. The Nazi ideologues put the printed word well behind speech as an instrument of mass-persuasion, and though very willing to use it, in forms varying from the quasi-respectable *Völkische Beobachter* to the obscene *Stürmer*, regarded it with something like contempt. (As, for instance, in the remark of Goebbels, himself an arch-practitioner and instigator of the directives which governed everything the German papers printed, that 'any person with the slightest spark of honour left in him will take good care in future not to become a journalist'.[218] But such extreme examples apart, it is probable that no newspaper in the world has not occasionally lapsed into candour and objectivity; nor, perhaps, is there any product of the book assembly-line, whether made to order in the socialist-realist manner or for the Hollywood hypermarket, which does not bear some traces of an individual's thoughts and feelings. Even if it be accepted that the dominant tendency of the printed word today is toward mass-manipulation in use and nullity in content, it is not the only possibility open, nor perhaps more than a temporary aberration in the history of print.

It may, indeed, be questioned whether this history has not already neared its end. The technical innovations of the 'electronic revolution' have, it is asserted, opened a prospect of communication and storage of information in which newspapers, books, and libraries will be obsolete and even the act of writing itself will be transformed and in some cases transferred entirely to machines. There can be no doubt that many operations in the storage, retrieval, collation and interchange of what has hitherto been in print will be performed in other ways, some of them already in use; only thus, it is said, can the enormous quantities of material be handled which result from the 'explosion' of all kinds of information. There has been, it is reckoned, a growth in printed information 'at an exponential rate, doubling perhaps every 15 years, at least since the days of Gutenberg',[219] and Gutenberg's methods can no longer deal with it. Nevertheless, whatever refinements are achieved in mass-storage and in using computers to collate what can no longer be systematised by the most capacious human brain, the change will not be absolute. At some point of most information-transmission, print, or some imitation of print (e.g. words projected on a screen), seems certain to survive: 'no matter what kinds of exotic technology we employ *people will still be reading.*'[220] What they will be reading may be influenced on the one hand by processes which can only accentuate tendencies to mass-production and standardisation; on the other by the huge resources of past and contemporary material which may readily be accessible through microfiche reproduction and other means. That it will be possible to have 'a whole library housed in a cabinet'[221] is an alluring prospect to the scholar, less so, probably, to the common reader; both may have doubts as citizens about the implications of centralised control and dependency on extremely elaborate, delicate and costly means.

It is clear that choices lie ahead which, if only for this last reason, the high capital cost of much of the 'new technology', will or ought to be matters of public policy. The centralisation involved in setting up huge computer-terminals, to which users would only 'plug in', the monopoly of information inherent in 'Ceefax' systems, the aesthetic consequences of mechanised writing-by-formula, the possibilities of 'multi-media' diversion piped into every home and available at the touch of a switch, point all too clearly towards control of means and manipulation of receivers or consumers: towards an audience ever more passive, less able to make or even to conceive of choice, less capable of connecting 'literature' (in whatever form it is presented for consumption) and real experience. The technical equipment for George Orwell's 'Minitruth' (the 'Ministry of Truth' in *1984* devoted entirely to the manufacture of lies), where 'history' is subject to constant revision for removal of inconvenient records, where every scrap of information can be centrally examined, censored, and 'processed' accordingly, and where the vacuous fantasies of 'prolefeed' can be turned out by machinery, is, it seems, on the threshold of availability. All it requires is government, or large-scale business organisation (one perhaps only formally distinguishable from the other) willing to invest in it.

It is important to remember, however, that Orwell foresaw or gave warning of such an eventuality *before* the means were available or even apparently feasible. That does not mean that he was gifted with extraordinary technical prescience, but that he could see a possible way that politics and culture were tending; without technical knowledge or much interest in such details he assumed for the purposes of satiric fiction that the techniques would come to hand. If in some respects we now seem nearer to Orwell's *1984* than makes the calendar comfortable to contemplate we should be clear that the dangers he set before us have moral and not technological causes. If the latter were the case his title date might as well have been 1450 as 1984; for certainly all that he imagined in the Ministry of Truth followed, technically, from then.

Before surrender to this dark fore-view, therefore, we may look back over the ground covered (however hastily) up to now and wonder how the uses of print, which in the beginning seemed to promise quite the opposite, can have been so far perverted—for whatever technical prodigies are imminent, they will not change the fundamental character of the first revolution wrought by print, in the dissemination of the word. We can say that the 'perversion' has not been in the instrument but in the uses to which it has been, and may be, put. The medium is *not* the message: printing showed itself from the start as in a sense neutral, used as has been noted for all the varied ends—oppression and rebellion, enlightenment and obscurantism—which language itself can serve. But, saying this, and rejecting the provocative paradox of the late Marshall McLuhan as quite inadequate even as historical slogans go, it is clear all the same that the printing machine has been, in the most extensive sense, a revolutionary tool; that almost at once the new medium began to bring about large and irreversible changes in society and culture; that like other mechanical inventions but perhaps more persistently than any other in the past 500 years of accelerating technical innovation it has apparently been endowed with a life of its own, invading and altering all human activities. What print has done is to potentiate language; it has even altered language (and to that extent, perhaps, it may be allowed to have modified the 'message'), but its real effect has been hugely to extend language's inherent possibilities. Any general view of printing, therefore, depends on the view of what language itself is for.

Speculative descriptions of the origins of language place much emphasis today on its emotional sources, as a means of communicating feelings and of eliciting appropriate responses, such as benevolence, anger or fear. On such a view, which tends also to emphasise the continuation of these functions in language, the purely rhetorical, at its basic and also its basest level, is a perfectly congruous use, and one which might be expected to predominate: words not, principally, as a means of conveying information but as persuasive noise.

It is necessary to challenge this account. The expression and communication of emotion have doubtless always been and certainly remain among the important functions of speech, but they cannot be the moving principle of language development (whether or not this is thought of as genetically determined), since if it were so there would be no reason for language to develop at all. Gesture, facial expression, and inarticulate sound can convey much between members of the same species, and all, perhaps, that is needful for social life at the level of feeling alone. What words can add is precisely that refinement and immense variability—using a limited range of sounds in an almost unlimited number of combinations—which makes general and, particularly, new information possible. It is, we may say, the infinite extent of information waiting in the real world for words to convey it that has caused language to grow and to keep on growing, immeasurably beyond the small repertoire of accepted signals in other social animals. Language is a means of learning, storing, and communicating what is the case in an unlimited number of situations—unlimited because, as they change, language can be modified or enlarged to meet them. But if to make statements about 'what is the case' is the fundamental purpose of words, it is necessary not only that they should be 'persuasive'—that goes without saying, indeed once a verbal form is accepted, to describe it as persuasive is mere tautology—but that they should be true. The very nature of language leads us to expect that the information conveyed by it will correspond with some reality. We also expect language to be true for all who hear or otherwise receive its messages: it is not a one-to-one means of communication but a *medium* which (however much meanings may be altered by the subjectivity of individual receivers) carries the same information to all who understand its given conventions.

Printing, therefore, has not been so neutral a means as appears, for these qualities of language are, so to speak, its predilection. To tell more people more quickly and more accurately what is the case—or, in the words of those who first began to use it and to extol its potentialities, to make 'learning' as common as possible[222]—was the obvious, 'natural', or, in the alternative formula of the time, God-given property of print. Print was not the message: the inherent message of language itself moved into print.

It is possible, consequently, to speak of those uses of the printed word which are devoted chiefly to persuasion and hypnosis strictly as perversion: it is language which has been perverted, and print secondarily as the means through which the proper information-bearing capabilities of language have so enormously enlarged. It is in print that the perversion is most obvious and where, as has been argued, it has its worst effect, for once we expected words in print to be even more certainly true than is naturally expected of words in general. Now we do not, and are left with a hiatus in communication, even a complete breakdown. But perversion, just because it is perversion—that is, a turning aside from proper function or purpose—is, however destructive, unlikely to be a permanent condition. Human society needs language as much as ever, and needs it to be truthful. It does not certainly follow (if we believe human beings to have free choice of any kind) that the need will be answered. But when it springs from so fundamental and lasting a part of human nature, to which the present dislocation and confusion of society themselves bear witness—for bad faith and lies, when endemic, make life intolerable—there is good reason to hope.

There are in fact plentiful signs of resistance to the malversation of language in print. These are partly in what, after 500 years of development, may be called conservative aspects of printing: the continued uses of print, in some form, as the most faithful and flexible means of scholarly record and exchange; the recognition that 'there is no other method as acceptable as reading from the printing page'[223] and that a great part of the reason for such superiority is the reliability of print, and the ease with which the accuracy of printed statements can be checked; in general book publishing, the preservation of continuous literary traditions and support, still frequently surviving market pressures, for the new work which grows out of it; in journalism the undoubted devotion of many individuals and some institutions, including parts at least of many publications, to disinterested inquiry and impartial reporting; among many readers, consequently, continued expectations of accuracy and cogency which have regulative force even when they are disappointed.

But if these are thought of as a dogged rearguard action fought against the tendencies of the time, there are other ways in which printing still keeps its adventurous, even revolutionary attributes. As, originally, the truly world-transforming power of print lay in the new scope given to 'mind' by a technical device, so some at least of recent technical innovations may have the same effect. One of the most important can hardly, perhaps, be called new: the typewriter has been in existence for more than 100 years, but it is only recently that it has come into its own as a means whereby the vital connection has been restored between print and the individual conscience. Censorship has produced its inevitable stepchild of clandestine writing and publication: in the USSR, where censorship and control of printing is more complete, probably, than anywhere else in the world[224] a literature which may well prove to be the most significant of our whole era has come to life out of apparent obliteration. It is true that the typewritten 'self-publication' (*samizdat*) by which these works have initially been uttered is necessarily very limited—no more, perhaps, than a few dozen copies in many instances—and has for that very reason been grudgingly permitted by authority. Even these small numbers, however, have allowed a whole literature to germinate and survive 'underground', and to emerge, at intervals and in variously more propitious circumstances, into the larger life of print proper.

If comparisons are made between such 'underground' writing and that which flourishes on the surface, with all the encouragements of financial reward and fashionable approval, in so-called open societies, it is tempting to suppose that censorship is in fact a blessing: that only under its rigours, and the severe penalties, including death, invited by those who defy or evade it, is literature purged of vanities and recalled to its true purposes. When a writer risks liberty or life he must have some powerful motive. The chief aim of censorship, the more clearly manifested as it becomes harsher and more extensive, is suppression of the truth: defiance of censorship springs from the overpowering desire, not only to discover what, in all its forms, the censors seek to hide, but to utter it. 'One word of truth', to quote the most illustrious (former) member of the Russian literary 'underground',[225] is what the writer longs to speak; evidently it is also what people long to hear.

A sombre view of contemporary literature in 'the West' may reckon it past redemption until, once again, it becomes dangerous to write with sincerity and conviction. In countries such as Britain, where censorship is reduced to a minimum, it is replaced by forces of fashion and mass-marketing, not apparently much less effective in reducing the bulk of what is published to empty uniformity. Just because it is less crushing than the uniformity imposed by State control it may be more corrupting; persuasion, equipped with material inducements and received opinions, may suggest that to speak 'in truth and conscience' is not risky but impossible.

Persuasion, however, proves no more omnipotent than censorship, and though the results are less spectacular, an irredentist literature exists here as well. Various forms of 'self-publication', or at least of minority-publication, have done much to preserve independence in different kinds of writing, perhaps most successfully in the journalism of news-letters and other periodicals of small though not always local circulation. Individuals and co-operative groups have found ways of book-publishing, again on a small scale, which put in print and permanency works whose value has nothing to do with the market. In these reactions to commodity-production new techniques have themselves played a part, not less important perhaps than was the handpress to the 'Republic of Letters' in which writers, scholars, publishers and printers combined their functions. It is true, no doubt, and a warning to bear in mind, that 'there will be no *samizdat* in a totally electronic system' of record and publication[226] but this side of such complete centralisation there are means now under development which might allow for less rather than more uniform control. Cheap and simple printshops are already easy for a few persons or even individuals to set up and operate. Authors may before long be able—although, admittedly, not without dependence on a larger system—to set up their work directly, and personally to see it through all manufacturing processes. Such 'do-it-yourself' communication might, it is suggested, do away with publishers altogether, or at least force a 'thorough re-examination' of their function, and help to overcome the effects of commercial monopoly.[227]

But though such methods and techniques seem as promising as others are threatening, the particular means used will be of less importance than the motives for using it. The view governing all that has been said in this brief survey is that quoted at the beginning, representing (it is said) a characteristically 'European' attitude to language and literature; that they are not governing institutions but 'tools' of society. Men use tools, and not (except in science fiction) tools men—although it is certainly the case, and a consequence of which the fantasies of science fiction present a mechanised allegory, that men's purposes are modified by the very tools they devise to achieve them. Printing with movable type was invented because men wanted to spread the word, and the way it has been spread, and the kind of word it is, have been profoundly affected by the machinery. But the word is still the reason for the machine's existence, and not the other way about—and is itself the instrument rather than the motive-force of social life, the way human beings live together. Words are the means by which they propose, or try to understand, ends for themselves; unless words are, or seek to be, truthful they will eventually lose their function, and all the means of spreading them will atrophy. Such an end to the story can hardly be reconciled with any general idea we may entertain of human existence.

Notes

1. *Imperial China*, ed. F. Schurmann and Ol. Schell (London 1976), p. 62
2. Robert Mandrou, *From Humanism to Science* 1480–1700, tr. Brian Pearce, London 1978, p. 308
3. Michael Clapham, *Printing*, in *The History of Technology*, ed. Charles Singer, vol. IV (Oxford 1947)
   The calculation is that 'a man born in 1453, the year of the fall of Constantinople, could look back from his fiftieth year on a lifetime in which about 8,000,000 books had been printed, more perhaps than all the scribes of Europe had produced since Constantine had founded his city in AD 330'.
4. Owen Chadwick, *The Reformation* in *The Pelican History of the Church*, (London 1964), p. 31
5. *From Humanism to Science*, p. 31
6. Plato, *Phaedrus*, tr. W. Hamilton, London 1973
7. Chadwick, *The Reformation*, p. 31
8. Quoted by E. H. Harbison, *The Christian Scholar in the Age of the Reformation* (New York 1956), p. 87
9. *The Adages of Erasmus*, tr. M. M. Phillips (Cambridge 1964)
10. *From Humanism to Science*, p. 28
11. Ibid, p. 29
12. E. G. Rupp, *Luther's Progress to the Diet of Worms* (Cambridge 1951), p. 54
13. A. G. Dickens, *Reformation and Society in Sixteenth Century Europe* (London 1968), p. 51
14. Quoted by M. H. Black in *The Printed Bible, Cambridge History of the Bible*, vol. III (Cambridge 1963)
15. Quoted by G. Strauss in *Nuremberg in the Sixteenth Century* (New York 1966)
16. John Foxe, *Book of Martyrs*, quoted by E. Haller in *The Elect Nation* (New York), 1963
17. F. F. Bruce, *The English Bible* (London 1961), pp. 37–8
18. Martin Luther, ed. E. G. Rupp and B. Drewery, *Documents of Modern History: Martin Luther* (London 1970), p. 122
19. *The English Bible*, p. 68
20. Ibid. p. 71
21. Ibid. pp. 70–1
22. Jasper Ridley, *John Knox* (London 1968), p. 239
23. *The English Bible*, p. 29

24   Ibid. pp. 78–9 and footnote.
25   S. Schoenbaum, *Shakespeare's Lives* (London 1970), p. 64
26   *The Poems of William Blake*, ed. W. H. Stevenson (London 1971)
27   Rabelais, *Gargantua and Pantagruel*, tr. Urquhart and Le Motteux, Book II, Chap. VIII
28   S. H. Steinberg, *Five Hundred Years of Printing* (London 1955), p. 88
29   Ibid. p. 262
30   O. Chadwick, *The Reformation*, p. 300
31   E. L. Eisenstein, *The Printing Press as Agent of Change*, 2 vols. (Cambridge 1979)
32   Eisenstein, op. cit. p. 145
33   Ibid. p. 143
34   The chief printer of the Marprelate tracts is believed to have been Robert Waldegrave, who was subsequently hunted for his life and took refuge in Edinburgh, where he was appointed King's Printer to James VI. He returned to England when James assumed the English throne, and printed a number of James's own writings, including the *Poeticall Exercises, Daemonologie,* and *Basilikon Doron.* See R. Dickson and J. P. Edmond, *Annals of Scottish Printing* (Cambridge 1890)
35   *A Remonstrance of Many Thousand Citizens,* 1646, from *Leveller Manifestoes of the Puritan Revolution,* ed. D. M. Wolfe (New York 1944), p. 114
36   Thomas Hobbes, quoted by Christopher Hill, *The Century of Revolution, 1603–1714* (London 1961), p. 154
37   Hobbes, *Leviathan,* chap. IV
38   Ibid. chap. XXXIII
39   Arise Evans, *An Echo to the Voice of Heaven,* 1653, quoted by C. Hill, *The World Turned Upside Down* (London 1972), p. 93
40   *The Century of Revolution,* pp. 154–5
41   Ibid. p. 160
42   *A Remonstrance of Many Thousand Citizens*
43   John Lilburne, *An Impeachment for High Treason Against Oliver Cromwell, Leveller Manifestoes,* p. 73
44   *Light Shining in Buckinghamshire,* 1648, from *British Pamphleteers,* ed. G. Orwell and R. Reynolds (London 1948), vol. 1, p. 75
45   William Erbery, *Testimony,* quoted in *The World Turned Upside Down,* p. 194
46   *Tyranipocrit Discovered,* 1649, from *British Pamphleteers,* vol. I, p. 95
47   John Warr, *The Corruption and Deficiency of the Laws of England,* 1649 quoted in *The World Turned Upside Down,* p. 273
48   Owen C. Watkins, *The Puritan Experience* (London 1972), p. 248
49   *The World Turned Upside Down,* p. 112
50   Ibid. p. 59
51   *Advertisements for the Managing of the Counsels of the Army,* 1647, from *Puritanism and Liberty,* documents edited by A. S. P. Woodhouse (London 1938), p. 398

52 *The World Turned Upside Down*, p. 63
53 R. Overton, *A Defiance Against All Arbitrary Usurpations*, 1646, quoted by D. M. Wolfe, *Leveller Manifestoes*, p. 322
54 *The Humble Petition of firm and constant Friends to the Parliament and Commonwealth*, 1649, From *Leveller Manifestoes*, pp. 327, 328–9
55 *The Century of Revolution*, line 92
56 W. Fox Bourne, *English Newspapers* (London 1887), vol. I, p. 34
57 *A Century of Revolution*, p. 216
58 *British Pamphleteers*, vol. I, pp. 182–3
59 John Milton, *Areopagitica*, from *Milton's Prose Writings*, ed. K. M. Burton, Everyman edition (London 1958), pp. 146–85
60 Samual Hartlib, *A Description of the Famous Kingdom of Macaria*, 1641, quoted by D. M. Wolfe, *Leveller Manifestoes*, p. 107
61 *Five Hundred Years of Printing*, p. 44
62 H. J. Chaytor, *From Script to Print* (Cambridge 1945), p. 123
63 Or a woman's! One consequence of printing, it is asserted, is that 'female writers also appeared . . . in noticeable numbers . . . Louise Labe, the rope-maker's daughter . . . Nicole Estienne, printer's daughter and physician's wife . . . and the Midwife, Louise Bourgeois . . .' (N. Z. Davis, *Printing and the People* (California, 1975), quoted by Eisenstein, op. cit.)
64 Eisenstein, vol. I, p. 84
65 Ibid. p. 121
66 *Five Hundred Years of Printing*, pp. 59–60
67 *Annals of Scottish Printing*, p. 10
68 *Five Hundred Years of Printing*, p. 202
69 *Annals of Scottish Printing*, pp. 292–304
70 Ibid. pp. 490–2
71 *Five Hundred Years of Printing*, p. 109
72 V. de Sola Pinto and A. E. Rodway, *The Common Muse, an Anthology of British Ballad Poetry* (London 1957), intro. p. 17
73 *The Euing Collection of English Broadside Ballads* (Glasgow 1971)
74 John Dryden, preface to *Fables Ancient and Modern*, 1700
75 *From Script to Print*, pp. 116–17
76 P. Earle, *The World of Defoe* (London 1976), p. 48
77 John Bowle: *Henry VIII* (London 1964), p. 268
78 *Five Hundred Years of Printing*, pp. 242–3
79 Ibid. p. 243
80 J. B. Williams, *A History of English Journalism to the Founding of the Gazette* (London 1908), p. 11
81 *Five Hundred Years of Printing*, p. 246
82 Robert Burton, *Anatomy of Melancholy*, ed. A. R. Shilleto (London 1896), vol. II, p. 94, vol. I, p. 15
83 A. Holland, quoted by J. B. Williams, op. cit. p. 14
84 James Shirley, *Dramatic Works and Poems*, ed. W. Gifford (London 1883)

85   B. Jonson, *Poems*, ed. I. Donaldson (London 1975)
86   B. Jonson, *Dramatic Works*
87   *Five Hundred Years of Printing*, p. 248
88   *A History of English Journalism to the Gazette*, appendix
89   *The Century of Revolution*, p. 154
90   *A History of English Journalism to the Gazette*, pp. 53, 56
91   *The Century of Revolution*, p. 136
92   Fox Bourne, *English Newspapers*, vol. I, pp. 32–3
93   George Kitchen, *Sir Roger L'Estrange* (London 1913)
94   *A History of English Journalism to the Gazette*, pp. 196–7
95   Quoted by Stanley Morison, *Ichabod Dawks and his News-Letter* (Cambridge 1931)
96   G. M. Trevelyan, *English Social History* (London 1942), p. 203
97   M. E. Craig, *Scottish Periodical Press*, 1750–1789 (Edinburgh 1931)
98   *Five Hundred Years of Printing*, pp. 251–2
99   Ibid. p. 252
100 W. G. Bleyer, *Main Currents in the History of American Journalism* (New York 1927), p. 44
101 *The Spectator*, 7 August 1712
102 William Warburton's Note to *The Dunciad*, Alexander Pope, Book II, line 315
103 Fox Bourne, *English Newspapers*, vol. I, p. 124
104 *The Spectator*, July 1714, quoted by Fox Bourne
105 *The Review*, January 1706, quoted by Fox Bourne
106 Quoted by Fox Bourne, pp. 109–11
107 Quoted by G. Kitchin, *Sir Roger L'Estrange*, p. 136
108 Quoted by Fox Bourne, pp. 111–12
109 Fox Bourne, pp. 118–19
110 Ibid. p. 128
111 Ibid. p. 158
112 Ibid. p. 217
113 Ibid. pp. 230–1
114 *Five Hundred Years of Printing*, p. 252
115 Bleyer, *American Journalism*, p. 76
116 Ibid. pp. 64–7
117 Ibid. p. 91
118 Ibid. p. 103
119 Dr Johnson, *Prose and Poetry*, ed. M. Wilson (London 1950), pp. 327–8
120 Ibid. extracts from *The Idler*, no. 31
121 Samuel Johnson, *The Rambler*, ed. S. C. Roberts (London 1953), p. 238
122 *The True Patriot*, 1758, quoted by Fox Bourne, pp. 133–4
123 E. P. Thompson, *The Making of the English Working Class* (Penguin Edition, 1968), p. 782
124 Ibid. p. 800
125 Quoted by E. Eisenstein, *The Printing Press as Agent of Change*, vol. I, pp. 115–16

126   *The Making of the English Working Class*, p. 805
127   Ibid.
128   T. L. Peacock, *Crotchet Castle*, chap. II
129   Fox Bourne, *English Newspapers,*vol. II, p. 54, note
130   Ibid. pp. 7–8
131   *The Times*, 20 March 1855, quoted Fox Bourne
132   *English Newspapers*, vol. II, p. 222
133   Ibid. pp. 230–1
134   D. C. Coleman, *The British Paper Industry*, 1495–1860 (Oxford 1958), p. 188
135   Ibid. pp. 258–68
136   Richard Baxter, *Baxterianae,*quoted Coleman.
137   *British Paper Industry*, p. 107
138   Ibid. p. 339
139   Ibid. p. 344
140   Information supplied by the British Paper and Board Industry Federation.
141   *British Paper Industry*, p. 209, my italics
142   *English Newspapers*, pp. 121–2, 254
143   W. G. Bleyer, *Main Currents in the History of American Journalism*, pp. 158–62.
      The *Sun* is also famous in newspaper history as the journal which published
      the 'Moon Hoax', in which a series of articles, purporting to have been drawn
      from the *Edinburgh Journal of Science*, reported the 'great astronomical
      discovery' of life on the Moon. This sold the paper so well that even after the
      hoax was exposed the *Sun*, whose declared motto was 'TRUTH', pretended to
      continue belief in it.
144   Ibid. pp. 190–1
145   Ibid. pp. 209–10
146   W. P. Davison, J. Boylon and F. T. C. Yu, *Mass Media*, New York, 1976, p. 11
147   *American Journalism*, pp. 326–7
148   *American Journalism*, pp. 339–40. The 'Kid', in the original drawings of R. F.
      Outcault, was a curious creature, with the body and limbs of a rather skinny
      child but the head, completely bald, of a newborn infant, even an embryo. A
      perpetual grin added to the expression of witlessness; his comments, in baby-
      talk, were, however, extremely 'cute'. Cf. Schulz's cartoon-strip, 'Peanuts'.
149   E. L. Godkin in the New York *Evening Post*, February 1898, quoted in *American
      Journalism*, p. 377
150   *Mass Media*, p. 13
151   *New York Journal*, October 1897, quoted in *American Journalism*, p. 371
152   *New York World*, December 1895, quoted in *American Journalism*, p. 350
153   *The Nineteenth Century*, May 1887, quoted by S. Morison, *The English
      Newspaper*, 1622–1932 (Cambridge 1932)
154   *The Star*, 1 January 1888, quoted in *The English Newspaper*
155   Ibid. 2 January 1888
156   *English Newspapers*, vol. II, pp. 368–9
157   *Mass Media*, p. 16

158 Ibid. p. 32
159 *Royal Commission on the Press: Final Report* (London 1977), pp. 270, 274
160 *Mass Media*, p. 22
161 Royal Commission on the Press, *Report*, 1949, p.164
162 Royal Commission on the Press, *Report*, 1977, p. 8
163 Royal Commission on the Press, *Report*, 1949, p. 5
164 Royal Commission on the Press, *Report*, 1977, pp. 8–9
165 Royal Commission on the Press, *Report*, 1949, p. 164
166 Royal Commission on the Press, *Report*, 1977, p. 8
167 Royal Commission on the Press, *Report*, 1949, appendices II, VII
168 Royal Commission on the Press, *Report*, 1977, p. 77
169 Ibid. p. 78
170 Royal Commission on the Press, *Report*, 1949, pp. 100–1
171 Ibid. pp. 101–2
172 W. P. Hamilton in *Wall Street Journal*, quoted in Royal Commission on the Press, *Report*, 1977, p. 10
173 Ibid. p. 11
174 Royal Commission on the Press, *Report*, 1949, p. 103
175 *The Times*, 22 November 1879, quoted Fox Bourne, *English Newspapers*, vol. II, p. 332. More recently *The Times* has not only acknowledged the inevitability of occasional error but has shown a scrupulousness in correcting it rare among contemporaries. In the early 1960s, during the editorship of Sir William Haley, a system was introduced of regularised 'Corrections', appearing always in the same part of the paper; an important argument for this innovation, introduced against some opposition, was that as 'a journal of record' *The Times* had a duty to 'keep the record straight' not only for current readers but for posterity. The example has not been widely followed.
176 Royal Commission on the Press, *Report*, 1949, pp. 103–4
177 Ibid. p. 104
178 Ibid. p. 127
179 Ibid. pp. 129–30
180 The survey carried out for the 1974–7 Royal Commission showed that 83 per cent of those questioned regularly read a daily newspaper; 66 per cent read a national morning paper, 9 per cent a regional morning, 34 per cent an evening, 43 per cent a local weekly. These figures overlap, of course, but the likelihood is that something near 100 per cent were reading a newspaper at least once a week. (Royal Commission on the Press *Report*, 1977, p. 87)
181 Royal Commission on the Press, *Report*, 1977, p. 89
182 Ibid. p. 90
183 John Houghton, *The Collection for Improvement of Husbandry and Trade*, 1692, quoted by G. N. Leech, *English in Advertising* (London 1966)
184 *London Gazette*, 1666, quoted in Encyclopaedia Britannica
185 Fox Bourne, *English Newspapers*, vol. II, pp. 214–16

186   R. and J. Lewis, *Politics and Printing in Winchester*, 1830–1880 (Winchester 1980), pp. 6–7
187   A comment in the *Daily Courant* of 1702, quoted by S. Morison in *The English Newspaper, 1622–1932* (Cambridge 1932), p. 318
188   W. G. Bleyer, *American Journalism, p. 249*
189   Ibid, p. 343
190   Ibid, p. 328
191   H. Straumann, *Newspaper Headlines. A study in Linguistic Method*, London 1938, p. 119. Compare a 1981 British example 'Old Soldiers Battle Church' (concerning a dispute between a local British Legion and an Anglican clergyman); and, in an eighteenth-century 'personal' advertisement, 'Wanted A Place A Woman'.
192   Headlines as percentage of editorial space on the main news page of three popular papers were given in the Royal Commission on the Press, *Report, 1949*, as follows: *Daily Express*: 1927, 24 per cent, 1937, 28 per cent, 1947, 33 per cent; *Daily Mail*: 20, 26, 27 per cent; *Daily Mirror*: 32, 29, 30 per cent. In 1981, the same papers had, in a representative week, an average of 41, 30, and 38 per cent.
193   S. Morison, *Politics and Script* (Oxford 1972), p. 316
194   Ibid. p. 336
195   *Newspaper Headlines*, p. 39
196   Editorial statement in the New York *Illustrated Daily News*, June 1919, quoted in *American Journalism*, pp. 423–4.
197   R. Harris and A. Selden, *Advertising and the Public* (London 1962). In 1961, according to these authors, out of a total advertising expenditure of £470m, £215m was spent on Press advertising, against £30m 'outdoor'; in the US in 1960, out of a total of $11,930m, $4,670m was Press advertising (newspapers and magazines), and $200m 'outdoor'.
198   Perhaps the oddest are when lengthy political statements appear as paid advertisements in papers which do not necessarily share their point of view. Thus the *News of the World* for 20 September 1981, carried as an advertisement a half-page of close print, 'On the Occasion of the 33rd Anniversary of the Founding of the Democratic People's Republic of Korea'. Immediately above it was a news story more in line with the journal's own interests, 'Ordeal at hands of hooded fiend'.
199   Martin H. Seiden, quoted in *Mass Media*, p. 72
200   *Politics and Script*. p. 330
201   Royal Commission on the Press, *Report*, 1977, p. 20
202   There are in fact a few social groups, such as the Vai-speaking people of Liberia, who have 'their own' script as well as the introduced printed literature of outside and dominant cultures (Arabic and English). They are thus 'multiliterate', and some, who have never learned to read print, present 'the truly rare phenomenon of literacy without education'. But these are exceptional relics of a generally irretrievable past. (See Neil Warren: *Universality and*

Plasticity: The Resonance between Culture and Cognitive Development, from *Developmental Psychology and Society,* ed. John Sants (London 1980).)

203 Thomas Whiteside, article on Book Publishing, *The New Yorker* 6 October 1980. Reprinted from *The Blockbuster Complex* by permission of Wesleyan University Press. This passage first appeared in *The New Yorker.* Copyright 1980 by Thomas Whiteside

204 Ibid.

205 Ibid. *The New Yorker* 13 October 1980

206 Ibid.

207 W. A. Evans, *Advertising Today and Tomorrow* (London 1974)

208 G. N. Leech, *English in Advertising* (London 1966)

209 Plato, *Gorgias,* tr. W. H. Hamilton (London 1960), p. 28

210 Ibid. pp. 31–2

211 *Advertising Today,* pp. 181–2

212 Ibid. pp. 19–20

213 Ibid.

214 H. Straumann, *Newspaper Headlines,* p. 32

215 Plato, *Phaedrus,* tr. W. H. Hamilton (London 1973), p. 93

216 *Gorgias,* p. 139

217 Leon Trotsky, *The Revolution Betrayed,* tr. Max Eastman (London 1937)

218 Quoted by Richard Grunberger, *A Social History of the Third Reich,* p. 498

219 J. M. Strawson, *Future Methods and Techniques* in *The Future of the Printed Word,* ed. Philip Hills (London 1980), p. 15

220 Ibid. p. 24

221 S. John Teague, *Microform Publication* in *Future of the Printed Word,* p. 136

222 John Florio, quoted by E. L. Eisenstein, *The Printing Press as Agent of Change,* p. 362

223 Teague, *Future of the Printed Word,* p. 140

224 Censorship is probably as complete in the People's Republic of China; too little is known in the West of any 'underground' literature which may have grown up under it.

225 Alexander Solzhenitsyn, who used this proverbial phrase, ('One word of truth outweighs the whole world') as the title of his Nobel Prize speech in 1970

226 Maurice B. Line, *Unprinted Word,* in *Future of the Printed Word,* p. 30

227 J. Strawhorn, *Future Methods,* in *Future of the Printed Word,* p. 23

Index